URBAN
REGENERATION
in the UK

PHIL JONES and JAMES EVANS

URBAN REGENERATION in the UK

2nd EDITION

Los Angeles | London | New Delhi
Singapore | Washington DC

Los Angeles | London | New Delhi
Singapore | Washington DC

SAGE Publications Ltd
1 Oliver's Yard
55 City Road
London EC1Y 1SP

SAGE Publications Inc.
2455 Teller Road
Thousand Oaks, California 91320

SAGE Publications India Pvt Ltd
B 1/I 1 Mohan Cooperative Industrial Area
Mathura Road
New Delhi 110 044

SAGE Publications Asia-Pacific Pte Ltd
3 Church Street
#10-04 Samsung Hub
Singapore 049483

© Phil Jones and James Evans 2013

First published 2013

Editor: Robert Rojek
Editorial assistant: Alana Clogan
Production editor: Katherine Haw
Copyeditor: Kate Harrison
Indexer: Jackie McDermott
Marketing manager: Michael Ainsley
Cover design: Francis Kenney
Typeset by: C&M Digitals (P) Ltd, Chennai, India
Printed by: MPG Books Group, Bodmin, Cornwall

Library of Congress Control Number: 2012944706

British Library Cataloguing in Publication data

A catalogue record for this book is available from
the British Library

ISBN 978-1-4462-0812-0
ISBN 978-1-4462-0813-7 (pbk)

Contents

About the Authors

Dr Phil Jones is currently Senior Lecturer in Cultural Geography at the University of Birmingham where he has been studying and teaching since 2000. His interest in urban regeneration stems from PhD work in historical geography, examining how past urban forms affect the contemporary city, looking in particular at post-war social housing. More recently Phil has worked on projects investigating walking and cycling, artistic methods and issues around the creative economy. He has also been Principal Investigator on four grants funded by UK Research Councils totalling over £1.6m.

James Evans is a Senior Lecturer in Environmental Governance in the School of Environment and Development at the University of Manchester. As a native of rural Oxfordshire but long-time inhabitant of first Birmingham and then Manchester, he has an abiding interest in the ways in which cities and their surrounding regions can become more sustainable. He currently leads three projects exploring these issues in relation to resilience, eco-city learning and living laboratories.

Acronyms

ABI	Area Based Initiative – refers to policy schemes tied to specific areas, as opposed to block grants given to local authorities for general purposes.
ASC	Academy for Sustainable Communities – a body originally administered by CLG with a remit to foster a culture of skills within the regeneration sector, although not itself engaging in training. Merged into the Homes and Communities Agency in 2010.
AWM	Advantage West Midlands – RDA for the West Midlands. Scrapped, 2011.
BCC	Birmingham City Council – local authority for Birmingham.
BID	Business Improvement District – a locally based initiative where businesses and property owners pay a voluntary additional tax to improve the environment of their local area.
BIS	Department for Business, Innovation and Skills – national government department, successor to the short-lived Department for Business, Enterprise and Regulatory Reform, which replaced the Department for Trade and Industry.
BRE	Building Research Establishment – a government agency conducting and coordinating research on construction technologies.
BREEAM	Building Research Establishment Environmental Assessment Method – a measure of the performance of developments against certain indicators of environmental sustainability. EcoHomes is a domestic version of BREEAM.
CABE	Commission for Architecture and the Built Environment – statutory body set up by DCMS and ODPM to promote high-quality architecture and planning. Merged into the Design Council, 2011.
CBD	Central Business District.
CIQ	Cultural Industries Quarter – district of Sheffield's inner city designated as a hothouse for the cultural industries.
CLG	Department for Communities and Local Government – successor to the ODPM, main government department for urban policy in England since 2006.
CPO	Compulsory Purchase Order – mechanism through which local authorities and other government bodies can acquire property against the wishes of the landowner.

CPP   Community Planning Partnership – Scottish agencies, successor to the
            SIPs, aiming to improve indicators of social inclusion in the top 15%
            most deprived neighbourhoods in Scotland.

CPRE   Campaign to Protect Rural England – charity and lobby group seeking
            to protect the interests of rural England. Formerly the Campaign for the
            Preservation of Rural England.

DBERR   Department for Business, Enterprise and Regulatory Reform – short-
            lived successor to the DTI, 2007–09. Replaced by BIS.

DCMS   Department for Culture, Media and Sport – central government depart-
            ment, which replaced the Department of National Heritage in 1997.

DETR   Department of the Environment, Transport and the Regions – precursor
            to ODPM, 1997–2001.

DoE   Department of the Environment – central government department
            1970–97, subsequently merged into the DETR and then into DEFRA,
            the Department for the Environment, Food and Rural Affairs.

DTI   Department for Trade and Industry – the body which was responsible
            for administering the RDAs. Rebranded as BERR in 2007 and subse-
            quently renamed BIS in 2009. The RDAs were phased out, 2010–11.

ECoC   European Capital of Culture – formerly European City of Culture, this
            EU funded scheme seeks to promote the cultural heritage of individual
            European cities. The award is made annually on a rotating basis to
            different member states.

EDC   Economic Development Company – non-statutory bodies established
            to coordinate strategies for economic growth within local authority
            districts. Many were set up as successors to Urban Regeneration
            Companies.

EEDA   East of England Development Agency – RDA for the east of England.
            Scrapped, 2011.

EP   English Partnerships – executive agency reporting to CLG. Significant
            landowner with a remit to help foster regeneration schemes across the
            UK in collaboration with local authorities, RDAs and other bodies
            (e.g. Pathfinders). Merged into the Homes and Communities Agency, 2008.

ERCF   Estates Renewal Challenge Fund – allowed local authorities to transfer
            individual estates into the ownership of housing associations. A smaller-
            scale version of LSVT, the scheme ran between 1995 and 2000.

ERDF   European Regional Development Fund – funds made available by the
            EU to help even out regional inequalities within member states.

ESF   European Social Fund – EU's structural programme responsible for
            increasing skills and employment opportunities.

ESRC   Economic and Social Research Council – the main body for funding
            social science research in the UK higher education sector.

EU   European Union – a supra-national body of European states which cooperate over certain aspects of social, economic and environmental policy.

GHA   Glasgow Housing Association – the housing association which took control of Glasgow City Council's housing portfolio following stock transfer in 2002.

GLA   Greater London Authority – a post-1997 replacement for the defunct GLC, with elections for the London Mayor taking place in 2000.

GLC   Greater London Council – a powerful local authority which operated across Greater London and was abolished by the Conservative government in 1986.

HIP   Housing Improvement Programme – during the 1970s and 1980s this was the mechanism through which local authorities were allocated permission by central government to spend money maintaining their stock of council houses.

ICT   Information Communications Technology – umbrella term for computing and telecommunications.

LAA   Local Area Agreement – agreements between central government, the local authority and LSP as to what the priorities are for action to improve local areas against floor targets for education, health and public safety. Scrapped, 2010.

LDA   London Development Agency – the RDA for London. This body was brought into the control of the GLA in 2010.

LDF   Local Development Framework – flexible planning document produced at the area scale by local authorities. The intention is that they should function in a similar fashion to a development masterplan.

LEP   Local Enterprise Partnership – much less well funded than the RDAs they replaced, these bodies were established in 2011 as partnerships between local authorities, businesses and third sector organisations, intended to boost economic growth within the English Regions.

LDDC   London Docklands Development Corporation – the Urban Development Corporation with responsibility for regenerating the area around what is now Canary Wharf, which operated between 1981–98.

LSC   Learning and Skills Council – responsible for planning and funding education and training in England for those not in the university sector. Scrapped, 2010.

LSP   Local Strategic Partnership – responsible for delivering the Neighbourhood Renewal national strategy. LSPs map directly on to local authority boundaries but lost a significant proportion of their remit with the scrapping of the LAAs in 2010 and some have been abolished by the host local authority.

LSVT   Large Scale Voluntary Transfer – introduced under the Conservative government this has been the main mechanism for transferring the ownership of local authority housing stock to the housing association sector.

NAO   National Audit Office – a parliamentary body responsible for auditing the work of government departments, executive agencies and other public bodies.

NDC   New Deal for Communities – established local organisations to tackle indicators of social deprivation in specifically targeted areas, with no remit for physical reconstruction. Funding ran through to 2011 but was not renewed.

NDPB   Non-Departmental Public Bodies – an alternative name for quangos, these are executive agencies reporting directly to government departments but with no democratic accountability.

NPPF   National Planning Policy Framework – simplified guidance for planning in England introduced in 2012 to replace the system of Planning Policy Statements.

NRF   Neighbourhood Renewal Fund – set 'floor targets' for improving indicators of social deprivation in the 88 most deprived local authority areas. Administered at local level by the LSPs, the scheme ran between 2001 and 2008.

NRU   Neighbourhood Renewal Unit – established in 2001 to oversee the government's Neighbourhood Renewal Strategy, administering the NDC, NRF and the LSPs. The unit was dissolved in 2008.

ODA   Olympic Development Authority – statutory body responsible for delivering the physical infrastructure for the 2012 Olympic Games.

ODPM   Office of the Deputy Prime Minister – responsible for urban policy for England 2001–06, replaced by the CLG.

OPLC   Olympic Park Legacy Company – body responsible for delivering the post-2012 Games legacy. Originally established as an arm of national government, after 2010 it was turned into a Mayoral agency reporting to the London Assembly.

PFI   Private Finance Initiative – a mechanism whereby the private sector builds and maintains a capital resource such as a school or a hospital and leases it back to the state for a fixed period, often 25 years, after which it reverts to state ownership.

PPG   Planning Policy Guidance – guidance notes issued to local authorities on a variety of planning related topics. Most of these were phased out 2004–06, and the remainder scrapped with the introduction of the National Planning Policy Framework in 2012.

PPP   Public Private Partnerships – partnership arrangements between the state and private enterprise to deliver a particular project.

PPS   Planning Policy Statements – successor to the Planning Policy Guidance notes, phased in from 2004. These were replaced by the much less detailed National Planning Policy Framework in 2012.

PSA   Public Service Agreement – introduced in 1998 these set targets for performance and value for money in public services.

Quango   Quasi-Autonomous Non/National Government Organisation – a term popular in the 1970s and 1980s to describe executive agencies funded by central government but operating at one removed from direct democratic accountability. In the regeneration sector the term was classically applied to the UDCs.

RDA   Regional Development Agencies – established 1998–99 with a remit to foster regional economic development. These bodies were a major source of funding at regional level, distributing resources from CLG and DTI/BIS. They were scrapped in 2010–11, replaced by the Local Enterprise Partnerships.

RP   Registered Provider – alternative name for RSL or housing association, used since 2008.

RPA   Regional Planning Authorities – unelected bodies in England which had overall responsibility for producing the regional spatial strategies (RSS) and overseeing the operation of the RDAs. Scrapped, 2010.

RSA   Regional Selective Assistance – discretionary grants available to encourage firms to locate or expand in designated Assisted Areas.

RSL   Registered Social Landlord – a body responsible for building and operating social housing whilst operating in the private sector with or without central government grants from the Homes and Communities Agency. Often used as an alternative phrase for housing associations. Since 2008 the preferred term has been Registered Provider (RP) of Social Housing.

RSS   Regional Spatial Strategy – overall plans for how land was to be developed within a region over a 15- to 20-year period. These superseded Regional Planning Guidance in 2004 and were scrapped by the Coalition Government in 2010.

SAP   Standard Assessment Procedure – a measure of a building's energy efficiency.

SCP   Sustainable Communities Plan – launched in 2003, this set out the Labour Government's long-term programme for delivering sustainable communities throughout England.

SEEDA   South East England Development Agency – RDA for south east England. Scrapped, 2010–11.

SIP   Social Inclusion Partnership – Scottish agencies with a remit similar to the LSPs, which attempted to coordinate the actions of other agencies operating in an area towards promoting social inclusion. These were phased out 2003–04.

SFIE   Selective Finance for Investment in England – a DTI scheme which
            funded new investment projects leading to long-term improvements in
            productivity, skills and employment.
SINC   Site of Importance for Nature Conservation – a national network of
            non-statutorily protected wildlife sites, generally administered by local
            authorities in partnership with nature conservation organisations.
SME   Small and medium-sized enterprises.
SOA   Single Outcome Agreement – agreements between local authorities
            in Scotland, Community Planning Partnerships and the Scottish
            government determining local responses to social and other needs.
SPD   Single Programming Document – a strategy document that maps
            priorities at the regional level with the objectives of the ERDF.
SPG   Supplementary Planning Guidance – produced by local authorities
            to cover a range of issues around a particular site, these are legally
            binding material considerations in subsequent decisions on planning
            permission.
SRB   Single Regeneration Budget – major national funding programme for
            urban regeneration, 1994–2001. Replaced by the Single Programme
            administered by RDAs which was abolished along with the RDAs in
            2010–11.
SuDS   Sustainable (Urban) Drainage Systems – umbrella term for a collection
            of technologies which attempt to slow, reduce and purify discharges of
            rainwater runoff.
TCPA   Town and Country Planning Association – founded by Ebeneezer
            Howard in 1899 as the Garden Cities Association, an NGO whose
            goal is to improve the social and environmental performance of the
            planning system in the UK.
TEC   Training and Enterprise Council – executive agencies which operated
            at regional level in the 1980s and 1990s with responsibility for foster-
            ing enterprise culture and economic development.
TIF   Tax Increment Funding – allows local authorities to borrow against
            predicted increases in business rates and tax income from proposed
            developments to fund key infrastructure and associated capital costs.
UDC   Urban Development Corporation – bodies set up by central government
            mostly during the 1980s to bypass local authorities and undertake
            specific localised projects levering in private capital, e.g. London
            Docklands Development Corporation.

URC   Urban Regeneration Company – pioneered in the late 1990s, these briefly became a central part of English regeneration policy following the 2000 Urban White Paper. They were established to act as coordinating bodies (with no significant resources of their own) to bring together local parties to produce development plans for an area/city. Many were subsequently reconfigured as Economic Development Companies.

UTF   Urban Task Force – body headed up by architect Richard Rogers which had a significant influence on early New Labour thinking on cities. Produced *Towards an Urban Renaissance* in 1999.

WCED   World Commission on Environment and Development – also known as the Brundtland Commission, its 1987 report produced one of the first definitions of sustainable development.

WEFO   Welsh European Funding Office – agency of the Welsh Assembly Government responsible for managing applications for funds from the European Union.

1 Introduction

OVERVIEW

- *Defining urban regeneration*: explores the origins of the term and how it has come to be used within contemporary policy.

- *Scale of change*: gives the context for regeneration, looking at the scale of development in the UK and examining the importance of sustainability as a guiding concept.

- *From boom to bust*: examines how wider global and economic trends have impacted on the way regeneration is carried out and the political response to this.

- *Scope and structure of this book*: provides a breakdown of the different chapters within the book.

- *How to use this book*: outlines some of the ways this book can help to develop an understanding of urban regeneration.

Introduction

For the decade leading up to 2008, towns and cities across the UK were undergoing a series of dramatic reconfigurations, the scale of which had not been seen since the 1960s. Shiny buildings in glass and steel seemed to spring up overnight and cranes dominated the skyline of our major cities. Older buildings and sometimes whole districts were razed to the ground to be replaced by new kinds of urban development. Terms like 'sustainable', 'mixed use', 'café culture' and 'waterfront redevelopment' became commonplace. The process profoundly transformed aspects of urban life – both the way towns and cities look and how we live in them. A spirit of optimism dominated the process, with regeneration seen as an important opportunity to rectify the mistakes of the past to create attractive, sustainable places for people to live, work and play.

During his time as Chancellor, Gordon Brown spoke of the need to end the cycle of boom and bust that had plagued the British economy since the end of World War II. The **credit crunch** of 2008 and subsequent recession put paid to the dream that the UK had entered a period of sustainable growth. Major building projects were suddenly put on hold or cancelled altogether as finance dried up and firms started to go bust. As the economy slowly starts to recover, regeneration activity is also starting to build up again, though in a somewhat less feverish way than at the height of the boom. The credit crunch injected a healthy dose of reality into the UK's overheated property market and gave an opportunity to think again about what regeneration is trying to achieve in terms of improving our towns and cities, rather than simply how regeneration can be used to maximise profits for private firms and individuals. In short, it is a very good time to be interested in urban regeneration. But what does 'urban regeneration' actually mean, how does it work and what does it do? These are the questions this book sets out to answer

Defining 'urban regeneration'

Cities are never finished objects; land-uses change, neighbourhoods are redeveloped, the urban area itself expands and, occasionally, shrinks. Pressure to change land-uses can come about for a number of reasons, whether it be changes in the economy, environment or social need, or a combination of these. The large-scale process of adapting the existing built environment, with varying degrees of direction from the state, is today generally referred to in the UK as urban regeneration. Some of the core elements of regeneration have appeared in urban policy before, albeit with slightly different labels. In post-war Britain there was a **discourse** of reconstruction, not only addressing areas which had suffered the destruction of wartime bombing, but also demolishing the large areas of slum housing that had been jerry built during the nineteenth century to house a growing urban industrial workforce. This post-war reconstruction was somewhat akin to urban renewal in the United States, wherein large parts of the inner cities were demolished and replaced with major new roads, state-sponsored mass housing and new pieces of urban infrastructure.

Urban regeneration is a newer concept, which arose during the 1980s and, as a label, indicates that the process is about something more than simply demolition and rebuilding. The urban sociologist Rob Furbey has written about the origins of the term, reflecting that 'regeneration' in Latin means 'rebirth' and embodies a series of Judaeo-Christian values about being born again. This notion was particularly appealing during the 1980s, when urban policy under Prime Minister Margaret Thatcher swung towards the **neoliberal** and was influenced by a very particular vision of Christianity, centred on the individual rather than the broader community. In a sense, therefore, regeneration – as opposed to mere 'redevelopment' – became akin to a moral crusade, rescuing not only the economy but also the soul of the nation. The phrase also functions as a biological metaphor, with run-down areas seen as sores or cancers requiring regeneration activity to heal the body of the city (Furbey, 1999).

One of the most significant figures in the early history of urban regeneration was Michael Heseltine who served as Secretary of State at the Department of the Environment between 1979 and 1983. This was a crucial period in the history of British cities, partly because Heseltine drove through the right-to-buy legislation which allowed tenants to buy their council houses at substantial discounts – a part-privatisation of social housing that massively increased owner occupation. Perhaps more significantly, Heseltine also led the government's response to the 1981 riots in the deprived inner city areas of Handsworth in Birmingham and Toxteth in Liverpool. Heseltine concluded that something dramatic needed to be done and there followed a series of policy interventions attempting to redevelop derelict and under-utilised sites, bringing economic activity and social change to deprived areas.

The Conservative approach during the 1980s doubtless had its flaws, but it set a trend for large-scale interventions reconfiguring the urban fabric of areas suffering from economic decline following the shift away from a manufacturing-led economy. From relatively modest beginnings in the 1980s, regeneration has become a tool applied in almost all urban areas in the UK, reaching a peak of activity in 2008 before the property bubble burst as a consequence of the global economic collapse.

Regeneration is, however, a somewhat ambiguous term. Some approaches to regeneration argue that it is necessary to tackle physical, social and economic problems in an integrated way. In practice, however, dealing with questions around social inequality and community cohesion tend to be separated off from regeneration. Indeed, under the New Labour governments, a separate discourse of neighbourhood *renewal* was devised to tackle social problems (not to be confused with urban renewal as practised in the United States during the 1950s–70s). Urban regeneration, meanwhile, has come to represent strategies to change the built environment in order to stimulate economic growth. It is in this area, rather than in community policy, that this book finds its focus.

The scale of change

Urban regeneration policies helped to create and shape the pre-2008 property development boom. The growth figures for UK construction since 1997 are quite startling (ONS, 2011). Using the value of sterling in 2005, the overall value of outputs from the construction industry in England grew from £51bn in 1997 to nearly £110bn in 2008. Although this figure fell back after the credit crunch, it was still £99.5bn in 2010. The scale of growth was similar in Scotland (£5.6bn in 1997 growing to £10.9bn in 2010), somewhat slower in Wales (£2.7bn in 1997 growing to £3.9bn in 2010) and trending downwards in Northern Ireland (£3.2bn in 2001, the earliest year available for this dataset, falling to £2.4bn in 2010). These numbers represent all construction activity, not just regeneration, but demonstrate just how quickly the UK has been building. Further, this growth in construction has been concentrated in urban areas. Although in land-use terms, only around 10% of the UK's land surface is urbanised, the percentage of total new residences built in urban areas grew from under 50% in 1985 to over 65% in 2003 (Karadimitriou, 2005).

The frenzy of building in UK towns and cities is not simply a product of economic growth, but reflects broader demographic shifts. People are living longer than ever before and, at the other end of the age scale, people are waiting longer to have children, both of which mean a decrease in average household size which, combined with a growing population means that the number of households is increasing rapidly. As a result, the number of households in England alone is predicted to rise from just over 21 million in 2004 to nearly 26.5 million in 2029 with 70% of that increase taking the form of one-person households (CLG, 2007b).

Table 1.1 shows the net annual increase in the number of homes in the UK, adding together new build and conversion of existing properties minus the rate of demolition. These data show fairly steady increases each year, with an unsurprising dip in the rate of growth after 2008. What is more interesting, however, is comparing this rate of growth as against forecasts for rates of household formation. Estimates for Scotland predict a net increase of households 2008–33 of around 19,250 per year, which is broadly in line with the rate of overall increase in housing stock (Scottish Government, 2010). Similarly, Northern Ireland is predicting an increase of around 8,100 households per year 2008–23, which is not dissimilar to its rate of stock increase (NISRA, 2010). More seriously, however, Wales is predicting household growth of 12,300 per year, 2006–31, well below the rate of stock increase (Statistics for Wales, 2010). In England the situation is even more acute, with a predicted 232,000 additional households per year 2008–33, far outstripping the number of new dwellings being added each year even at the most frenzied point of the economic boom (CLG, 2010).

Table 1.1 Number of dwellings added to total housing stock per year.

	England	Wales	Scotland	NI
2003	144,000	7,000	18,000	11,000
2004	155,000	8,000	19,000	5,000
2005	169,000	8,000	21,000	14,000
2006	187,000	8,000	19,000	8,000
2007	198,000	10,000	22,000	7,000
2008	208,000	8,000	22,000	17,000
2009	166,000	7,000	17,000	7,000
2010	129,000	6,000	14,000	9,000

Source: DCLG Live tables on dwelling stock (http://www.communities.gov.uk/housing/housingresearch/housingstatistics/housingstatisticsby/stockincludingvacants/livetables/, accessed 22 September 2011).

The overall shortage of dwellings in England is one of many complex issues that drove high rates of house price inflation up to 2008. There was a range of other factors at work, including rising professional salaries, historically low rates of interest, the increased willingness of banks to lend more money to people with much less **equity** and, quite simply, a belief that house prices would keep rising which encouraged people to pay higher and higher sums for property. Nonetheless, the underlying structural shortage of housing became a real source of concern under the Labour governments 1997–2010. The Treasury in particular was concerned that housing shortage was acting as a brake on economic growth, particularly in the overcrowded south east. A series of policies were pursued to help increase the level of house-building, including reforms to the planning system. A target to increase house-building in England to 200,000 new properties per year (HM Treasury, 2005) was, only briefly, met at the peak of the boom. The broadly neoliberal politics of the UK puts an emphasis on the private sector to deliver on housing targets with a belief that reducing state regulation will allow the housing market to find a 'natural' balance of supply and demand. Unfortunately, relying on the private sector does not work well at a time when the housing market is sluggish and banks are less willing to lend. There is also little incentive for house-building firms to greatly increase activity if the intention is to reduce the price of their end product. Generations of politicians in England have failed to square this circle; periodic economic down-turns cool house price inflation, but do nothing for the underlying structural problems in the English housing market.

A great deal of the growth in the overall number of households is being driven by increasing numbers of people living alone. In England the prediction is that by 2033, 19% of the population will live alone, compared to 14% in 2008 (CLG, 2010). In Scotland this demographic transition is even more dramatic with single-adult households predicted to increase from an already high 38% in 2008 to 45% by 2033 (Scottish Government, 2010). This has huge significance for the kinds of homes that are required. This is less of a problem in Scotland, which has a much greater tradition of people choosing to live in apartments. In England, however, the idea of the *house* is deeply embedded in the culture. While there has been a boom of apartment building since the late 1990s, the English do not seem to have fully embraced this housing form.

The boom in apartment construction, however, wrought a tremendous transformation upon English cities. High-density living in the heart of the city came back into fashion for the English middle classes who had largely abandoned the city core after the mid-nineteenth century. Unlike the Scots, apartment dwelling for the contemporary English middle class is very much a 'young' stage in the lifecourse. In the Netherlands, new inner city developments are built as large, airy apartments designed for families, with new schools to serve the incoming population. In England, new-build apartments tend to be well appointed but quite small, with a predominance of one and two bedroom units not designed with families in mind. At the same time, local authorities have not responded to the trend for inner city living by building new schools for incoming populations. Existing schools within the English inner cities tend to be of poorer quality and middle-class parents generally use their higher incomes to move to areas with good schools. Thus more than a decade of redevelopment in the core of English cities has left them with transitory populations of younger professionals, who stay for a few years to enjoy the bright lights and amenities of the city centre, before moving out to raise children in the suburbs. English city centres now have a *population*, but little in the way of *community*.

Of course there is more to urban regeneration than the rebuilding of city cores – a point that is directly addressed in Chapter 7 which considers regeneration in the suburbs. Nonetheless, it is the city centres that have grabbed the headlines and the imagination. Cities have gone to considerable efforts to re-image their central areas to make them more attractive to visitors and help to build the city as a brand in an attempt to generate inward investment. Stepping out of the train station in Sheffield in the mid-1990s visitors were greeted by a rather grim view of bus stops, a busy road and no obvious way into the city centre. Today there is a plaza paved in natural stone, an iconic curving fountain and a highly legible pedestrian routeway leading into the heart of the city. Similar transformations have taken place across the UK, with cities competing to produce iconic buildings (Selfridges in Birmingham, the Wales Millennium Centre in Cardiff, the Shard on the South Bank in London), create new public spaces and put on spectacular events.

These physical transformations of the urban fabric are seen as a critical part of the symbolic transformation of a city's fortunes into the kind of place where people want to come to live, play and do business. Cities increasingly see themselves as competing in a global marketplace making branding – writ large in steel and glass – a crucial part of their strategies for economic development. This does, of course, open cities up to the criticism of putting style before substance, or even form before function. One architectural critic reviewing Colchester's new Firstsite gallery, for example, commented that despite being a stunning building, the dramatic curved walls were not particularly well set up for the hanging of art (Moore, 2011).

The *where* of regeneration is fairly straightforward to understand: concentrating on previously developed ('brownfield') land in urban areas in order to generate growth. In turn, understanding the broader political and economic context allows us to understand the *why* of regeneration: in a global economy where cities are competing to attract inward investment, making those cities an attractive place to live is paramount. Perhaps the more important question that this book seeks to answer is *how* that regeneration takes place. A key part of the answer to this question is the rise of sustainability as a core concept. Arguably, putting sustainability at the heart of urban policy is the most important change in the transition from urban redevelopment into something we now describe as urban regeneration. Developing from an obscure concept in the late 1980s, the principles of sustainable development and the need to balance economic, social and environmental factors cut across not only urban regeneration, but UK government policy in a whole range of areas. While the concept of sustainability is notoriously difficult to pin down, it implies a commitment to protecting the environment and ensuring equal access to social and environmental services as well as economic development (see Chapter 5). The idea of 'quality of life' has become common parlance, as the political agenda has subtly shifted toward creating environments in which people want to be. Urban regeneration therefore not only acts as a vehicle for reinventing the economies and tarnished reputations of declining industrial cities, but simultaneously helps deliver on a government commitment to sustainability. Related to these trends, urban regeneration has been caught up in the wider '**new urbanism**' movement that emphasises high-quality design and well-planned spaces (see Chapter 6). Another important new element in discussions of regeneration is the desire to create more 'resilient' cities which are better able to cope with the shock of changes to the wider economy and environment. In the aftermath of the 2008 credit crunch and ensuing financial crisis, questions of **resilience** have gained a new importance (as will be discussed in Chapter 8).

From boom to bust

One of the challenges of studying urban regeneration is that it is not an isolated process. Cities are affected by wider economic, political and environmental factors. The fortunes of cities are tied to the fortunes of nations and, ultimately, the global economy. This has a much longer history than simply considering the credit crunch of 2008 and its after-effects. Over the course of the twentieth century, cities in the Western world suffered from the loss of traditional industries that were either undercut by cheaper products from East Asia, or withered by the decline in colonial power. Across Europe and North America, urban regeneration began in earnest from the 1980s as an attempt to ameliorate the negative effects of de-industrialisation and enable cities to attract new investment in the global economy. The goal of policy was to direct development and investment towards those areas in which it was most needed. Left to their own devices, developers would chose to locate developments on the cheapest land in areas with the highest demand. In the UK context this would result in pressure to relax constraints on greenfield development, particularly around London and the south east. At its heart, therefore, regeneration is a political strategy using a whole range of planning regulations and other policies to encourage developers to invest in run-down and derelict urban areas that the 'invisible hand' of the market would otherwise ignore.

The dangers of allowing urban policy to be driven by what the market 'wants' were amply demonstrated by the out-of-town development boom of the late 1980s and early 1990s. Large numbers of these developments were permitted under the free-market-inspired Conservative government of this period. Although economically successful in themselves, out-of-town developments damaged the economies of central cities while at the same time increasing car dependency and seriously disadvantaging those poorer communities dependent on local shops and services. In fairness to the Conservative government of the time, the problems raised by this strategy were recognised and measures put in place to restrict out-of-town development as the 1990s progressed. It was, however, the Labour government that came to power in 1997 which really brought a sea change in attitudes towards planning and development in UK towns and cities. **Brownfield** sites ('previously developed land') within existing urban areas became the key strategic target for meeting housing and development needs. This strategy was given formal expression in 2000 when Planning Policy Guidance note 3 was released, setting a target for local authorities to build 60% of new housing on brownfield sites. This 60% target gave a significant boost to the urban regeneration agenda by forcing local authorities and developers to look first to target sites within existing cities. Although estimates of total amounts of brownfield land are notoriously inaccurate, its distribution follows the geography of **deindustrialisation** and hence much of this land is located in urban areas. Derelict land is frequently considered an eyesore and its redevelopment is a critical element in regeneration, replacing an undesirable land use with high-quality housing. The definition of what comprises a brownfield site is drawn rather broadly, however, and can include some rather surprising types of land uses, not simply derelict industrial sites (a point that will be returned to in Chapter 5).

The 60% brownfield target helped shift the location of sites for new housing so that the majority was built in existing urban areas (Aldrick and Wallop, 2007). In turn this reinforced a new tendency for developers to build apartments rather than houses within cities in order to maximise the number of residential units fitted onto a development site. This helped local authorities meet their housing targets and enabled developers to maximise the returns from the purchase of expensive inner city land. What was clear, however, was that the policy emphasis on using more expensive brownfield sites was caught up in the property boom that developed from the late 1990s and which ran until the credit crunch of 2008. During this period, the proportion of new apartments being built each year grew rapidly in England, despite its lack of a flat-dwelling tradition, rising from 12% of new homes in 1997, to 46% in 2008, before falling back to 30% post-credit crunch in 2010 (CLG, 2011b). After 1997 developers had much less freedom to build the kinds of properties they could easily make money from (large houses on greenfield sites, out-of-town shopping centres, etc.). Nonetheless, 1997–2008 was still a highly profitable period, properties even being built for which there was no traditional market.

Up to 2008 it seemed as though urban regeneration was an unstoppable machine, with ever more ambitious schemes being dreamed up and delivered. Schemes that a dispassionate observer might have seen as marginal, rapidly sold out 'off plan' before a single brick was laid. Indeed, pre-selling became a major mechanism through which developers generated the necessary **capital** to actually deliver their projects (Boddy, 2007). Symbolic of the feverish atmosphere that prevailed prior to 2008, it was even possible to 'flip' apartments bought off plan, selling on for profit before these buildings even existed. During the pre-2008 period, a great many people chose to **buy-to-let**, with the intention that rental income from tenants would cover the mortgage payments, while rapidly increasing property prices would yield a profit when the property was sold. A survey of private landlords undertaken by CLG in 2008 revealed that some 70% saw increasing property value as generating some or all of the profit from their investment (Leyshon and French, 2009). Clearly this model only works if house prices continue to increase. As a result of the credit crunch of 2008, however, UK house prices fell sharply, with the price of apartments hit particularly hard. Subsequently prices stagnated as the market remained sluggish. The finances of regeneration have therefore needed to be rethought with pre-selling and buy-to-let no longer such attractive options to drive sales.

The credit crunch is the most dramatic example of how regeneration is tied into broader economic and social processes. The global banking system was thrown into crisis in 2008 as the subprime mortgage scandal in the United States started to unravel and 'safe' investments proved to be part of a giant pyramid scheme. Those banks that survived the immediate crisis found themselves having to improve the ratio of cash assets to their outstanding loans in order to make them resilient to further economic shocks. In turn this made banks more reluctant to lend money except where the loan was backed with significant capital assets. Developers needed to bring more to the table; for individuals, mortgages of more than 90% of house value were suddenly hard to find. The phenomenon of some banks being willing to loan house-buyers more than 100% of the property's value (instant negative equity built on an assumption of continuing price rises) disappeared overnight. The buy-to-let market has been hit particularly hard by these changes, because its growth was highly leveraged and dependent on asset price rises which are no longer automatic in the current market. Meantime, repossession of homes in the UK peaked in 2009 at 47,900 properties (up from an unusually low 8,200 in 2004), but has since fallen. Indeed, figures for possession cases passing through the courts, the first stage in a repossession, fell sharply in 2010–11 to around the levels seen in 1995 (CLG, 2011c), suggesting some stability following a brutal cull of the most over-exposed households.

It needs to be emphasised that urban regeneration activity did not suddenly come to a halt after 2008. Many of the fundamentals underpinning regeneration activity remain the same. There is still a structural housing shortage in England that creates a market for house-building. The principle of reusing brownfield sites remains paramount. There is still money to be made from putting derelict land into new uses. Nonetheless, there are differences from what happened during the boom times and there have been different political responses to the changed financial circumstances. The **Coalition government**, elected in 2010, has introduced a series of reforms which change how regeneration operates, based on a distinct ideological approach compared to previous Labour regimes. Scrapping the regional development agencies (RDAs), for example, means that the large quantities of public money these bodies used to catalyse large schemes across England are no longer available. The intention is that the private sector should pick up the slack, though with continuing economic uncertainty this intention seems somewhat optimistic. Meanwhile, the Scottish National Party's rise to power in Holyrood since 2007 has seen a distinct approach developing in Scotland, with a much greater emphasis on using public money to redress social justice issues such as housing inequality. The political landscape therefore has a major impact on how regeneration is delivered and the form it takes. These are issues that will be examined in detail in the next chapter.

The scope and structure of this book

A book of this kind has a lot of ground to cover. Historically, our focus begins with the emergence of 'urban regeneration' as a serious policy domain in the early 1980s but concentrates on developments since the Labour government came to power in 1997. While various precursors to regeneration are mentioned where necessary, there is no space for a more general history of urban development. Similarly, while much regeneration practice involves drawing on successful ideas used in other countries, the focus here is on the UK. The UK is, of course, a country of many parts, with distinct legal-political substructures for England, Wales, Scotland and Northern Ireland. In terms of the case studies used to illustrate the discussion, examples have been drawn from these four regional blocks, although inevitably with greater weight given to England, being significantly larger in population and economic activity than the other three combined. Given the scale of regeneration activity in the UK over the past quarter century, it would be impossible to mention every interesting scheme which has been undertaken. While there is some degree of regional balance in the case studies chosen, there are inevitably omissions, particularly in terms of the smaller towns, whose regeneration schemes have tended to receive less attention and are often less innovative than those of the larger metropolitan areas.

Within the UK field of regeneration there is a vast amount of published material, and the proliferation of academic journals focusing on regeneration is a good barometer of scholarly interest in the topic. But, despite its importance, urban regeneration does not fit neatly into existing disciplinary and sub-disciplinary categories, not least because it spans social, economic and environmental dimensions. Regeneration is driven by applied practice, rather than academic research. As a result, research tends to be scattered across a variety of disciplines, from more obvious ones such as urban studies and planning, to regional studies, public policy, property development and engineering.

For the same reasons, regeneration involves a bewildering range of government departments, agencies and organisations all of which release reports, papers and research within the field. Government policy changes rapidly, as do the responses from various stakeholders. Further, many of the key organisations frequently change their names, making it even harder to keep tabs on the sector. For example, the government departments responsible for environment and communities were re-shuffled and renamed four times between 1996 and 2006. This pace of change can make it difficult for all but the most enthusiastic to keep up with moves in the sector.

This book aims to contextualise the regeneration agenda and synthesise existing research in a systematic way to provide a reference text for this important field. It is aimed primarily at an academic audience, as there are an increasing number of university courses dealing with urban regeneration. The book is designed for third year undergraduates, postgraduates and academics and will take the reader through the basic context of regeneration into state-of-the-art research. Accordingly, the topics have been chosen to reflect core themes from the academic literature, rather than to act as a practical guide on how to 'do' regeneration. So, for example, we have not chosen to cover the legal dimension of regeneration – while these aspects play a crucial role in work on the ground, the technical elements are probably of less interest to a general academic audience. We have also aimed to strike a balance between covering the wider context for regeneration, while retaining a focus on regeneration itself. Transport, for example, though playing a major role in where and how regeneration can be undertaken, is not covered separately. Similarly, while social issues are discussed to provide context for urban regeneration policies and case studies, these are not given chapters in their own right. A number of texts already cover these issues in more depth than is possible in a general review of regeneration activity and these are indicated where appropriate.

The remaining eight chapters of this book each cover a distinct aspect of regeneration with illustrative case studies used throughout. Chapter 2 deals with the policy framework, detailing the legislative context in which urban regeneration operates. A brief overview is given of post-industrial policy approaches during the 1980s and early 1990s, before moving on to critically review urban policy during the **New Labour** boom and how this has shaped the contemporary urban regeneration landscape. Chapter 3 considers issues of governance, in order to understand the political processes through which urban regeneration is actually delivered. The notion of partnerships, which is central to contemporary regeneration, is critically analysed. Chapter 4 explores the strategies for economic growth that underpin urban regeneration through the idea of the 'competitive city'. The chapter identifies key funding streams and approaches to urban economic regeneration and examines their success.

Chapter 5 tackles the issue of sustainability, which has become a central concept in all discussions of contemporary regeneration. Key social and environmental policies are reviewed and different approaches to integrated planning are assessed. Chapter 6 considers the visual transformation of the cityscape, examining issues of design and cultural elements of regeneration. A number of key tensions are explored surrounding architectural innovation and the retention of heritage as well as questions of culture and identity. Chapter 7 charts the extension of the urban regeneration agenda beyond central cities, asking whether a distinctly suburban mode of regeneration has evolved. Chapter 8 examines how the principles of regeneration operate on the mega-scale, looking at how large projects such as the Olympics can be delivered in a mature capitalist economy. The final chapter – Conclusions – then summarises and integrates the key themes that span each chapter, and explores the future direction of developments within the sector.

How to use this book

This book has a number of features that are intended to make it easier to use. Most importantly, it makes extensive use of case studies to demonstrate how concepts and policies work in practice. The case studies are primarily drawn from academic research and are used to think critically about the advantages and disadvantages of different ways of doing urban regeneration. The book aims to give detailed descriptions and explanations of how urban regeneration works, while also questioning dominant approaches. At the start of each chapter there is an overview, summarising the contents, arguments and overall structure of the chapter. Within each chapter the sections end with a list of key points, while the chapters themselves conclude with annotated reading lists that highlight key academic texts for each of the concepts addressed, and further reading about the wider ideas that frame regeneration. These lists allows the reader to undertake further research in specific areas of interest.

In addition to an index, the book also has a glossary of academic terms that are used, and an annotated list of acronyms to help guide the reader through the 'alphabet soup' of multiple agencies and policies. While the book has been designed as a coherent whole, with key concepts and cases cross-referenced within the text, each chapter can also be read as a stand-alone learning aid.

2 Policy Framework

OVERVIEW

This chapter details the legislative context in which urban regeneration operates

- *Introduction: origins of the neoliberal shift*: gives a brief overview of how neoliberal approaches came to dominate contemporary urban regeneration policy.

- *Innovations during the New Labour period, 1997–2010*: explores the legacy of the New Labour governments and the development of now taken-for-granted policy innovations.

- *Contemporary policy in England*: examines the framework for English urban regeneration since New Labour lost power in 2010.

- *Devolution*: explores the policy landscape developed by powerful devolved governments in London, Scotland, Wales and Northern Ireland.

Introduction: origins of the neoliberal shift

The minutiae of urban policy can be a rather dry subject, but it is of critical importance to the way in which actors in the regeneration process are able to operate. For over 30 years now the political context for urban regeneration has been broadly neoliberal. The election of Margaret Thatcher in 1979 crystallised an emerging belief that the state could no longer be the primary actor in the redevelopment of cities. Instead the philosophy was one of market forces guiding the private sector to invest, with the state intervening only as far as it created the conditions for the private sector to step in.

There was an important political context in which this neoliberal shift took place. The financial crises of the 1970s were accompanied by swingeing cuts to public spending – a situation which seems very familiar today. The Conservatives took office in 1979 determined to further rein in the public sector which was seen not only as inefficient, but also as giving too much power to the labour unions. Many city councils were controlled by the Labour party, which at that time was fighting its own internal battle against 'militant' hard left tendencies, played out in cities like Liverpool. **Thatcherite** urban policy was directed towards greatly reducing the power of these local authorities as part of a broader assault on the political left. This did not, however, automatically mean that the private sector entirely took over urban redevelopment, but rather that central government took much more control over spending at local level, sidelining those Labour councils.

Competitive bidding

As part of the 1980s' Thatcherite reforms, a new principle was introduced to determine the level of funding that central government gave to local authorities to undertake urban redevelopment. The maintenance and regeneration of local authority housing estates had been funded through the Housing Improvement Programme (HIP), which left local authorities free to determine where they spent resources allocated within a block grant. While HIP was retained, new competitive bidding regimes were introduced which required councils to put proposals together for redeveloping individual estates and areas. These proposals would be evaluated alongside proposals from other local authorities within the region and funding allocated to the projects deemed most 'deserving'.

Schemes like Estate Action resulted in large injections of cash for relatively small areas, resulting in a kind of 'grand slam' approach to redevelopment. Local authorities had an incentive to put their most deprived areas into these competitions to increase their chance of winning funds against less deprived estates within other local authority areas – a kind of ugliness contest. This actually helped certain very deprived areas as there had been a tendency among some local authorities to concentrate resources on less run-down areas where they felt the money would do more good. The problem was that these competitive schemes were funded by reducing the overall HIP allocation, which meant overall cuts in general maintenance. This resulted in considerable neglect and decline of areas which were not successful in the competitions, with local authorities not permitted by central government to divert revenue from other areas into maintenance.

The Estates Action scheme was primarily targeted at upgrading areas of run-down council housing, but the principles of area-based initiatives and competitive bidding which it developed became the model for more general funding in what, from the mid-1980s, was beginning to be called urban 'regeneration'. The City Challenge scheme contained an element of physical renewal in areas of council housing, but had a broader remit to foster the economic redevelopment of the target area. Rebecca Fearnley (2000) has examined a City Challenge funded scheme based in the Stratford area of Newham in south London, which was seen by the government as one of the most successful of these projects. Fearnley notes that the Stratford scheme, which ran from 1993–98, had some significant successes, such as an overall increase in housing satisfaction as well as decreases in reported crime and fear of crime in the area. She argues, however, that the scheme focused on issues which were comparatively easy to tackle, such as physical renewal of the housing stock. Indeed, in terms of economic regeneration, while much work was done increasing the employability of residents, the scheme was much less successful at actually attracting employers to the area to increase the number of jobs available.

One of Fearnley's overall criticisms of City Challenge was that it mostly worked through the existing structures of local service delivery – local authorities and schools – and was much less successful at bringing in and nurturing community-led organisations and projects. In more recent urban policy there has been a much greater emphasis on the need to successfully bring the community in to the process, something which began under the New Labour governments and continued under the Coalition government after 2010. If there is one fundamental shift that came out of the move to a neoliberal approach in the 1980s and 1990s, it was the need to bring together multiple actors – community, private sector and various state agencies – in order to undertake regeneration. To give a simple example, it is no use bringing new employers into an area if the schools are not producing students with the necessary skills to fill the jobs. This central idea of bringing partners into regeneration projects will be discussed in more detail in the next chapter where questions of governance are addressed.

New institutional structures

As well as setting the general parameters for how central government funding schemes now operate, the neoliberal approach of the 1980s and 1990s had major implications for how regeneration would be organised. There was a greatly expanded use of arms-length executive agencies, sometimes referred to as '**quangos**' (quasi-autonomous national/non governmental organisations) or as Non-Departmental Public Bodies (NDPBs). These organisations wield considerable power, but answer only to the relevant Minister, rather than having any direct line of democratic accountability. In terms of urban regeneration, perhaps the most important quangos set up under Thatcher were the urban development corporations (UDCs).

The UDCs were parachuted into chronically deprived urban areas to bypass local authorities and attempt to stimulate a process of physical and economic renewal. Between 1981 and 1992, 14 of these bodies were set up, the first ones being London Docklands and Merseyside. They were limited life organisations and all were wound up by the late-1990s, with the exception of Laganside Development Corporation in Belfast, which ran until early 2007. The London Docklands Development Corporation (LDDC) was probably the best known, investing heavily in new infra-structure projects to help lever in major new private office developments. In spite of the collapse of the office property market in the late 1980s, which briefly left Canary Wharf looking dangerously like a white elephant, there is little doubt that there has been a radical improvement in the physical infrastructure and economic activity in the area – which was, after all, the main aim of the UDCs.

The LDDC was finally wound up in 1998 and produced a series of publications examining its own achievements. Reviewing these studies, Florio and Brownhill (2000) note that the somewhat heroic accounts of dramatic changes to the area brush over the considerable tensions that the LLDC created. The primary problem was that it represented the *redevelopment* of the area, not its *regeneration* – existing socio-economic problems in the area were not helped by the creation of a shiny new office cluster. Indeed, the argument is that the developments actually increased social polarisation by creating islands of extreme wealth while leaving untouched large neighbouring populations suffering acute poverty. For all of this criticism, however, it is interesting that the UDC model was revived in order to meet some of the needs of the 2003 Sustainable Communities Plan, discussed below.

The UDCs that came after the Docklands and Merseyside development corpora-tions were considerably less well funded and it was clear that the model was really too expensive to be more generally applicable. By the 1990s, there was a degree of pragmatism among the British political left that the neoliberal agenda was here to stay with Labour-controlled local authorities accepting that they had to work within these strictures. In turn, under John Major's premiership, there was a soften-ing of the stance on local authorities and a rehabilitation of these bodies as partners in the regeneration process. With their powers greatly curtailed there would be no return to councils being able to take on much of the process themselves, but unlike the UDCs they not only had expertise in physical redevelopment but also in com-munity issues such as education, health and social welfare.

Continuity in neoliberal approaches

1997 and the election of a ('New') Labour government is as much a watershed in British politics as the election of Margaret Thatcher's Conservatives in 1979, but this was not necessarily immediately obvious at the time. Committed to the

Conservatives' spending plans during that early period in order to reassure middle-class voters, there was no sudden abandonment of neoliberal policy principles. In the first few years, key Conservative policies were retained, in particular the Single Regeneration Budget and attempts to move local authority housing out of council control and into the housing association sector.

The Single Regeneration Budget (SRB) was introduced in England in 1994 and drew together a series of different funding strands, with the idea of reducing complexity in the system. Unlike projects based around the UDCs or funding schemes such as Estates Action, the SRB Challenge Fund was not exclusively targeted at areas of acute deprivation. In the first three rounds of SRB funding, spending in the 99 most deprived areas amounted to £122.50 per head. The remainder of the country was not forgotten, however, with £21.30 per head spent in the remaining 267 districts designated 'non-deprived' (Brennan et al., 1999: 2074). Indeed, having rolled together a number of different programmes, the types of projects which received funding could vary enormously, which was a significant advantage for taking a **holistic** approach to tackling complex socio-economic-environmental problems in an area.

SRB was originally administered by the now defunct Government Offices for the Regions. These bodies were essentially regional branches of central government and, indeed, were staffed by a rotating group of civil servants on secondment from Whitehall to ensure that they were not 'captured' by local interests. As such the SRB remained something which was very much controlled by central government. Although the scheme was scrapped in 2001, projects continued running for several years afterwards. Subsequently, funds were administered directly by the Regional Development Agencies (RDAs) as part of a 'single pot', which operated along similar principles.

The SRB and single pot were fundamentally predicated on competitive bidding, demonstrating that this principle was not abandoned by the New Labour administrations 1997–2010. More controversial than the continuation of competitive bidding under New Labour was the acceleration of the programme of Large Scale Voluntary Transfer (LSVT). In neoliberal terms this was a logical extension of right-to-buy legislation, which had reduced the overall size of council housing stock by encouraging sitting tenants to purchase their homes at a significant discount. Under LSVT, local authorities were encouraged to transfer the ownership and management of their remaining council housing to housing associations. These housing associations, though eligible for public sector grants and regulated by the public sector, are effectively private sector bodies that can borrow private finance – their activity does not therefore show up in measures of public spending/borrowing.

Some councils had assumed that with Labour returned to power in 1997, the very tight restrictions on how much could be spent maintaining their housing stock would be eased and the transfer policy scrapped. Such assumptions were rapidly scotched. Transfers required a vote in favour from tenants and the primary attraction was that transfer would bring with it a significant injection of new funds – with the implicit threat that housing stock would continue to be neglected for lack of resources if left with the local authority. The rate of transfers, which had stayed below 50,000 housing units per year prior to 1997, topped 100,000 a year between 2000 and 2002. Indeed, of 133 tenant ballots between 1999 and 2004, only 16 resulted in a rejection of the transfer proposals (Ginsberg, 2005).

LSVT and the fact that local authorities are simply no longer permitted to build new homes has significant implications for urban regeneration. Where housing stock has not been transferred it is now very difficult to undertake significant changes to the physical infrastructure of council housing areas. Birmingham, which rejected stock transfer in 2003, struggled to find investment for run-down areas of council housing. Glasgow, on the other hand, voted in favour of transfer, which made it much easier to work on strategic schemes of demolition and rebuilding such as that associated with the bid to host the 2014 Commonwealth Games in the East End area of the city.

Key points

i) Under the Thatcher governments local authorities were partially bypassed as agents of urban redevelopment, with urban development corporations used to lever in non-state partners and finance.

ii) The principle of competitive bidding for central government grants has become a key element in resource allocation, creating the suspicion that this allows the central state to set local priorities.

iii) The election of a Labour government in 1997 saw the acceleration, rather than reversal, of these principles of partnership and competition.

Innovations during the New Labour period, 1997–2010

One of the most important changes which occurred during the New Labour period was the devolution of powers to the constituent nations of the UK, establishing the Scottish Parliament and the Welsh and Northern Ireland Assemblies. This action meant that different policy approaches began to be taken in the four countries. In this section we focus on how New Labour governments subsequently shaped regeneration policy in England – Scotland, Wales and Northern Ireland are each dealt with separately at the end of this chapter.

As noted above, the New Labour period did not see an abandonment of the Thatcherite emphasis on bringing a variety of partners into any regeneration process. Indeed, this was greatly expanded, with significant implications for the governance of regeneration, which will be discussed in the next chapter. Where Thatcher's governments expanded the number and variety of arm's length agencies dealing with regeneration, the New Labour period was characterised by a multiplication of state agencies until they reached dizzying heights of complexity. This process was made even more opaque by the tendency which developed to rebrand and repackage these agencies on a very regular basis, such that even experts found it difficult to keep track of the different policy initiatives and responsible bodies. A symbol of this complexity was the fact that yet another arm's length executive agency, the short-lived Academy for Sustainable Communities, was set up in 2005 to build capacity within local communities and other non-state actors to actually understand how the different bodies and initiatives fitted together in order to make regeneration happen.

The unresolved tension between regeneration and communities

New Labour's first term (1997–2001) saw a whole variety of exciting and innovative urban policies being floated. This was the era of the integrated Department of the Environment, Transport and the Regions (DETR), the Urban Task Force led by internationally renowned architect Richard Rogers, and the establishment of the Commission for Architecture and the Built Environment (CABE). But where the early rhetoric talked about regeneration as a holistic concept, bringing together built environment, transport, communities and regional development, in practice the alignment of physical redevelopment and social policy was more imagined than real. Indeed, during New Labour's second term (2001–05) the regeneration portfolio was reshuffled into the Office of the Deputy Prime Minister, which lost control over transport, regional growth and the environment. In 2006 there was yet another reorganisation, creating the Department for Communities and Local Government (CLG). Thus regeneration moved from being part of a holistic, integrated super-Ministry, with the backing of politically powerful Deputy Prime Minister John Prescott, to being in a weak department with a narrow portfolio headed by a succession of somewhat mediocre Ministers.

Although CLG retains responsibility for planning policy, the change of name to 'communities' is quite significant as it de-emphasises the macho world of altering physical forms. Instead the new name reminds us that the point of urban regeneration is not new buildings and townscapes, but rather that reforms to the physical environment are just one part of making life better for *people* – improving society and communities. Nonetheless, in the rough, tough world of struggles for power between different branches of the civil service, 'communities' does have a rather weak feel to it.

This book is primarily focused on regeneration as it affects the built environment, and the New Labour period saw a clear splitting off of physical regeneration from what became known as the 'renewal' of communities. This changing discourse under New Labour diluted the notion of regeneration as a holistic pursuit of improvements to society-environment-economy. There were some attempts to address this split, most notably through the Housing Market Renewal Pathfinders (see below), although with relatively limited success.

The major initiatives under the community 'renewal' portfolio were directed through the Neighbourhood Renewal Unit and associated fund which operated between 2001 and 2008. This fund targeted the 88 most deprived localities in England, spending £2.88bn (Neighbourhood Renewal Unit, 2007). Running in parallel to this was the New Deal for Communities (NDC), which was intended to produce a local response to local problems, tackling five key indicators of social deprivation: unemployment; crime; educational under-achievement; poor health; and problems with housing and the physical environment. There were problems, however, not least because the NDCs were not allowed to spend their funds on large-scale rebuilding programmes and so could do little for problems with housing and the environment. Again, this indicates the problem of the lack of joined-up working that remained unresolved during the New Labour period. Indeed, there was considerable under-spend of NDC resources as locally agreed targets were subsequently rejected at national level. As Imrie and Raco (2003: 27) noted, 'Communities are often "shoehorned" on to local policy initiatives according to central government guidelines … limiting the effectiveness of programmes on the ground.'

In many ways the NDCs typified a tension under New Labour between the rhetoric of bottom-up community empowerment and the setting of very rigid, centrally driven priorities for what issues could and could not be tackled. A culture of management through targets pervaded the New Labour years, not just in regeneration and community policy. Perhaps the most extreme example of this came with the Local Area Agreements. These evolved from a Treasury-driven concept of 'floor targets', where minimum standards were set in different areas and which local authorities were required to meet (Bailey, 2003). These targets were agreed locally through the Local Strategic Partnerships (LSPs), unelected bodies sitting across the same boundaries as local authorities. The Local Area Agreements (LAAs) were set up in 2007 to essentially act as a contract between central government, the LSP and the local authority to determine what indicators of communities under stress were the priorities for being tackled in a local area. This is a highly bureaucratic response, requiring a very large amount of paperwork and with a tendency to find ways of meeting the target, rather than addressing the problem which underlies the target. The LSPs thus became very powerful in setting the priorities for spending in an area, not least because they were responsible for distributing some of the funds coming down to local areas from central government. To reiterate, these bodies were unelected and the targets that they set were not subject to review by the local population that they were being applied to. Perhaps unsurprisingly, the LAAs were among the first things to be scrapped by the incoming Coalition government in 2010, which was committed to a dramatic simplification (and reduction) of public funding.

Urban Task Force, Urban White Paper

When it comes to transforming the physical infrastructure of cities, some of the approaches that are now taken for granted are legacies from the early New Labour period. The Urban White Paper, *Our Towns and Cities: The Future* (DETR, 2000) remains thus a very important document. It was partly based on the report of a Task Force commissioned by Deputy Prime Minister John Prescott to look at urban policy. Their report *Towards an Urban Renaissance* (Urban Task Force, 1999) reflected the optimism of the period and had a strong leaning towards the importance of high-quality design – unsurprising given the involvement of internationally renowned architect Richard Rogers. Praise was lavished on cities such as Barcelona, combining high-density housing, high standards of urban design and vibrant cultural identity. The Urban Task Force report was not without its critics (detailed by Cooper, 2000) and while the emphasis on urban design did find its way into the subsequent White Paper, it was not top of the priority list. Instead, issues of local involvement in decision-making, an emphasis on partnership working and a reinvigoration of local and regional government were emphasised first.

Perhaps the most important thing that came out of both the Urban Task Force report and the subsequent White Paper was a clear commitment to sustainability being at the heart of urban policy. Sustainability as a *concept* will be discussed in more detail in Chapter 5, but given its centrality to contemporary policy it must be briefly mentioned here. As the White Paper argued:

> We also have to bring together economic, social and environmental measures in a coherent approach to enable people and places to achieve their economic potential; bring social justice and equality of opportunity; and create places where people want to live and work. These issues are interdependent and cannot be looked at in isolation … That is why moving towards more mixed and sustainable communities is important to many of our plans for improving the quality of urban life. (DETR, 2000)

Note the close link between communities being 'mixed' and therefore 'sustainable'. Mixing is not only about demographics – income, age, family structure, ethnicity, etc. – but also about that live/work/play mix in the built form that the Urban Task Force stressed. This holistic notion of sustainability integrating economic, social and environmental concerns had a relatively coherent bureaucratic form under the DETR, but in the reorganisation after the 2001 election this integration was lost. Even though urban policy under the Coalition government has since diluted the meaning of sustainability still further, it is nonetheless impossible today to talk about regeneration without talking about sustainability.

Reforming planning policy

Planning policy has been significantly changed under the Coalition government since 2010, but there are also some clear continuities. The now defunct *Planning Policy Statement 1: Delivering Sustainable Development* stated that:

> Plans should be drawn up with community involvement and present a shared vision and strategy of how the area should develop to achieve more sustainable patterns of development. (ODPM, 2005c: 3)

This kind of statement has much in common with the Coalition government's emphasis on local decision-making and community involvement. Indeed, note the interdependence of strong, involved communities and sustainability within this discourse. While New Labour and the Coalition government have had quite different visions on how this should function in practice, both deploy similar rhetoric about the need to actively pursue sustainable development through community involvement.

One can see similar continuities in the Planning and Compulsory Purchase Act, 2004. Some of its innovations – in particular the Regional Spatial Strategies – have subsequently been scrapped. Other elements, however, have had a more lasting impact. Local Development Frameworks were introduced which were designed to give individual local authorities more flexibility in setting their priorities for development – although previously these had to be compatible with Regional Spatial Strategies. Since the abandonment of regional-level planning, Local Development Frameworks have become key documents determining the direction of planning at a local level.

The intention of the 2004 Act was to give developers more clarity and certainty about what local priorities were, in order to cut down the amount of time proposals languished within the planning system. This streamlining agenda was partly driven by the Barker Reviews. Again, these are significant because they foreshadow much of what the Coalition government talks about in terms of the direction for planning, in particular the emphasis on growth. Work on the Barker Reviews began in 2003 when Kate Barker, an economist and member of the Monetary Policy Committee, was asked by the Chancellor and the Deputy Prime Minister to produce a review of housing supply in the UK. When this review was commissioned, UK house prices had been rising steeply for a number of years and the Treasury was concerned that this was causing the economy to overheat, while the ODPM was concerned about affordability.

The first Barker report, *Delivering Stability: Securing our Future Housing Needs* (Barker, 2004) argued that housing supply was not being mapped onto demand. Allocations of housing land had hitherto been allocated by local authorities based on population projections rather than necessarily reflecting demand. The concern was that where areas had low demand, too much housing land might be released for development, while high-demand areas might see local authorities refusing further planning permissions in a given development cycle where their existing demographic targets had been met. Barker proposed that allocations of housing land should be more closely related to the market price of land.

The principle of land prices informing releases of housing land was subsequently adopted and informed the production of the Regional Spatial Strategies and, through them, the Local Development Frameworks. It is significant that, even under New Labour, the Treasury began to play a major role in determining planning policy, putting an emphasis on market mechanisms and economic expansion. The use of market mechanisms was quite controversial as it was seen as further encouraging the growth of the south east of England, where there is clearly a high market demand for development land, even in the aftermath of the credit crunch with house prices having stabilised. Lobby groups such as the Campaign to Protect Rural England were quick to express the belief that the need to forecast market needs up to 20 years ahead of time is problematic. If demand is not as high as forecast, the CPRE argued, house-builders will simply build at low densities to fill up the 'surplus' land (CPRE Oxfordshire, 2006).

Regardless of objections from the usual suspects, a second document, the *Barker Review of Land Use Planning* (Barker, 2006) swiftly followed. This was in the same vein as the housing review in that it called for a more market-determined view on organising the release of land for more general development. Indeed, there was also a view that, in certain circumstances, some reconfiguration of the green belt surrounding urban areas might be appropriate. The obvious critique of this was that if not carefully managed it could lead to a return to the boom of out-of-town shopping centres that occurred in the late 1980s. There is, after all, a clear market for such developments, although it would work against more general policy aims of revitalising urban centres and reducing reliance on car-based transport. The review also called for significant changes to the planning process in an attempt to give developers a clearer sense of what was required and thus speed up the processing of applications, with a slow planning process seen by the Treasury as a major brake on economic development. Again, much of the second Barker report resonates strongly with the reforms to planning policy that came about with the release of the Coalition government's *National Planning Policy Framework* (CLG, 2012e).

Coordinating public and private sector activity

One of the defining characteristics of the New Labour period was the dramatic growth in size and complexity of quangos operating at a variety of different scales, whilst at the same time placing an imperative on regeneration activity to bring together public and private sector as well as the community. There were a number of different attempts to find ways of coordinating activity across these different bodies. One of these attempts came through reviving an older model, the Urban Development Corporation. This decision was interesting because the UDCs, the most Thatcherite of regeneration tools, have always proved tremendously divisive, not least because they bypassed local authority control. The UDCs also placed an emphasis on physical regeneration over social and were always open to the accusation of being little more than state-sponsored **gentrification**. Nonetheless, UDCs became central to the delivery of development in the Thames Gateway (see Chapter 8) although both Thurrock and Thames Gateway Development Corporations were earmarked for closure in 2010 as part of the '**bonfire of the quangos**' (see below).

Urban Regeneration Companies (URCs) have been a somewhat less controversial vehicle for coordination at a local level. These were considered key to the delivery of the Urban White Paper, 2000, and at their height some 23 were operating in England, though at the time of writing only four remain. Unlike the old Urban Development Corporations, they were not set up with the assumption that the local authority has failed and therefore needs to be bypassed — in fact local authorities were seen as key partners. The idea was that the URC should set out a **masterplan** for the regeneration of a specific area, which would guide public sector investment in infrastructure and lever in private capital. URCs themselves do not have significant resources, simply acting to bring the other agents together with a clear focus on physical redevelopment rather than community renewal. The URCs have, however, been involved in very significant projects. The Sheffield One URC, for example, helped crystallise plans to transform the old rail and bus stations into a much more attractive point of entry to the city. Liverpool Vision, one of the first URCs, was involved in the dramatic transformation of the Ropewalks district into a cultural quarter as well as in the vast Paradise Street redevelopment in the commercial core.

Many of the original URCs (including Liverpool and Sheffield) have subsequently been transformed into Economic Development Companies (EDCs), with an emphasis on economic development rather than physical planning. Nonetheless, the geography of the URC/EDC model is interesting. With a few exceptions, these bodies are disproportionately concentrated in the northern former industrial heartlands, suggesting that these areas still face major challenges requiring state intervention. Because these bodies did not attract large-scale public funding to begin with, they seem likely to continue despite cuts. Indeed, with reductions in public spending, collaboration between public and private sector to help deliver regeneration is ever more crucial, meaning that agencies for coordinating this activity at local level are likely to continue in some form under the Coalition government even if they end up being called something different.

The rise of 'design-led' regeneration

In 1997, the country clearly had a distinct problem dealing with a very troubled **legacy** of post-war urban design which needed to be addressed. Simply knocking down the worst of the1960s buildings does not, in itself, solve the problem of poor design and there were major questions about the quality of buildings that had been erected in the name of regeneration during the 1990s. The Urban Task Force thus had a distinct design-led flavour and there were other reforms in the first New Labour term that emphasised the importance of good quality architecture and spatial planning in UK cities. The Royal Fine Art Commission (RFAC) had been set up in 1924 and had the power to call in and comment on development plans – though it had no statutory power to enforce changes. In 1999, RFAC was reborn as CABE (Commission for Architecture and the Built Environment). Alongside the Urban Task Force, CABE was closely associated with the personal interests of the Deputy Prime Minister John Prescott, and its creation brought with it a clearer remit to promote high-quality design, both through commenting on major development plans and providing advice to developers and various public bodies. As with RFAC, however, CABE's advice was not statutorily binding and its main power was in naming and shaming poor design through its Design Review Comments, a role it retained after its merger with the Design Council in 2011.

During the New Labour period the emphasis on good design was arguably more successful in helping to spur a succession of flagship buildings by name architects, rather than increasing the quality of everyday architecture. Nonetheless, there were some attempts to improve quality more broadly through the use of design coding, piloted by CABE. This was subsequently adopted into English planning policy and remains a principle within the new National Planning Policy Framework (CLG, 2012e), though there is a presumption against local authorities using codes to be too prescriptive about acceptable designs in a given neighbourhood.

Construction policy

Where the Urban Task Force is perhaps the most visible symbol of New Labour's aspirations for UK cities, it was Sir John Egan's Construction Task Force which has arguably had a more lasting impact. Sir John was not a construction industry insider and his review highlighted concerns with the flexibility of the building industry, in particular the difficulties faced when introducing new practices and new technologies as well as the kinds of training needed by construction workers and managers to help meet these new challenges. Egan particularly identified the advantages of longer-term partnerships between construction firms and developers, noting the cost and quality advantages that these arrangements brought to the housing association sector (Construction Task Force, 1998). The original review has fed into a broader Egan agenda supported through Constructing Excellence, a cross-sector body which draws on both public and private funds to promote best practice. The construction industry has a major role to play in meeting targets on sustainability because of the very large impact that construction has on the environment. By helping to restructure how the industry operates, the Egan agenda encouraged the much wider application of new technologies and practices which has driven more sustainable construction.

This agenda of sustainable construction has also been driven by a progressive tightening up of the Building Regulations, with ever more stringent standards of insulation and energy use. The Regulations have also been altered to minimise other environmental impacts of new construction, such as reducing the quantity of surface water runoff through the use of sustainable drainage systems (SuDS). The Building Research Establishment also drove this agenda through its Environmental Assessment Method (BREEAM) and the EcoHomes standards. Many of these ideas were subsequently absorbed into the CLG's Code for Sustainable Homes, launched in 2006. Level 6 of that Code is for homes which are effectively carbon neutral, in that they generate sufficient energy from renewable sources to 'pay back' any energy they draw from the national grid. New Labour subsequently set a target for all new buildings to meet level 6 of the Code by 2016.

In practice the industry has struggled to meet this target and the Coalition government subsequently redefined what 'carbon neutral' meant in the context of housing to make it easier to achieve. Regardless of the compromises, this remains a significant policy aspiration, indicating that issues around sustainability and climate change that arose under New Labour remain at the heart of government policy.

The Sustainable Communities Plan

Some of the most lasting physical legacies of the New Labour period came about as a result of the Sustainable Communities Plan. It was launched in February 2003 and prioritised interventions in:

- The 20% most deprived wards in England
- Former coalmining areas
- Growth areas in the south east (Milton Keynes and the south Midlands, the London-Stansted-Cambridge-Peterborough Corridor, Thames Gateway and Ashford)
- The northern growth corridor
- Strategic areas of brownfield land
- The Housing Market Renewal Pathfinder areas. (ODPM, 2003)

The Plan document was not uncontroversial, not least because it proposed an additional 200,000 homes in the 'growth areas' in the south east of England, most notably in the Thames Gateway area. To many critics then, the Sustainable Communities Plan therefore gave a mandate to 'concrete-over' the south east while doing little to rebalance economic growth across the English regions.

The main tools introduced by the Sustainable Communities Plan for attempting to encourage growth in economically stagnant areas were the Housing Market Renewal Pathfinders. These bodies, which operated between 2003 and 2011, were perhaps the ultimate expression of the tensions inherent in New Labour's attempts to regenerate communities whilst sticking to a profoundly market-informed approach. Twelve Pathfinders were set up covering fairly small areas in the Midlands and the north of England where it was deemed that the housing market was near collapse resulting in abandoned houses and a decayed physical environment. The Pathfinders had a remit to restart the housing market by making their operating areas more attractive to homebuyers. This was mostly to be achieved through demolition of obsolete homes and reconstruction with new housing and other infrastructure. On one level, this was quite an enlightened initiative, recognising the very different challenges faced in certain parts of the country compared to the high-demand south east (see Box 2.1).

BOX 2.1   BRIDGING NEWCASTLEGATESHEAD PATHFINDER

As one of the nine Housing Market Renewal Pathfinders established by the Sustainable Communities Plan, Bridging NewcastleGateshead (BNG) covers the inner areas of both Newcastle and Gateshead. The conurbation is still feeling the effects of post-industrial decline and is being hit particularly hard by cuts imposed by the Coalition government as its economy is heavily dependent on the public sector. The BNG was intended to run for 15 years, but was closed down in 2011, just halfway through its planned lifespan. The Pathfinder was responsible for an area containing 140,000 people and 77,000 dwellings, of which 47% were socially rented and 40% owner-occupied. Vacancy levels were at 7%, which is comparatively high, and there was a 6% population decline between the 1991 and 2011 censuses (Leather et al., 2007: 134).

During its lifetime, the BNG demolished 2,855 properties, created 348 new dwellings and improved a further 6,888. The second phase of the project had been intended to see the delivery of a further 4,000 properties, but the collapse of the housing market after 2008 and subsequent abolition of the BNG meant that this was never realised. The future of the sites purchased and cleared with a view to creating attractive new properties remains in some doubt (Bridging NewcastleGateshead, 2011).

Between 2003 and 2011, £2.24bn was allocated to the Pathfinders, making it a very substantial programme. The Pathfinders were also expected to draw in resources from other public sector funding streams, such as the Neighbourhood Renewal Fund and the New Deal for Communities, suggesting a concern with wider social issues as well as physical redevelopment. Stuart Cameron (2006) argued, however, that the Pathfinder initiative shifted from its initial concern with communities suffering housing abandonment. Instead, the focus became a more general drive to 'modernise' areas to fit in with broader regional economic policy through reviving the housing market, rather than prioritising the particular needs of individual communities/areas. Over the first five years of the policy, 16,000 properties were demolished, but only 3,700 new homes were built (HCA, 2011). The rhetoric was of improving quality, rather than quantity, in areas of low demand, but there was an understandable suspicion by local communities that a land grab was taking place, clearing out deprived communities to make room for wealthier incomers. As early as 2005, CABE's review of how the Pathfinders were progressing talked about the need to work at a sub-regional level and consult carefully with communities to identify the source of problems in particular areas (CABE, 2005a). Any programme which seeks to physically reconfigure an area and bring in new residents is always open to the charge that it represents little more than gentrification and this accusation dogged the Pathfinders.

The Pathfinders were symbolic of New Labour's failure to rebalance economic growth from the overheated south east towards more deprived regions. Their funding was abruptly cut in 2011, leaving only a small pot of transition money to help residents who had been left in areas which had already been partly demolished pending redevelopment (CLG, 2011a). The Pathfinder programme was set up with good intentions, but the tension between community need and a market-based approach was never resolved and, given the very large amount of funding they absorbed, it is little surprise that they were unceremoniously axed as part of the Coalition government's crusade to reduce public spending.

Key points

i)   The split between community renewal and physical regeneration emerged at an early stage in the New Labour period and was never resolved.

ii) The Treasury-driven Barker reviews made market demand a key mechanism for informing medium-term local planning strategies.

iii) The idea of bringing together public and private sector (as well as communities) to undertake regeneration became firmly entrenched under New Labour, resulting in a whole series of executive agencies which attempted to coordinate this activity.

iv) The Sustainable Communities Plan drove large-scale building programmes in the south east and major reconstruction projects in the Pathfinder areas. This was one of the most controversial legacies of the New Labour period.

Contemporary policy in England

Traditional **Keynesian economics** suggests that during a recession public spending needs to be maintained, or even increased, in order to stabilise the economy and allow growth to restart. The election of the Conservative-led Coalition government in May 2010 brought the New Labour period of high public spending to a close. The new government came to power with an ideological commitment to cut public spending in order to eliminate the budget deficit thus rejecting Keynesianism and returning to a fundamentally neoliberal economic approach. This has had a series of knock-on effects for urban regeneration policy. Prime among these has been the so-called 'bonfire of the quangos' and the rise of the linked concepts of the **Big Society** and **Localism**.

The bonfire of the quangos and creation of the LEPs

The proliferation of executive, arm's-length agencies was one of the defining characteristics of the New Labour government and was highly controversial. Liberal Democrat members of the Coalition government were concerned with the lack of democratic accountability inherent in these bodies, while Conservatives have a more general commitment to reducing the size of the state. In October 2010 there was a headline-grabbing initiative to scrap 192 of these 'quangos' (BBC, 2010). Looking below the surface a little, only around half of these were actually being completely abolished, others having their functions merged or reabsorbed into government departments (see Box 2.2). Nonetheless, from a regeneration point of view there was one major change – the demise of English regional government – and a series of smaller changes as different agencies were merged, shuffled and scrapped.

BOX 2.2   EXECUTIVE AGENCIES REPORTING TO CLG REVIEWED IN THE 2010 'BONFIRE OF THE QUANGOS'

Advisory Panel for the Local Innovation Awards Scheme	**Abolish**
Advisory Panel on Standards for the Planning Inspectorate	**Abolish**
Architects Registration Board	**Retain**
Audit Commission for Local Authorities and the National Health Service in England	**Abolish** – transfer function into private sector

(Continued)

BOX 2.2   *(Continued)*

Building Regulations Advisory Committee	**Retain**
Commission for Administration (also known as Local Government Ombudsman)	**Retain**
Community Development Foundation	**Abolish** – transfer function to charitable sector
Firebuy	**Abolish** – transfer functions into CLG
Homes and Communities Agency	**Retain and reform**
Independent Housing Ombudsman Ltd	**Retain**
Infrastructure Planning Commission	**Abolish** – transfer functions into Planning Inspectorate
The Leasehold Advisory Service	**Retain**
London Thames Gateway Development Corporation	**Abolish** – transfer functions to local authorities
National Housing and Planning Advice Unit	**Abolish**
National Tenant Voice	**Abolish**
Olympic Park Legacy Company Ltd	**Abolish** – transfer to the Mayor of London's office
Ordnance Survey	**Retain**
Rent Assessment Panels / Residential Property Tribunal Service	**Abolish** – transfer function to Ministry of Justice
Standards Board for England	**Abolish**
The Office for Tenants and Social Landlords (also known as Tenant Services Authority)	**Abolish** – transfer functions into Homes and Communities Agency
Thurrock Development Corporation	**Abolish** – transfer functions to local authorities
Valuation Tribunal for England	**Abolish** – transfer function to Ministry of Justice
Valuation Tribunal Service	**Abolish** – transfer function to Ministry of Justice
West Northamptonshire Development Corporation	**Abolish** – transfer functions to local authorities

The regional tier of government in England, established under New Labour, never operated in a coherent fashion, particularly after the failure to establish meaningful and directly elected regional assemblies. The (unelected) assemblies had already been scrapped toward the end of the New Labour period, but the Coalition government went further by removing the Regional Government Offices, the Regional Development Agencies (RDAs) and the Regional Spatial Strategies. Almost nothing of the New Labour experiment in English regional government now remains, with the exception of London, discussed below.

The RDAs were a major conduit for spending government money at the regional level, taking a strategic role in: planning; funding area-based redevelopments (flagship buildings in particular); coordinating large infrastructure projects; and managing local bids for European funds. Their replacement, the Local Enterprise Partnerships (LEPs), have much smaller resources available to them and a more restricted remit. Local authorities and businesses were invited to collaborate in putting bids together to become a LEP 'whose geography properly reflects the natural economic areas of England', according to the Local Growth White Paper (BIS, 2010: 12). This quote reflects the discourse coming out of the Coalition government, that English regional government had been arbitrarily imposed and did not reflect the realities of local needs and priorities – indeed, acting as an expensive brake rather than an enabler of local economic activity.

Where the RDAs had significant power independent of the local authorities within the region, it is anticipated that the LEPs will play more of a coordinating role *between* local authorities and local businesses. This includes collaborative working on infrastructure projects, particularly transport, and attempts to strategically plan in areas such as housing provision within the LEP region, pooling local authority resources to maximise returns. Nonetheless, where the RDAs had very deep pockets, with substantial allocations of funding from central government to spend regionally, the LEPs will not act as a major funder in their own right for local projects. This represents a very large cut in public funding for regeneration. The LEPs will coordinate bids to the new Regional Growth Fund, a £1.4bn pot set to run from 2011 to 2014 and allocated on a competitive basis by the Department for Business, Innovation and Skills (BIS). The Regional Growth Fund is, however, primarily concerned with providing investment in job creation by private enterprise, rather than activity directly connected to physical regeneration. Outside London, the Homes and Communities Agency will take on some of the responsibilities for regeneration that the RDAs held, but without substantial increases in funding available.

The Homes and Communities Agency is a good place to start when considering the other changes to regeneration policy brought about by the bonfire of the quangos. The Agency was another creation toward the end of the New Labour period, merging the land and development interests of English Partnerships and the social housing remit of the Housing Corporation. The Coalition government has retained the body, though slashed its administrative budget and passed its responsibilities for London over to the Greater London Authority. Although still responsible for the

£4.5bn Affordable Homes programme (2011–15), it has also suffered major cuts, including £1.9bn of schemes being scrapped in 2010 (Johnstone, 2010). This had a major impact on a variety of regeneration projects in social housing areas, such as Birmingham's Lyndhurst estate and Southwark's Aylesbury estate.

Another New Labour innovation closed by the Coalition government was the Sustainable Development Commission. Established in 2000, it was intended to be a UK-wide watchdog on issues around environmental sustainability, reporting not only to Westminster, but to the governments in Wales, Scotland and Northern Ireland. One of its key roles was in monitoring how well sustainability targets were met on the government's own land and property, effectively pushing the government to act as a champion of more environmentally friendly approaches to the built environment. Guidance was also produced on a range of issues from energy efficiency and transport to resource use and education. The body was finally wound up in 2011, leaving the government without an independent advisor on sustainable development. This is significant because, as we shall see in the next section, a major overhaul has placed sustainable development (broadly defined) at the heart of the planning system.

Big Society, Localism and the reformed planning system

The Big Society is a concept that confused voters on the doorsteps in 2010. The origins of the term are murky and its definition ambiguous, but it was a major plank in the Conservative manifesto at the election and found its way into the subsequent Coalition agreement. At its core, the Big Society seeks to transform public services, asking communities themselves to become more directly involved, in some cases actually taking over delivery of local services. This fits into the broad neoliberal commitment to reducing the overall size of the state, accompanied by a somewhat moralistic belief that an individual's 'dependence' on the state is inherently wrong and instead communities ought to be encouraged to look after themselves.

Although the Big Society was condemned on the political left as a smokescreen for savage cuts to the public sector, it nonetheless represents a sea change in thinking about the relationship between state and society. Regeneration and, in particular, planning policy have been significantly rethought as part of the process of attempting to realise the Big Society. The two most significant manifestations of this were the Localism Act, 2011, and the reformed *National Planning Policy Framework* (CLG, 2012e).

The Localism Act, 2011, has much wider concerns than regeneration, but some elements have significant knock-on effects. Since the end of World War II the power of local authorities in England has been significantly eroded, leaving them considerably weaker in many ways than comparable public bodies in Europe and North America, with extremely high levels of control imposed by central government. In a major philosophical change, the 2011 Act gave local authorities the freedom to undertake *any* activity not explicitly prohibited by law. This general power of competence, it is hoped, will promote innovative working by local authorities who would previously have feared sanction from Whitehall if they stepped outside the centrally dictated list of permissible activities. Potentially this gives more freedom to local authorities to find new ways of 'doing' regeneration in their areas, though the effects of this are yet to be seen in practice.

The Act has a number of interesting mechanisms which operate at the (vaguely defined) 'community' scale. Community Right to Buy gives locals the right to intervene when a community asset (village hall, playing fields, etc.) is due to be sold off. Communities are given the opportunity to put a bid together and raise the funds to buy and manage the asset themselves. Where Parish Councils do not exist, residents can establish Neighbourhood Forums to draw up Neighbourhood Development Plans and even produce Neighbourhood Development Orders, outlining the kinds of development they want in their area. Neighbourhood Forums can also deploy the Community Right to Build mechanism which encourages communities to work together with a developer to come up with a plan for new housing, business premises, community assets and so on in their area. A local referendum can then be held to approve the plans drawn up which, although not statutorily binding, must be taken into account by the local planning authority when considering whether or not to allow the development to go ahead. The intention is that local communities will thus be able to have the kinds of development they want in their locality (Layard, 2012).

Putting a project together, whether for saving a community asset or creating new buildings, is, however, an incredibly complex and time-consuming business. The principle of increased local control is relatively uncontroversial, but the practicalities of actually delivering this element of the Big Society are somewhat problematic. Indeed, the Regional Centres of Excellence, which were established in 2003 to assist communities in developing the skills to engage with regeneration programmes, were scrapped as part of the bonfire of the quangos in 2010. The danger therefore is that the only people who will be able to engage with this element of the Big Society are wealthy, articulate, middle-class professionals with time on their hands. The other flaw, particularly for the Neighbourhood Forums, is that building anything tends to be very controversial, making it difficult first to get a coherent proposal together with a developer, and second to get it approved in a local referendum. As such, it is unlikely that these mechanisms are ever going to be extensively used, but they do offer a potentially interesting route for some communities to take a little more control over their locality.

A reform which is having a more significant impact is the scrapping of the Regional Spatial Strategies. Although not formally withdrawn until the Localism Act, 2011, was passed, local authorities were instructed to ignore the Regional Spatial Strategies from 2010. These were one of the most controversial elements of English regional government under New Labour because, among other things, they set house-building targets for each local authority. The lack of democratic account-ability underpinning these documents was seen as particularly problematic. Although local authorities were part of a negotiation process, ultimately these documents were written at regional level, had statutory force and imposed targets. Nonetheless, while there were significant flaws in the New Labour approach to regional planning, these documents did allow for more strategic considerations to be taken into account, such as regional growth and the need to create suitable infrastructure to support this. The cooperative approach between local authorities intended to be fostered by the Local Enterprise Partnerships represents a weakening of the capacity for more stra-tegic decision-making on planning across local authority boundaries.

Another major strategic change was the scrapping of the Infrastructure Planning Commission. This was a late period New Labour invention, establishing a strategic body at arm's length from the government, which was therefore nominally impar-tial, to undertake decisions on major projects such as airports, roads, rail, power stations, and so on. The idea was to speed decision-making, partly in response to the painfully slow process of approving plans to build Heathrow Terminal 5, which took eight years from first submitted plan to approval. The Commission was scrapped as part of the Localism Act, 2011, with final approval of decisions returned to the rel-evant Secretary of State. The trade-off here is between a direct line of democratic accountability on major planning decisions and non-partisan review of how schemes contribute to strategic planning priorities. Both positions have merits, although the fact that the third runway at Heathrow was controversially signed-off by Ministers in 2009, just before the Commission was given control over airport expansion, suggests that there may be some merits to independent review. (The third runway decision was subsequently reversed by Ministers as one of the first actions of the Coalition government in May 2010.)

Alongside the Localism Act there was a major reform of planning guidance for England, scrapping the 24 Planning Policy Statements/Guidance Notes which cov-ered a variety of different topics including greenbelts, biodiversity, town centre developments and flood risk, to name just a few. These documents which, with supplements, represented a substantial quantity of text, were replaced by the *National Planning Policy Framework* (CLG, 2012e). This is a much shorter document, summa-rising some elements from the previous statements. The concept of 'sustainable development' is key to the Framework; however, the definition of sustainability that it uses is not one that would please a 'deep green' activist. Issues of sustainability will be discussed at length in Chapter 5, though it is important to note that this docu-ment does acknowledge the need to address economic, social and environmental sustainability together. Nonetheless, the order in which these three elements of sustainability are listed is telling.

According to the *National Planning Policy Framework*, the purpose of the planning system is to deliver *growth*, but to do so only in accordance with the principles of sustainable development. This emphasis on growth is significant because it leads to the most important change that this document represents – that planning should operate on the presumption that projects applying for planning permission should always go ahead so long as they meet the principles of sustainable development. This *presumption of development* places a great weight of responsibility on the concept of 'sustainable development' to prevent the worst excesses of unrestrained growth. Responding to the initial draft of the Framework, the National Trust argued that the emphasis on growth ran the risk of returning to 1930s-style **urban sprawl** (National Trust, 2011). Though significantly shorter than the documents it replaces, the Framework still contains many of the previous checks and balances, particularly the greenbelts surrounding urban areas which have been highly effective in preventing major expansions of existing urban areas since the 1950s. Nonetheless, the presumption of growth does represent a significant shift, the consequences of which will probably not become clear until the economic conditions favour a return to large-scale house-building.

Key points

i) Cuts to public spending and an attempt to reduce the bureaucratic complexity surrounding regeneration have led to a dramatic simplification of the number of agencies and funding streams working in this area.

ii) The Local Enterprise Partnerships are intended to produce a more collaborative approach to regional development, but they lack the generous funding that was available to the old Regional Development Agencies.

iii) Discourses of the 'Big Society' and 'Localism' put the emphasis on communities taking much greater control over and responsibility for planning issues.

iv) Reforms to the planning system place an emphasis on growth and a presumption of permission being granted so long as the development is considered 'sustainable' – although the meaning of sustainability has been somewhat diluted.

Devolution

Perhaps the most significant long-term shift signalled by the 1997 election was devolving a degree of power to Scotland, Wales and Northern Ireland – something which had been fiercely resisted by Conservative administrations. Unlike the largely botched attempt at creating regional government in England, devolution to the Celtic fringe proceeded very smoothly, in part perhaps due to the fact that real power was on offer. Each of the three regions had previously been controlled by a dedicated government department at Westminster, and although there was some variation from English policy – particularly in Scotland – there was an overall coherence. Since the new Welsh and Northern Ireland Assemblies and Scottish Parliament have been established there has been more of an opportunity for regionally distinctive policies for urban regeneration to be devised and this has happened to various degrees in different areas.

Conversely, the English regional assemblies had no democratic mandate, few powers and little role beyond strategic planning. The exception to this was in London where a new regional government was established with a powerful, directly elected Mayor and Assembly with a wide range of powers. Unsurprisingly, therefore, London's governing structures survived the Coalition government's 2010 bonfire of the quangos relatively intact – doubtless helped by the fact that the Mayor at that time was Boris Johnson, a popular and charismatic member of the Conservative party.

London

When New Labour came to power in 1997, London had not had a city-wide government since the Greater London Council was scrapped by Margaret Thatcher in 1986. Following a local referendum, the Greater London Authority (GLA) was established in 2000, comprising an Assembly and a Mayor elected by all Londoners – giving the Mayor the largest personal mandate of any politician in the UK. Labour rebel Ken Livingstone was the first Mayor, followed by the election of Conservative Boris Johnson in 2008 and again in 2012. The individual London boroughs retain significant powers, however, meaning that the GLA has no remit on a number of key issues, for example, education.

The main job of the elected Assembly members is to hold the actions of the Mayor to account. The Mayor was originally given direct control over four key bodies: Transport for London; the London Development Agency; the Metropolitan Police Authority; and the London Fire and Emergency Planning Authority. The London Development Agency, which played a similar role to the RDAs in the rest of England, was folded into the GLA administration as part of the Coalition government's reforms to public sector bodies in 2010. At the same time, the GLA also gained control over the London remit of the Homes and Communities Agency, which gave it significant land resources and powers over the funding of social housing. Indeed, the abolition of the Olympic Park Legacy Company led to a further transfer of powers into the GLA.

The result of these changes is that where sub-national government in England generally was significantly weakened by the reforms imposed by the Coalition government, the GLA's powers were actually strengthened. The Coalition government had planned to expand the model with more directly elected mayors across English cities, but this has proved unpopular at the ballot box. Of ten English cities that held a referendum on the issue in 2012, only Bristol voted in favour and even there by a narrow margin on a very low turnout.

Scotland

Of the new governments established in the constituent countries of the UK after 1997, Scotland's is by far the most powerful. Scots voted overwhelmingly in favour in a referendum both on devolution and granting tax-raising powers to a devolved Parliament. Since 1999, Scotland has therefore had a measure of independence, though not full sovereignty. Scotland is, however, quite a divided country between the highly urbanised central belt around Glasgow and Edinburgh and the largely rural highlands and islands. The densely populated central belt thus has a significant role in the electoral politics of Scotland, comprising half of the country's population and economic activity (Bailey and Turok, 2001), as well as providing the power base for the rival Labour and Scottish National Parties. Since devolution, Scotland has been governed first by a Labour–Liberal Democrat Coalition then, between 2007 and 2011, a Scottish National Party (SNP) minority administration. This has resulted in a much more pragmatic, consensual approach to policy-making north of the border, preventing both partisan and central belt interests from dominating. The SNP majority government elected in 2011 offers the potential for a still more distinctly Scottish approach to policy, with an independent Scotland as a desired end point.

The Scottish Parliament oversees the Scottish Government (previously the Scottish Executive), which deals with the day-to-day delivery of policy. Prior to devolution, the Westminster-controlled Scottish Office established a number of quangos such as Scottish Homes to tackle aspects of regeneration. Where quangos proliferated under New Labour in England, post-devolution most of these functions were being taken back into direct control under the Scottish Government. One major quango remains, Scottish Enterprise, which essentially acts as a regional development agency for the country. The focus is primarily economic development, but this body has put resources into a number of key strategic regeneration schemes – for example, the redevelopment of the Clyde Waterfront.

The Scottish Government is organised into a number of Directorates, which tackle different themes, overseen by a cabinet-style system of Ministers drawn from Members of the Scottish Parliament (MSPs) belonging to the governing party. From a regeneration perspective, the most important Directorate is Governance and Communities. Each Directorate has a number of sub-directorates, dealing with specific issues, such as those for Planning, Housing and Regeneration and the Built Environment. Since 2007 the balance of power between the Scottish Government and the individual local authorities in Scotland has been shifted following the agree-ment of a Concordat. This dramatically simplified the funding made available to local authorities, giving much more freedom to determine spending locally, work-ing in line with a Single Outcome Agreement (SOA) drawn up between the local authority and the Government. These SOAs cover a number of areas, not simply regeneration, and are overseen by Community Planning Partnerships. These operate in the same fashion as England's Local Strategic Partnerships, coordinating between different public and private agencies as well as, nominally, communities.

Devolved government does not mean that Scotland ignores trends in wider policy circles, just that the details of application can differ. A good example of this is with the notion of cultural clustering. The economic arguments behind this will be discussed in more detail in Chapter 4, but, put briefly, there is a belief, influenced by the ideas of Richard Florida (2002), that cities in which both traditional and alternative cultural resources abound will attract economic growth through the 'creative' industries. Cities and regions across North America and Europe have thus been looking at ways of nurturing these cultural resources. The Scottish Government produced a National Cultural Strategy which seeks to encourage the growth of cultural clusters within Scottish cities, both facilitating existing ones, such as in Glasgow, and developing new ones, such as in Dundee. While this policy is not without its critics (see, for instance, McCarthy, 2006), it does reflect an attempt to give a regional spin to a 'fashionable' policy idea – something that has been facilitated by devolution.

There have also been circumstances where the Scottish Executive directly takes on a policy structure from England. In terms of urban regeneration, the most noteworthy adoption has been that of the urban regeneration company (URC) model. Six URCs were established in Scotland following an evaluation of the English and Welsh URCs which indicated that the private sector was more willing to invest in these areas because the presence of a URC indicated a willingness by local public sector actors to work together in a coordinated way. Riverside Inverclyde URC, for example, has been championing a major development around the historic James Watt Dock, levering in investment from developers Peel Holdings for a refurbishment of the historic Sugar Warehouse and securing public funds for a new £2.2m access road to the site (Fergus, 2011).

Wales

Where Scots were given the opportunity to vote in favour of setting up their own Parliament, Welsh voters were only offered an Assembly, with fewer powers. Furthermore, the Welsh were not given the opportunity to vote on whether the Assembly would have the power to vary taxation within the Principality. Prior to 2007 there was no separate executive branch of government with all powers held by the Welsh Assembly, a somewhat clumsy arrangement indicating the relatively limited nature of Welsh devolution as originally conceived. Once established, however, the Welsh Government began to take more direct control over policy-making within the principality. Following a referendum in 2011, the power of the Welsh Government to propose legislation to the Assembly has been extended in 20 areas including matters around planning, housing and economic development.

Because the passing of powers to Wales has progressed somewhat more slowly than in Scotland, regeneration policy has not yet deviated far from English approaches. This said, the Welsh Development Agency, the quango responsible for economic development, was merged back into the Welsh Government in 2006, foreshadowing the scrapping of the English regional development agencies in 2010. The Welsh Government currently follows a similar structure to Scotland, with a series of Directorates overseeing sub-departments, with Ministers drawn from Assembly members providing the political direction.

Functions connected to regeneration are spread across a number of different Directorates and Departments. The Housing, Regeneration and Heritage Department sits within the Sustainable Futures Directorate, but economic development and transport functions sit within the Business, Enterprise, Technology and Science Directorate. In terms of the social aspects of regeneration, Wales has been operating the Communities First scheme since 2001, which targets pockets of high deprivation with relatively small-scale interventions to address local needs in terms of skills, youth training, food cooperatives and so on. Addressing issues of physical infrastructure, the Welsh Government provides capital grants, particularly targeting Renewal Areas within individual local authorities.

On the larger scale, Wales has adopted the urban regeneration company (URC) mechanism, but only one such body has ever been set up. Newport Unlimited URC is currently coordinating a series of major projects to transform the central area of the city by 2020 as well as areas around disused portions of the Llanwern steel works and junction 28 of the M4 motorway. The model of multiple partners coming together to deliver this quite radical reconfiguration of Newport is in line with how the URCs operate both in England and Scotland.

Northern Ireland

Devolution in Northern Ireland has been a somewhat more tortuous process as it was tied to a peace process attempting to resolve tensions between elements within the protestant and catholic communities. The Belfast, or 'Good Friday' agreement signed in 1998, paved the way to a referendum on a system predicated on the sharing of power between the largest parties of the Unionist and Nationalist communities. Urban regeneration is thus caught up in a unique political context in the UK and is set up with very rigorous procedures to ensure that neither community is seen to be gaining an unfair advantage in terms of public policy and public spending. Progress in the development of regeneration policy within the province was hampered by the suspension of the Northern Ireland Assembly 2002–07 due to protracted arguments between the different political parties over the direction of the peace process.

The Northern Ireland Executive leads the formulation of policy, with scrutiny by the Assembly. In a significant difference from the situation in most democratic systems, Ministers are not selected from the largest party (or parties in the case of a coalition) but rather by the d'Hondt system. This means that Ministers are selected proportionally from all parties with a significant number of seats in the Assembly. This was a key element in making the Good Friday Agreement work, preventing sectarian interests from dominating government. The main result of this is very careful juggling of different priorities across the different parts of the Executive falling under the remits of different parties. An example of how the province's history uniquely affects urban policy is that communities in Northern Ireland are able to draw on funds from the **EU**'s Peace II programme. This scheme is designed to promote ongoing peace-making efforts in formerly conflict ridden parts of the EU and funds up to 75% of costs for urban renewal and neighbourhood development projects.

Interestingly, in Northern Ireland regeneration falls squarely under the Department for Social Development, suggesting that the split between social and physical regeneration is less apparent in the province. In order to ensure that neither protestant nor catholic communities are seen to be benefiting 'unfairly' from initiatives designed to tackle social need, multi-criteria scoring has been introduced to set priorities. These scores are derived from census data and weighted according to a complex set of multi-scaled calculations which go right down to the Enumeration District level. Brian Robson of Manchester University produced the first of these scoring tools in 1994 and this was subsequently revised by Michael Noble of Oxford University in 2001 (Northern Ireland Assembly, 2002). The 'Noble Index' is thus a key tool in implementing the 2003 People and Place strategy for Neighbourhood Renewal. Thirty-six areas have been targeted for action based on their scores, mostly concentrated in the two major urban centres, with 15 in Belfast and 6 in Londonderry/Derry. The People and Place strategy stresses the importance of engaging local people with meaningful participation in the renewal process as well as attempting to ensure that the renewal does not further the process of community segregation.

Evidence of this need to ensure meaningful community engagement was even apparent in the Laganside Urban Development Corporation, in spite of the UDC model being overwhelmingly driven by a physical infrastructure and economic development agenda. Laganside Corporation proudly boasted that between its inception in 1989 and ceasing operations in 2007 it secured:

- Over £900m of investment in the area
- 14,200 jobs
- 213,000m² of office space
- 83,000m² completed retail/leisure space
- Over 700 completed housing units. (Laganside Corporation, 2007)

At the same time, however, the Corporation also funded community projects within its area and its annual reports are run through with assessments of how the organisation and its actions comply with legal requirements to promote tolerance and equality. In Northern Ireland, community, politics and physical renewal truly cannot be considered separately.

Key points

i) Devolution has resulted in regional regeneration powers being subjected to much closer democratic scrutiny.

ii) Regional devolution has driven some innovative approaches to regeneration, although there are significant common threads, particularly around sustainability and community engagement.

iii) Meaningful devolution of powers has driven a much closer integration of social policies with physical regeneration than is the case in England with its parallel discourse of community 'renewal'.

Further reading

A key problem with a chapter of this kind is that it dates rapidly. Government web-sites are one of the only ways to really keep abreast of the latest policy initiatives, as well as providing relatively easy access to policy reviews commissioned from external agencies. For an insight into some of the ideas on good design, mixed use and sustainable communities that have become the norm within policy it is worth revisiting the original Urban Task Force report. Imrie and Raco give a good general overview of New Labour urban policy. Jordan gives interesting insights into the contrasts between the policy approaches of New Labour and those emerging under the Coalition government, and Bradbury and Mawson's edited collection is a heavyweight review of the impact of devolution on UK policy, with specific sections on planning.

Bradbury, J. and Mawson, J. (eds) (2006) *Devolution, Regionalism and Regional Development: The UK Experience* (Routledge, London).

Imrie, R. and Raco, M. (2003) *Urban Renaissance? New Labour, Community and Urban Policy* (Policy Press, Bristol).

Jordan, B. (2011) *Why the Third Way Failed: Economics, Morality and the Origins of the 'Big Society'* (Policy Press, Bristol).

Urban Task Force (1999) *Towards an Urban Renaissance: Final Report of the Urban Task Force Chaired by Lord Rogers of Riverside* (DETR, London).

3 Governance

OVERVIEW

This chapter explores ideas of governance which are used to understand the political processes through which urban regeneration is delivered. The following areas will be covered:

- *Definition: from government to governance*: examines what governance means and why it is important for urban regeneration.

- *Understanding the state*: breaks down the idea of 'the state' as a single body and looks at the complex arrangements of state institutions involved in cities.

- *Different forms of governance*: looks at the debates between scholars on how different relationships between the state and non-state sectors can be theorised.

- *The new institutionalism*: examines how the structure of institutions themselves can have a significant effect on how governance takes place.

- *Community involvement*: examines the place of the community in governance arrangements between state and non-state sectors.

- *Regional regeneration and the European Union*: highlights the growing importance of the EU for regeneration and explores whether this represents an undermining of national state power over the process.

Definition: from government to governance

In English, the word govern has a number of meanings, both as noun and verb. Government can be taken to represent the institution charged with the act of governing – where it becomes synonymous with '*the state*'. It can also be used to mean the actions of that institution – what the state seeks to achieve. Governance, in turn, refers to the process of *delivering* the aims of the state (Newman, 2001). The act of a government agency paying welfare benefits to the unemployed, for example, can be considered as governance, as it is delivering part of the state's social agenda.

Not all of the state's aims are delivered by its own agencies, however. Increasingly non-state actors are being brought in to help deliver services which the state does not wish to be directly involved with. One of the more controversial examples of this is the public-private partnership, where a private contractor bids for the right to build a new capital resource (for instance, a hospital) and lease it back to the public sector over a fixed period, whilst retaining responsibility for its maintenance. The public sector is then free to concentrate on more core activities with no need to have separate competence in construction and maintenance which are already available in the private sector.

The concept of governance is therefore very useful in looking at ways in which a whole range of actors are involved in the delivery of policy. This is particularly true for urban regeneration where the idea that it should be directly delivered by the state alone is unrealistic because of its large-scale and diverse remit as well as high costs. While the state sets a framework in which urban regeneration takes place, a large number of actors, from developers and construction firms through to charities and local communities, are involved in the actual process of undertaking a regeneration programme.

Understanding the state

A monolithic state?

As the discussion above suggests, the notion of governance raises all kinds of issues about 'the government' as an institution in itself. While an over-arching concept like 'the state' includes all the formal institutions of government, it does tend to make us think of the state as a single entity. Clearly this is not the case. The state can be broken down into a number of different scales (local, regional, national) and into different types of institution, for example, central government departments as against quangos/executive agencies which operate at arm's length from central government. Supranational government, in particular the European Union, are also of critical importance and further muddy the waters of the concept that the state is a singular, monolithic entity speaking with one voice.

Given that the direct effects of urban regeneration are felt most acutely at local level, local authorities play a critical role in initiating and managing the processes. Even a local council is no coherent entity speaking with one voice. Regeneration projects need to coordinate the different agendas of different council departments. The aims of an economic development department trying to maximise economic activity in a city may come into conflict with a planning department which has to enforce a set of planning rules laid down by central government.

Local councils are run by directly elected councillors who have a political mandate and direct accountability to their constituents. There can, however, be some tensions where a local council is controlled by one political party while central government is controlled by one of the opposing parties. In some parts of the UK there is an intermediate tier of regional government. The Scottish Parliament, Welsh Assembly, Northern Ireland Assembly and London Assembly are directly elected bodies. These differently mandated regional governments play a significant role in urban regeneration, in particular through acting as the regional planning bodies. In the English regions there is some degree of cooperation on strategic planning through the Local Enterprise Partnerships, though these lack any statutory powers in this area.

Even before one considers national government, therefore, it is clear that 'the state' as it affects urban regeneration is an exceedingly complicated and tangled series of overlapping institutions with more or less accountability at the ballot box. Since the devolution of powers to Scotland, Wales and Northern Ireland, the UK government based in Westminster has had much less direct control over issues relating to urban regeneration in these areas. The Department for Communities and Local Government (CLG) is the crucial Department of State so far as regeneration in England is concerned, laying down overall policy frameworks within which the other state institutions have to operate – for example, publishing the *National Planning Policy Framework* (CLG, 2012e), which governs the direction of planning policy. CLG also oversees the Homes and Communities Agency, which has significant interests in land development and social housing, as well as a number of executive agencies such as the Urban Regeneration Companies and Economic Development Companies which operate at a local level.

Hollowing out?

Bob Jessop (1994), examining the changes to the political system in the post-war period, talks about the state being 'hollowed out'. National governments still carry the appearance of having their powers intact but in fact aspects of their responsibilities have been removed (like hollowing a log) through being passed upwards to supranational bodies (for instance, the European Union) and downward to local and regional governments. This process is sometimes referred to as **glocalisation** (Swyngedouw, 2004) and has significant implications for the governance of regeneration in the UK. Britain has traditionally had a very strong central government, something that was reinforced during the 1980s under Margaret Thatcher's premiership in an attempt to undermine the power of local authorities. Continental Europe has a much stronger traditional of regional government, and funding streams established by the European Union tend to bypass national governments. European resources have become an increasingly important component of funding for local regeneration projects since the 1990s.

European Union funding is tied to certain criteria, which often involve levering in private sector resources and meeting certain targets in terms of involving local stakeholders. This means that the relationship between different parts of the state and different non-state stakeholders has become critical in urban regeneration. The idea of governance is thus exceedingly useful as it provides a framework for understanding the relationships between the different actors involved in the delivery of policy aims.

Third sector or 'shadow state'?

Despite the fact that the state is a multi-faceted institution and does not speak with one voice, there are concerns that where the state enters into relationships with non-state actors, the aims of the state will dominate. This is particularly the case where the state hands responsibility for delivery of services over to charitable, community and voluntary groups – sometimes referred to as the '**third sector**'. Such groups can become particularly dependent on that state funding stream and thus vulnerable to having their core interests shifted in line with what the state wants – the threat being that funds will be withdrawn otherwise.

Jennifer Wolch (1990) used the term 'shadow state' to describe this phenomenon where actors in the 'third' sector (i.e. neither public nor private) are captured by the state while formally remaining separate from it. In urban regeneration a good example of this is the housing association or registered provider of social housing (RP) sector, which provides affordable housing to people on lower incomes. There is a large amount of funding available for RPs from the Homes and Communities agency – a central government quango. This funding is dependent on those RPs delivering certain policy aims, such as the kinds of houses they build, where they build them and what environmental standards they comply with. Indeed, there has been some argument that the need to comply with performance indicators, laid down centrally as part of a broader trend towards target-driven management in the public sector, has in fact harmed the business performance of RPs and their social mission (Sprigings, 2002).

In terms of the governance of urban regeneration, therefore, there are two main fears for the third sector. The first is that while they might have been brought on board to meet funding requirements for inclusion, their voices will simply be drowned out when big decisions over resource allocation are being made. The second, and perhaps more pernicious, is that those organisations will be 'captured' by the way they have become involved with the process and the source of their funding.

Reproducing the aims of the state agents, becoming their shadow, these organisations are moved away from their core mission and, indeed, can stop playing the role they were nominally brought in to play, i.e. to provide a different kind of input to the project. This problem is particularly acute in an era of public sector funding cuts and the Big Society, where captured third sector organisations are being asked to continue playing the same roles on behalf of the state, but without the funding they had grown used to getting in order to support those functions.

Key points

i) The state no longer seeks to deliver all its policy aims directly through its own agencies.

ii) 'The state' is no single entity, but speaks with numerous voices with different interests.

iii) The development of European-level government and increasingly powerful regional government has led to arguments about the power of the central state being 'hollowed out'.

iv) A criticism of using 'third sector' bodies to deliver policy is that those bodies can end up merely reproducing or 'shadowing' the policies of the state, losing their individual expertise and becoming highly vulnerable to public funding cuts.

Different forms of governance

A great deal of work on what governance meant at a local level was undertaken during the 1990s in a programme of research funded by the Economic and Social Research Council (ESRC). In critiquing some of this work, the public policy expert Jonathan Davies (2001) came up with a useful typology of different forms of governance: governance by government; governance by partnership; and governance by regime. To these we can add governance by networks, an idea associated with that ESRC research programme and particularly Rod Rhodes (1997). Each of these is explored in turn though it should not be assumed that one is necessarily 'better' than another. Different forms of governance may be more or less appropriate depending on what the state is attempting to achieve in a given set of circumstances.

Governance by government

Governance by government is perhaps the most straightforward model. Essentially, the aims of government are delivered by the government itself. As discussed above, governments are very large institutions operating in a variety of guises and at different geographic scales, hence it can be appropriate for different parts of the state, with different remits, to work together on particular projects.

In the redevelopment of cities, this model tended to apply during the period of the post-war reconstruction up until the early 1980s. At this time, local councils had considerably more self-determination when it came to decision-making and spending than they do today. Local councils are considered as part of 'the state' as it is broadly defined and the working relationship between central and local government fits the governance by government model. Major housing and reconstruction programmes undertaken in the 1950s and 1960s were carried out by local authorities through grants and subsidised loans provided by central government. Indeed, many local authorities even directly employed their own teams of construction workers to carry out some of the building work.

The notion that the state should do this kind of work itself is clearly affected by the socialist ideals which formed a strong undercurrent in the post-war reconstruction. There were, however, undeniable problems with inefficiency and corruption in some, though by no means all, parts of the post-war programme. High-profile scandals included T. Dan Smith, former Chair of the housing committee in Newcastle, and Alan Maudsley, former Birmingham City Architect, who were both jailed on separate corruption charges in the 1970s. These scandals gave ammunition to those who opposed the socialist model of the state providing. The Conservative central government under Prime Minister Margaret Thatcher which was elected in 1979 broke the post-war political consensus. Thatcher argued that the state was an inefficient means of delivering services – a belief which was most famously acted upon in the privatisation of many state-run businesses, including the major utilities.

The Thatcherite attack on the state as service provider went beyond the waves of privatisations. Local authorities, condemned as corrupt and inefficient, had severe restrictions imposed on how they could raise and spend revenue. The big post-war state housing programmes were brought to an end through the slashing of grants and subsidies to local government. Clearly the state did not completely stop delivering services under Thatcher, but there was a clear ideological shift away from the idea that the state should deliver its own aims wherever possible to one in which it was felt that the state should only be involved in those areas where other sectors of society could not deliver that service better. As a result, the governance of the UK was broadened out from the governance by government model.

Governance by partnership

The second model of governance discussed here is where the state brings in partners to take some of the responsibility for delivery. If, under Thatcherism, the government was not going to deliver on all its policy aims itself, then external agents had to be brought in. This change of emphasis should be taken alongside a growing notion that urban *redevelopment* needed to be thought of as a more all-encompassing, holistic model of *regeneration*, acknowledging that the city is a hugely complex entity with a diverse range of problems which the state acting alone could not remedy. Non-state actors, in both the private and charitable sectors, were acknowledged as having a variety of expertise and resources which could be productively harnessed. In the 1980s, most of the emphasis was on drawing in private sector finance, with an increased recognition of the usefulness of the non-profit third sector emerging during the 1990s.

Though the idea of securing private sector investment came to prominence under Thatcher, it was not entirely absent before. When redeveloping Britain's city centres, local councils had long been working in partnership with development companies and other private actors to deliver new shopping centres and other resources. In the 1980s, a language of **levering in** private finance emerged, using public money to attract investors to areas which would otherwise pose too high a risk to developers. This was the era of the Urban Development Corporation (UDC), well-funded public sector bodies operated at arm's length from the central government which used a variety of economic incentives, particularly major **infrastructure** programmes combined with tax breaks to bring developers into run-down areas. The London Docklands Development Corporation, which operated between 1981 and 1998, invested heavily in infrastructure and was involved in building the Docklands Light Railway, 115 kilometres of new roads and reclaiming 826 hectares of land and water in the area. The construction of the now hugely economically successful Canary Wharf development, which was seen as somewhat high risk at the time, created a major new centre of business and professional services in an area of London which had suffered major job losses during the recession of the early 1980s.

The Thatcherite model of partnership was very much driven by the belief that the private sector, through the regulating mechanism of the market, knew best and that if a scheme was good for business then it would be delivering on the aims of the government. While schemes like Docklands did a lot to regenerate physical infrastructure, they can be criticised for not having tackled some of the more intractable social problems in Britain's inner cities. Merely bringing in private sector finance, therefore, was not enough to achieve a more all-encompassing *regeneration* of an area – former dock workers were unlikely to find employment in the finance houses attracted to Canary Wharf. During the 1990s there was an increasing recognition that alternative actors needed to be brought in to the process; charities, voluntary bodies and the local communities themselves (the 'third sector') began to be seen as partners in the regeneration process.

The increased inclusion of the third sector in the 1990s does not imply that such organisations began to dominate the process – governance 'partnerships' are not an exchange of equals. Davies, in fact, uses the word 'partnership' to imply that the state remains the dominant actor in this mode of governance. The 1990s were significant for a swing back towards involving local authorities – still very much part of the state – in regeneration. One of the reasons the UDCs had been set up was because the Thatcher government did not trust local authorities to deliver its policy aims. Indeed, there was a hope in the 1980s that regionally based Training and Enterprise Councils (TECs) would take the lead on local regeneration schemes, effectively bypassing local authorities. The TECs were designed to build relationships with local businesses and voluntary agencies to tackle unemployment and skills shortages; in practice they were not equipped to lead regeneration schemes. The Major and Blair governments of the 1990s took a much less hard-line approach to local authorities, accepting that they had considerable expertise and local knowledge which made them well placed to coordinate locally based regeneration projects.

Governance by networks

It was in this context that the local governance programme of the Economic and Social Research Council was operating during the mid- to late 1990s. The leading figure in this programme was Rod Rhodes, who defined governance as '*self-organizing, interorganisational networks*' (Rhodes, 1997: 53, emphasis in the original). The word 'network' is quite useful as it suggests the bringing together of a series of different actors to accomplish a task, though not actually putting together a single over-arching body – each of the different actors remains independent. In this context, the 'network', as distinct from 'partnership', implies that the state does not dominate the process. In practice, however, weaker actors such as community groups, tend to have much less influence over the process than those actors bringing political power or financial muscle to the project.

The distinction between networks and partnerships is somewhat blurred – just how much state involvement in a project transforms it from a network into a part-nership? It is perhaps not worth getting caught up in the semantic argument, but to try to examine just what powers the state has over a particular regeneration project – it clearly remains a very important player, although it is important to re-emphasise that 'the state' is no single entity. Certainly, central government still provides a great deal of funding for regeneration projects, both directly and through quangos such as the Homes and Communities agency in England. Similarly, the involvement of local authorities in individual schemes gives the state considerable control over the process. Indeed, one can critique Rhodes' notion that these networks are 'self-organising' by the fact that it is often the state, at either the local level or through an executive agency, which brings together a network to produce a particular project, coalescing around a funding stream related to particu-lar state aims. This was certainly true of the Single Regeneration Budget (1994–2001), where projects were generally led by local authorities, but when bidding for these resources they were required to demonstrate that a network/partnership had been set up with a range of actors to create a more inclusive project (see Box 3.1). As a result, in terms of the actual implementation, the introduction of a network of non-state actors into the decision-making and delivery process means that unexpected outcomes are inevitable.

BOX 3.1   EXTRACTS FROM THE GUIDANCE GIVEN TO ORGANISATIONS BIDDING FOR THE SINGLE REGENERATION BUDGET ROUND 6

The SRB is a flexible programme which supports schemes which have a mix of the following objectives:

- improving the employment prospects, education and skills of local people;

- addressing social exclusion and improving opportunities for the disadvantaged;

- promoting sustainable regeneration, improving and protecting the environment and infrastructure, including housing;

- supporting and promoting growth in local economies and businesses; and

- reducing crime and drug abuse and improving community safety.

Bids must be supported by partnerships representing all those with a key interest from the public and private sectors and from local voluntary and community organisations. The make-up of partnerships should reflect the content of the bid and characteristics of the area or groups at which it is aimed. In some cases, existing partnerships will put forward bids; in others, new partnerships (or adaptations of existing ones) will be formed.

Source: CLG (2006b)

Governance by regime

The idea of urban regimes was developed in the United States through the work of Stephen Elkin (1987), examining the city of Dallas, and Clarence Stone (1989) looking at Atlanta. Both authors examined in great detail the development of a long-term relationship between the city council and local businesses to promote the economic development of the city as a whole. A lot of this activity coalesced around land-ownership and development, but also took in social issues – for example, business leaders in Atlanta were active in pressing the city authorities to desegregate its schools in 1961, feeling that this would be good for business in the longer term.

Urban regimes, in Stone's model, work at a macro scale of policy – such as race relations – rather than on specific detail. By definition this is a long-term type of relationship between the local state and business interests. There have been various attempts to apply the idea of regimes to the UK. There are, however, some significant differences between the political model in the UK and the US, particularly in the relationships between local councils and local business leaders, which tend to be less overt in the UK. The involvement of non-state actors in urban regeneration in the UK tends to take the form of medium-term relationships based around specific projects. In terms of regeneration there does not seem to be the same kind of long-term strategic overview involving the private sector which could be characterised as forming a regime-type relationship. Looking for examples of regime governance in urban regeneration would seem, therefore, to be somewhat of a red herring.

Case Study: Park Central, Birmingham

A former council estate, abutting the southern edge of Birmingham's central business district, Park Central is a good example of the kinds of innovative governance arrangements which are now required to deliver urban regeneration. The initial impetus for the scheme, unusually, came from a highly coordinated campaign by local residents who wanted to see some money being spent on their estate to improve its run-down environment. The Labour-controlled local authority initially resisted a proposal to apply for a central government funding stream which would have moved the estate into the ownership of a third sector housing association. The Labour government elected to Westminster in 1997 did not scrap the scheme and the local party, somewhat reluctantly, agreed to authorise a bid after all. This scheme, the Estates Renewal Challenge Fund (ERCF), gave the housing association ownership of the properties and their **curtilages** as well as a large grant to meet refurbishment costs. The council's bid to the scheme was approved by the government and tenants voted in favour of leaving the public sector.

When the estate was in council ownership it clearly represented the governance by government model. The fact that local authorities have been starved of funding for maintaining their housing stock – and prevented by central government from independently raising revenue to do this – meant that this governance arrangement had become increasingly problematic. Schemes like the ERCF *forced* local authorities into a different mode of governance for housing, accepting that central government wanted social housing services in their cities to be moved into the partnership mode.

The housing association that was set up to take control of the housing stock in the area was called Optima Community Association – this stress on 'community' was deliberate, emphasising that the organisation was more than simply a housing provider, but was trying to improve all aspects of community life. The separation from the local authority was not a clean break, however. Several of the senior staff positions were recruited from inside the city council's housing department. At the same time, while Optima took ownership of the properties and their curtilages, the city council retained ownership of the public realm – not only roads and pavements but also a very large park which ran through the area.

This land-ownership question became significant as Optima looked at ways to raise revenue to build new homes – the ERCF only paid for refurbishments. Optima were always going to demolish some properties and thus had land available to sell to a developer. In an outcome which was never anticipated when the original bid for the ERCF resource was made, Optima and the city council cooperated in producing a more integrated masterplan for the area – changing the size and shape of the park, demolishing more property than originally anticipated and creating a sizeable development parcel. Rather than selling off land piecemeal, the idea was to get a development company to come on board as a partner in redeveloping the site as a whole.

On some levels, Optima had attempted to distance itself from the city council when attempting to bring developers on board. An indicative masterplan was commissioned by Optima to give developers some idea of what kind of scheme they wanted, rather than simply giving out copies of the city council branded supplementary planning guidance. The development was thus distanced from the bureaucratic control of the local authority and the poor reputation of council estates. At the same time, however, it was made clear to developers that with the city council having a landholding interest, the partnership would be able to access the city's powers of compulsory purchase to smooth the process of land assembly.

While the Park Central scheme was a response to general aims of both the local and national state to improve the area, when it came to the detail Optima produced something quite different from what was originally envisaged by the remit of the ERCF programme. Optima acted as the centre of a network of agents acting somewhat independently of the state. At the same time, however, Optima ensured that this network was sufficiently closely tied in to state mechanisms, particularly at local government level, to ensure that it could access some of the state's powers – particularly over compulsory purchase and land assembly.

After a lengthy bidding process, Crest Nicholson were chosen as the development partner and they quickly drew up a masterplan for the site. As the scheme progressed, Optima received income from land sales to the developer – helped by the fact that the bulk of the scheme was completed before the collapse in the housing market in 2008 – with a proportion of new residential units let out to its tenants. Existing residents were also involved in the development process, for example helping to determine what kinds of facilities would be available in the redesigned park (Figure 3.1). While by no means perfect, the scheme has had significant successes which can in part be put down to the cooperative and mutually beneficial relationship between the different partners.

The relationship between Optima, its tenants, the city council and the developer is a medium-term one, coalescing around a particular project – Park Central. As such it does not possess the characteristics of a regime; it is neither sufficiently long term, nor is it looking to the more general interests of the wider city's development. It does, however, provide an example of how a partnership arrangement can work, both through making use of the state's power, but at the same time going beyond the specific remit of funding schemes and accessing the ideas and expertise (and resources!) of external agents (for more details of this case study see Jones and Evans, 2006).

Figure 3.1   The transformation of an inner city estate. Top: Birmingham's Lee Bank, with low-quality park in 2000. Bottom: the rebranded 'Park Central', with new flats surrounding a high-quality park in 2007.

Key points

i) A series of different models have been devised to describe the kinds of relationships between the state, private and third sectors in order to deliver policy. These range from governance by government (where the state delivers its own services) to governance by regime (where the state and non-state sectors work together in a very long-term, stable relationship to promote mutual interests).

ii) The debate over the precise role of the state in governance arrangements is very contentious, with Davies in particular arguing that in the UK the state remains a dominant *partner* in the regeneration process rather than behaving as merely one actor in a network of involved parties.

iii) In the UK today, regeneration schemes can only take place where a variety of different actors from both the state and non-state sectors have been involved, although in practice it is often state actors which take the lead.

iv) The Park Central case is relatively unusual in that it is led by a third sector body. Although it originated from a city council project and was originally funded by a national state scheme, it has established considerable independence from the regeneration programme which was originally envisaged. This demonstrates the problem of attempting to apply just one model of governance – the real world has a tendency to be messy!

The new institutionalism

The idea of the new institutionalism came out of a paper by the political scientists James March and Johan Olsen written in 1984. In 'The new institutionalism: organizational factors in political life' March and Olsen noted a revival in political science studies looking at institutions themselves exerting a significant influence on how political life operates and decisions are made and put into practice. The new institutionalism reacted against trends in political science in the 1960s and 1970s to downplay the importance of state institutions in how society operates, preferring a behavioural model looking at the role of the individual. The state, in effect, was reduced to acting as a reflection of society, rather than actively shaping society to its own agenda. This approach brought with it a particular attention to the importance of shifting social class structures in the post-war period – changing class structures subsequently being reflected in changing political landscapes and institutions.

Non-institutional interpretations of society emphasise the role of the individual. So the behaviour of markets, for example, is seen as the consequence of interlinking decisions by individuals to buy and sell according to their personal preferences. New institutionalism accepts some of this argument but suggests that rational choice by individual actors is not the only mechanism at play. In setting up institutions, which are of course composed of individuals, society creates a layer of regulations, rituals and ceremonies through which an institution acts. Procedures are established through which individuals in an institution react to certain events. These procedures become ritualised such that they become a purpose in their own right.

Inertia is a very powerful force here – 'we've always done things this way' – meaning that institutional responses do not change quickly to reflect the current state of society as the non-institutional, behavioural argument would suggest. In turn, through the way in which they operate, those institutions can have a profound effect on shaping society. As March and Olsen (1984: 739) comment:

> Empirical observations seem to indicate that processes internal to political institutions, although possibly triggered by external events, affect the flow of history. Programs adopted as a simple compromise by a legislature become endowed with separate meaning and force by having an agency established to deal with them…

The impact of this kind of institutional structure on decision-making is outside the conventional understanding where people act to further their interests, depending on whether they have the power to do so and the constraints imposed by the existing legal framework.

New institutionalism therefore suggests that political preferences are shaped by education, indoctrination and experience – thus acknowledging the significant effect of institutional structures in shaping decision-making. This is, therefore, critical in terms of governance as decision-making is fundamentally shaped by the institutional structure of both state and non-state actors. In this light, the Thatcherite shift towards giving the non-state sector a much more prominent role in the delivery of services can be seen as even more dramatic as it overturned a series of institutional structures within the state that had been built up over several decades. New institutionalism also highlights the important effects of how governance arrangements are made, whether they be partnerships, regimes or networks, as these arrangements themselves are shaped by the principles under which they operate – the mission statement of a regeneration partnership, for example, can fundamentally shape the direction a redevelopment takes and how the actors within that partnership behave.

In theorising new institutionalism, March and Olsen suggested some three possible avenues of exploration. The first was the *policy martingale*. The idea of the martingale – a concept in probability theory – comes out of a gambling practice where a player with a one in two chance of winning a particular game doubled their stake with every losing bet – the idea being that they would eventually win back their money. March and Olsen use this idea to suggest that chance plays a major part in the policy process and that, when a decision is made, this has a fundamental effect on the subsequent direction of policy-making. Essentially one can conceive of the decision-making process as a series of forked branches with incremental decisions, influenced by random factors, pushing the process in one direction or another. Hence even in nominally identical political systems a particular set of circumstances will result in different sets of decisions being taken. This will in turn shape that decision-making process in particular ways and institutional responses will develop around this.

The second theoretical model March and Olsen identify is that of *institutional learning*. Where an institution feels that a decision taken has produced a successful outcome, they are more likely to reproduce that decision in the future. At the same time, institutions adapt their expectations of what constitutes 'success' based on their past performance. Hence if a particular regeneration project is judged to be a success, not only will an institution be more likely to do similar things in the future, it will also be more likely to redefine itself as an organisation which attempts to carry out projects of that nature. This can lead to a somewhat conservative decision-making process and make it very difficult to move in new directions.

The third of these models is that of the *garbage can*. This assumes that problems, possible solutions, decision-makers and opportunities flow through the policy system independent of each other and come together at random in a specific time and place. Hence the way in which a decision is taken is entirely dependent on the chance coming together of particular decision-makers facing a particular problem with particular resources available to them. This model has certain attractions, though it is difficult to unpick the details of how this actually happens on the ground, particularly where it is hard to get access to the decision-makers sitting in particular meetings as decisions are made and acted upon.

When March and Olsen wrote their article back in 1984 their central message was that institutions themselves, and the way they handled decision-making, had a significant impact on the process beyond the 'rational' choices of the decision-makers as individuals. At the time this was quite a significant break with behaviouralist models which emphasised individual choices. Today, however, the importance of institutions in the policy-making process is widely acknowledged such that Pierson and Skocpol (2002: 706) could declare that 'we are all institutionalists now'.

Case Study: the Greater London Authority

London, as Britain's biggest city, poses particular problems for regeneration (Imrie et al., 2009). The Greater London Authority (GLA) is an excellent case study of how institutional arrangements can play a critical role in how policy is delivered. The old Greater London Council (GLC) had been abolished by Margaret Thatcher in 1986 – partly because it was seen as a vocal opponent of Conservative central government. This left the governance of London to the individual boroughs, lacking an over-arching body to coordinate strategic activities. The resulting bureaucratic mess went unresolved until New Labour came to power in 1997, creating the GLA and giving it a directly elected Mayor as its head. In the race to become Mayor of the new body, the old socialist stalwart and former GLC leader Ken Livingstone ran as an independent following a successful **Blairite** campaign to stop him from gaining the official Labour party nomination. In May 2000, Livingstone defeated Frank Dobson, Tony Blair's preferred choice, and was elected Mayor of London by a comfortable, if not overwhelming, margin. He was allowed to rejoin the Labour party in 2004 and won another four-year term, this time as the official party candidate, in May of that year. In 2008 he was replaced by Conservative Boris Johnson, but during his time in office he fundamentally shaped the GLA as an institution and the role of the Mayor for future administrations.

Livingstone's capacity to irritate Prime Ministers aside, the formal institutional arrangements in which the GLA operates are very interesting. The Mayor is directly elected by the population of the London city region – producing by far the largest personal mandate of any elected politician in the UK. While the GLA is also comprised of an elected Assembly, its powers are in holding the Mayor to account, rather than playing an active role in policy-making – the Mayor alone having executive power. This combination of constitutional authority with the electoral mandate gives the Mayor considerable personal power within the remit of the GLA.

When defining that remit, however, there was a tension between whether the new London authority would be based on the model of a local authority – as with the GLC before it – or something more akin to the devolved regional governments being set up in Scotland and Wales. Travers (2002: 781) has argued that the civil servants in the Scottish Office and Welsh Office had an incentive to ensure the new institutions being set up in Edinburgh and Cardiff had as many powers as possible, as they would be transferred to administer the new bodies. Those Whitehall departments which shared responsibility for issues relating to London, however, would lose out on powers to administer these if a powerful London assembly was established and thus there was more incentive to retain as many powers as possible within their own departments. As a result, the GLA's formal powers were originally quite restricted. A series of existing bodies and funding streams were rolled together and the GLA was given control over transport, strategic economic development, police, fire and emergency planning.

The formal powers only tell part of the story, however. The Greater London Authority Act, 1999, which established the GLA, defined the body as having a general purpose of promoting the social, economic and environmental development of London. The GLA therefore has a *general* responsibility to act in particular areas except where explicitly required not to – a power of general competence not given to ordinary local authorities until the Localism Act, 2011. Thus while the GLA is explicitly forbidden to reproduce activities being undertaken by statutory authorities such as health or education, it does have the authority to work in partnership with these bodies to promote the general well-being of the city.

With a general power of competence, an elected Mayor with a considerable personal mandate and not weighed down by institutional traditions ('we've always done it this way'), there was considerable freedom to shape the role and direction of the GLA. This freedom was enthusiastically grasped by Ken Livingstone, who modelled the institution to suit his interests. As Thornley et al. (2005) note, the agencies which were rolled into the GLA had already been working on strategic planning for the city and attempted to push these agendas into the formal London Plan which was produced by the GLA. Instead, the Plan was dominated by the personal, political vision of the Mayor who was able to stamp his authority on the newly coalescing institutional structures. Thornley et al. also argue that, by virtue of being involved in the process of setting up the GLA, business interests have managed to establish close links into the GLA decision-making process. Indeed, a discourse of promoting 'competitiveness' is now central to the Mayor's remit. A visible symbol of this is the canyon of high-rise commercial and residential developments that sprang up along the river frontage during the first decade of the twenty-first century, with Livingstone committed to augmenting London's reputation as a world city and *the* place to do business, a commitment shared by his successor Boris Johnson.

Key points

i) New institutionalism revived an earlier model of seeing institutions themselves as having a major role to play in how societies function – something which had been undermined by fashionable 'behaviouralist' approaches in the 1970s.

ii) 'We've always done it this way' – once procedures and systems are set up for carrying out a particular activity, institutions can be very reluctant to do things differently. This can have serious implications for how rapidly changing circumstances can be responded to.

iii) The establishment of a new tier of government in London created an opportunity to establish a new institutional structure, in turn creating a new way of 'doing' regeneration in the capital.

Community involvement

As will be seen in Chapter 8, one of the stories behind the London Olympics development was in the streamlining of compulsory purchase powers under the Planning and Compulsory Purchase Act, 2004. This legal change applied to all of England and Wales and is interesting because it indicates that the state has a willingness to crush local opposition to a particular regeneration scheme if that project is seen as a priority. Despite this, a discourse of community involvement is still central to the rhetoric of contemporary urban regeneration. Indeed, this emphasis on community engagement can be seen as a reaction to the property-led, public-private partnership approach of the 1980s that produced schemes such as London Docklands. Through the 1990s, first through City Challenge and then the Single Regeneration Budget, central government funding for regeneration projects became tied to involving local community stakeholders. This has become even more critical with the rhetoric of bottom-up, community-led development as part of the Coalition government's localism agenda.

Where a partnership or network of organisations is established to respond to a particular funding stream, as discussed above, not all of the actors within that network can be considered as equals. Where a community lacks a well organised body to speak with one voice, or where competing community organisations have very different visions for the area, it is difficult to deliver a scheme with which most people are happy. Indeed, community voices can end up simply being marginalised, leaving behind instead a rather ambiguous discourse of communities being 'empowered' by the process but in practice having little influence over proceedings (Atkinson, 1999).

Academics examining the involvement of local communities in decision-making have created typologies, or ladders with different levels of community participation. The idea of a ladder was devised by Sherry Arnstein (1969), a planner, who perceived three tiers of participation (Figure 3.2). Non-participation occurs where community voices are manipulated or are given a forum to discuss issues ('therapy') without actually having any impact on the process. More tokenistic involvement could include simply informing the community of the decisions which were being made and the issues at stake or engaging in a formal consultation process which would not necessarily result in any change to the process. Placation, though still tokenistic, would involve giving hand-picked members of the community seats on various decision-making boards. More realistic degrees of citizen power come through making communities a partner in decision-making or actually delegating power down to the communities to be the majority decision-maker over particular issues. At the top of Arnstein's ladder was some form of citizen control, for example, a neighbourhood corporation with managerial control over, for example, a school. This degree of involvement has many resonances with the notion of the Big Society, with citizens taking direct control over public services.

The accusation levelled at regeneration projects is that for all the rhetoric of community involvement, the degree of citizen participation generally comes rather low down on Arnstein's ladder. Local Strategic Partnerships, for example, although having significant input from community groups, are fundamentally undemocratic bodies and largely invisible to the general public despite having been a conduit for central government funding streams. Indeed, in recent years there has been somewhat of a retreat from direct community involvement in partnerships bidding for funds. Where the Single Regeneration Budget (1994–2001) and Single Pot (2001–11) placed an emphasis on community partnership, severe cuts to the quantity and type of public funding available under the Coalition government has eroded this. One element of this is the folding together of different area-based, top-up funding streams into the Local Services Support Grant. This is paid directly to local authorities

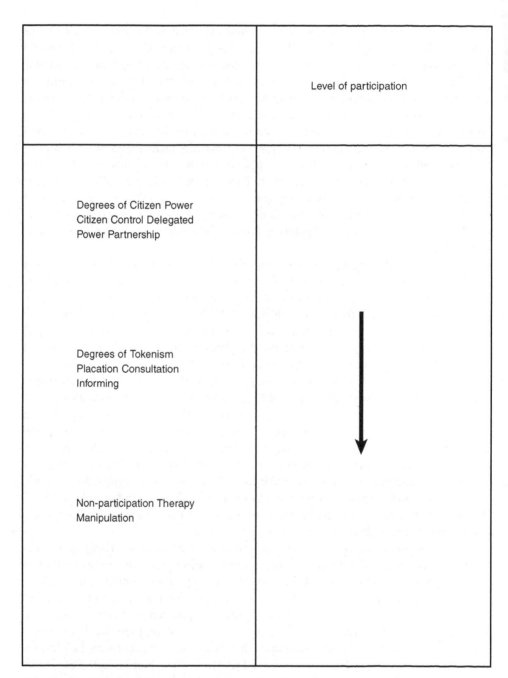

Level of participation

Degrees of Citizen Power
Citizen Control Delegated
Power Partnership

Degrees of Tokenism
Placation Consultation
Informing

Non-participation Therapy
Manipulation

Figure 3.2 Sherry Arnstein's ladder of citizen participation in decision-making. Nearly 40 years on, participation in UK urban regeneration seems all too often to be located towards the tokenistic end (derived from Arnstein, 1969).

and is not ring fenced, meaning that councils are free to spend the money on priorities that they determine locally. Thus communities looking for resources to spend on local projects are competing with a wide range of other priorities in drawing down funds from the local authority, rather than being much-needed partners in targeted funding schemes. Major ring fenced funding pots do still exist, but are much less community-focused. Thus bids to the Regional Growth Fund coordinated by the Local Enterprise Partnerships must concentrate on job creation in the private sector, while the Homes and Communities Agency's Affordable Homes scheme is focused on the registered providers of social housing, rather than on the tenants they serve.

BOX 3.2 ELEPHANT LINKS COMMUNITY FORUM

A regeneration programme proposed by Southwark Council in the late 1990s combined a Public Private Partnership undertaking physical regeneration and a £25m seven-year Single Regeneration Budget (SRB) application looking at environmental improvements and tackling social exclusion. Although a Stakeholders' Forum was established to help shape the SRB bid, much of the work was done by the Council and presented to the Forum late in the process, causing some community representatives to threaten to withdraw their support.

The SRB funding was granted in 1999 and a Community Forum, eventually including 63 local tenants' and residents' groups, was established to be one of the partners. The Forum had some successes, securing resources so that it had a more professional organisational capacity and gaining a voice on the physical regeneration programme which was running in parallel to the SRB process. There were, however, conflicts within the Forum and even walk-outs by key groups, and the Council stepped in to counter the 'unruly' behaviour of the Forum, withdrawing its resources. At the same time, the large physical redevelopment programme was cancelled in 2002, with the Council looking to break up the project into more manageable pieces and attempting to bypass the involvement of the Community Forum. The Council even went to Court to require the Forum to return key documents relating to the original project.

Source: North (2003)

Even where schemes do exist with a significant 'community' element, the bureaucratic complexity of the bidding process effectively restricts the leadership of bids to the local state and well-funded third sector organisations, meaning that the involvement of the actual community in community projects can be more apparent than real. The system therefore brings with it the potential for a cynical local authority to simply use a community group as a purely nominal partner in order to access a funding stream. At the same time, the very notion of a single 'community' voice is somewhat ridiculous, making it difficult to fit 'the community' neatly as an actor into a process with private and public sector partners (see Box 3.2 for a troubling example of how community involvement in a project can go sour).

Key points

i) While there is an emphasis on getting communities involved with regeneration projects, in practice the community is often the weakest partner, particularly where there is not a well organised community body with a clear agenda (very difficult to produce in practice).

ii) Increasingly the community aspects of regeneration are being hived off into a discourse of 'renewal', involving separate bodies such as local strategic partnerships. This breaks down the idea that regeneration is a holistic approach which does not simply focus on bricks and mortar.

iii) There has been considerable difficulty in moving community involvement into the more meaningful 'participation' areas of Arnstein's ladder and away from merely keeping communities informed of what is happening.

iv) Changes to the funding landscape under the Coalition government make meaningful community engagement with schemes more difficult than ever.

Regional regeneration and the European Union

Since 1975 the European Union (at that time named the European Economic Community) has been providing funds to sub-national regions of the member states under the European Regional Development Fund (ERDF). Objective 1 funding tackles structural change in severely economically deprived areas. Objective 2 funding tackles specific socio-economic change particularly relating to industrial and rural areas. Where regions are deemed to qualify for these funding streams, quite considerable extra resources are available outside the ordinary local and national state sources. The availability of EU funding, bypassing national governments, forms part of Jessop's argument about the hollowing out of the central state and the process of glocalisation discussed above.

The semi-autonomous regional governments in Scotland, Wales and Northern Ireland carry the responsibility for coordinating bids by local authorities and others to the ERDF. In England these bids are coordinated by regional teams within the Department for Communities and Local Government (CLG). This represents an attempt to regain control over EU funding at national level, as previously these bids were coordinated by the regional development agencies. Bids can be made by private and voluntary sector organisations as well as local authorities and the Local Enterprise Partnerships but permission to submit bids will be tightly controlled by Westminster. This shift of emphasis is interesting because it somewhat undermines the notion of glocalisation.

Parts of the West Midlands fall under the Objective 2 classification and the region has been successful in leveraging ERDF funding for numerous projects. To take a couple of examples specifically related to urban regeneration, the Burslem area of Stoke was granted £1.2m in 2011 to part-fund a comprehensive redevelopment of abandoned and historic buildings in the town centre. In the Craig's Croft area of Solihull, £4.3m was approved to establish a business incubator centre for both commercial and social enterprises to create jobs in a deprived area currently undergoing a major long-term regeneration programme (AWM, 2011). These schemes must be matched with resources from other sources including national and local funding streams, public and private sector. (In the Craig's Croft case, Solihull Metropolitan Borough Council funded the other half of this £8.6m scheme.) As a result, bidding for ERDF funding is highly complex, requiring coordination between different agencies, a great deal of technical expertise and support, and access to additional sources of funding.

In Wales, since 2000, bids to the ERDF have been coordinated by the Welsh European Funding Office (WEFO). Taking account of all European funding streams, Wales secured £1.55bn in the period 2007–11, which is a significant sum of money for a country of around three million people (WEFO, 2011). This funding reflects the significant structural problems which continue to be faced by the Welsh economy following the collapse of the mining and industrial sectors in the 1980s, as well as considerable expertise in leveraging EU funding which has built up within the principality. EU resource was a significant contributor to the redevelopment of Cardiff as it was established as the Welsh capital. Nonetheless, while the Cardiff Bay project did attract around £7m from the ERDF in the 2000–06 round of funding, this was dwarfed by the £496m in UK government funding via an urban development corporation and the £1.14bn brought in from the private sector (Cardiff Harbour Authority, 2007). While EU funding can be extremely important, therefore, it is rarely the sole source of revenue on a project and often only pays for quite small elements in a much larger programme.

Key points

i) The European Union has become increasingly important as a source of finance for regeneration projects, although in practice projects require a portfolio of different funding sources.

ii) The importance of the EU for funding adds some weight to the 'glocalisation' argument that national governments are increasingly being bypassed, although in practice, in England and Wales, overall control over bids to the EU are regulated by central government.

Further reading

Governance is a diverse and complex topic. Newman provides a helpful introduction to the development of governance in the UK since the election of the Labour government in 1997. Davies' exploration of urban regeneration and regimes provides a good critique of Rhodes' work on network governance. March and Olsen have written a useful summary of the development of the new institutionalism in the 20 years since they devised the term. Haus and Erling's article is an excellent, critical pan-European comparison of approaches to community involvement in urban governance, and Marshall's article provides a good examination of the impact that European funding programmes are having on how local authorities organise themselves.

Davies, J. (2001) *Partnerships and Regimes: The Politics of Urban Regeneration in the UK* (Ashgate, Aldershot).

Haus, M. and Erling, K. (2011) 'Urban leadership and community involvement: ingredients for good governance?', *Urban Affairs Review*, 47(2): 256–279.

March, J. and Olsen, J. (2005) *Elaborating the 'New Institutionalism'*. Arena Centre for European Studies Working Paper No.11 (University of Oslo, Oslo).

Marshall, A. (2005) 'Europeanization at the urban level: local actors, institutions and the dynamics of multi-level interaction', *Journal of European Public Policy*, 12(4): 668–686.

Newman, J. (2001) *Modernising Governance: New Labour, Policy and Society* (Sage, London).

4 The Competitive City

OVERVIEW

This chapter identifies key approaches to the economic regeneration of cities attempting to recover from deindustrialisation, and explores the outcomes of current schemes through a series of case studies. The chapter is structured as follows:

- *Deindustrialisation and the competitive city:* discusses the decline of British cities and the subsequent competition to attract investment in the new economy, setting urban regeneration within this context.

- *Funding economic regeneration:* outlines the key policies and funding mechanisms used to drive economic regeneration.

- *Regenerating cities in practice:* uses a series of case studies to demonstrate and evaluate the economic success of urban regeneration.

- *The financial crisis and its impact on regeneration funding:* considers the implications of the global financial crisis and the credit crunch for urban regeneration.

- *The entrepreneurial city:* explores how cities are responding to the knowledge economy, discussing the role of training and enterprise policies in regenerating cities.

Deindustrialisation and the competitive city

Deindustrialisation and globalisation

While the symptoms of urban failure are poverty, crime and dereliction, the underlying causes tend to be economic. In order to understand the palliative of urban regeneration, it is first necessary to appreciate the economic problems afflicting British cities that created the need for it. The modern British city emerged in the industrial era of the eighteenth and nineteenth centuries, and the waning of the British manufacturing sector in the second half of the twentieth century has been the main cause of their decline. Industry in North America and Europe was undercut by cheaper and often superior goods produced by emerging countries in the Far East, such as Japan, Korea and Taiwan, with lower labour costs and often more efficient production processes (Dicken, 2003). This trend has continued apace with China's emergence as the largest global manufacturing power, overtaking the USA for the first time in 2011 with 19.8% of global output (Marsh, 2011).

The effect of post-war deindustrialisation on British cities has been devastating. From the closure of steel plants in Sheffield in the 1980s and the rapid decline of the motor industry in the West Midlands to the rationalisation of chemical plants on Teesside and the loss of ship-building from Newcastle, high levels of unemployment became synonymous with urban life. Between 1971 and 1981, Britain's cities lost 34.5% of their manufacturing industry, equating to almost one million jobs. Birmingham lost nearly 60,000 jobs between 1981 and 1992, which represented a decrease of over 11%, compared to a regional average loss of just 0.7% and a national *gain* of 5% (Duffy, 1995). At the same time, new businesses preferred sites located outside major cities, which afforded the space to build the larger integrated assembly lines required by more sophisticated production processes. This was in stark contrast to the urban areas vacated by industry that were characterised by antiquated buildings, obsolete infrastructure and high levels of pollution. The development of the motorway network from the mid-1950s compounded the problems of cities, as components and products could be moved around easily without needing centralised rail stations and storage depots.

The deindustrialisation of cities in the UK was accompanied by an equally dramatic loss of population. From the 1930s onwards, there was a selective migration of the wealthier and more educated middle and upper classes out of Britain's industrial cities to rural locations, suburbs and new towns. As Table 4.1 shows, the trend of urban population loss in the 1960s, 1970s and 1980s was uniform across all major UK cities, although the cities of Liverpool, Manchester and Glasgow were hit particularly heavily. The upturn between 1991 and 2010 coincides with the rise of urban regeneration policies and in-migration from the so-called A8 eastern European nations after they became full members of the EU in 2004. It is worth noting however, that Liverpool, which has been the subject of intense regeneration activity in the last 30 years, continues to struggle and barely grew in the first decade of the twenty-first century as other cities boomed.

Selective out-migration in the second half of the twentieth century tended to leave poorer, less skilled populations in UK cities. The negative effects of this movement only became acutely felt in the 1970s and 1980s when industrial decline accelerated, leaving these populations workless. Further, new retail and leisure developments tended to mirror the geography of consumer spending power, abandoning the city centre for out of town locations near to major road networks.

At the same time as manufacturing industry shifted to the Far East and the emerging Tiger economies of South East Asia, Western economies became increasingly dominated by the service and financial sectors. The emergence of the so-called 'new economy' was based on services, communication, media and biotechnologies, and tended to be characterised by information and knowledge-intensive activities. Some commentators believed that the new economy would spell the end of cities, suggesting that if money and information could be sent instantaneously via the internet between locations anywhere in the world there would be no need for the concentrations of people and industry that characterise cities. We were offered a future in which everyone would be able to work at home (or in the Bahamas, or, indeed, anywhere they wanted).

But such predictions failed to materialise. In fact, rather than cities becoming obsolete, the new economic era heralded the advent of greater metropolitan dominance by an elite group of global cities such as Tokyo, New York and London. The urban theorist Saskia Sassen (1994) argues that cities have remained necessary because the work of global integration has to be done *somewhere*. Analysts tend to distinguish between codified knowledge that is widely available, for example through the internet, and tacit knowledge that is generally closely guarded by individuals

Table 4.1 Population change by percentage in British cities since 1900 (Hart and Johnston, 2000; Office of National Statistics, 2002; 2012; Scottish Neighbourhood Statistics, 2012).

City	1901–51	1951–61	1961–71	1971–81	1981–91	1991–01	2001–10	2010 pop.
Birmingham	+49.1	+1.9	−7.2	−8.3	−5.6	+0.7	+6.0	1.0m
Glasgow	+24.9	−2.9	−13.8	−22.0	−14.6	−4.7	+2.4	592k
Leeds	+19.3	+2.5	+3.6	−4.6	−3.8	+5.1	+11.7	799k
Liverpool	+10.9	−5.5	−18.2	−16.4	−10.4	−2.8	+1.3	445k
London	+25.9	−2.2	−6.8	−9.9	−4.5	+10.5	+9.1	7.8m
Manchester	+8.3	−5.9	−17.9	−17.5	−8.8	−2.1	+27.0	499k
Newcastle	+26.1	−2.3	−9.9	−9.9	−5.5	−0.1	+12.3	292k
Sheffield	+23.0	+0.4	−6.1	−6.1	−6.5	+2.5	+8.2	555k
UK	+32.1	+5.0	+5.3	+0.6	+0.02	+2.3	+6.0	62.3m

(Lever, 2002). While codified knowledge can furnish information concerning markets, services and processes that are valuable, it does not necessarily confer a competitive advantage, as technically everyone can access it. Tacit knowledge concerning investment and innovation is often only passed on through face-to-face interactions, in order to ensure confidentiality and the correct interpretation of information. Such knowledge confers a competitive advantage, and tends to be associated with high-level financial and technological industries. While the Global Cities hypothesis has been criticised, it is generally accepted that cities in which these face-to-face interactions and innovations can easily occur have enjoyed economic success. Cities able to train, educate and retain workers in the new economy reap the economic benefits of being the venue where high-worth individuals work and play.

As command points for controlling the new economy, global cities have much more in common with each other than they do with other cities in their own country, creating massive imbalances in wealth between cities (and parts of cities) that get a share of the global pie and those that do not. The concentration of wealth in the south east of England around London is testament to this phenomenon. France is also characterised by a growing economic gap between Paris and the rest of the country, referred to in the popular press by the phrase '*Paris et le desert Français*' (Paris and the French desert). But while national policy has traditionally made noises about reducing regional imbalances, some groups are now calling for global cities like London to receive preferential treatment as they contribute so much to the national economies of which they are a part.

The new economy and the competitive city

Regeneration policy in the UK has been framed by the emergence of global cities and the new economy. As manufacturing industry shifted to overseas locations, cities began to move their attention towards encouraging an alternative basis for their development in the new economy. Within the context of deindustrialisation and de-population, the main goal of regeneration is to generate employment, preferably in the form of middle- to high-income jobs in the service sector. While relatively footloose in terms of material demands, service industries tend to cluster in areas that provide attractive living and business environments (we will return to the idea of clusters later). Cities seeking to stimulate economic growth have competed with one another to attract such industries, with the result that they must 'sell' themselves as desirable locations within the new economy.

The idea of competition between cities formed the basis of a major five-year research programme called 'CITIES: Competitiveness and Cohesion', which began in 1997 and was funded by the UK government. The programme suggested that cities are commonly understood to be competitive if they offer a place in which it is cheap to do business, or if they have a mix of attributes that is more attractive to key industries (Begg, 2002). Although the idea of urban competitiveness is fairly vague, the research identified three conceptual approaches to its measurement:

economic outputs (such as income, unemployment and growth);
measures of success (such as visitor numbers and student population); and more
general indicators relating to the quality of life of residents. Although some econo-
mists have argued that it makes little sense to think of territorial units such as cities as competing in the same way as, say, firms might (Krugman, 1996), processes
whereby cities bid for funds or high-profile sporting or cultural events are
undoubtedly here to stay, and city leaders are becoming ever more obsessed with
league tables ranking the 'best' cities in which to live or do business, and regeneration schemes as the means by which to climb them.

In order to woo businesses and visitors, cities have sought to establish cultural
attractions around theatre and the arts, shopping facilities, and sports and conference
facilities. Creating these environments goes hand-in-hand with large-scale infrastructure planning. An effective modern transport system is necessary to allow easy
commuting, access to attractions and to reduce the negative effects of congestion
and air pollution. Information Communications Technology infrastructure is
increasingly critical, providing broadband to modern offices, private homes and
schools, and in public spaces. Regeneration projects need to be planned, financed
and executed in order to ensure that new facilities are located in the right place with
the right mix of land uses.

Professor of Regional Economic Development, Richard Florida (2002), has
taken these arguments further, claiming that only those places able to attract what
he calls 'the creative classes' will prosper in the new economy. He defines this
category as a select group of people who are employed in 'science and engineering, architecture and design, education, arts, music and entertainment, whose
economic function is to create new ideas, new technology and/or new creative
content' (ibid: 8). This emergent class is distinct from service sector workers more
generally because they are primarily paid to create rather than to execute orders
and are typified by very high levels of education and human capital. At the cutting
edge of the new economy, Florida identifies the emergence of a 'knowledge
economy', in which the most valuable asset is information and know-how. Florida
claims that workers in key growth industries such as IT and biotechnology are
increasingly important drivers of economic growth, as they tend to earn twice as
much as average service sector workers. Amongst this class of people, specific
lifestyles that incorporate individuality, self-expression and openness to difference
are highly valued, as these moral norms and desires are seen as inseparable from
creative work. The **creative class** seeks what he calls an 'experiential lifestyle'
which offers a range of creative experiences that complement their less con-
strained working arrangements.

Cities have traditionally been diverse places, home to the widest ethnic and
demographic cross-sections of society, and urban planners and marketers play on
these legacies. Mixed land uses are complemented by efforts to impart historical
identity to regenerated areas and provide individual lifestyle environments such as
loft style apartments with home office space, and boutique retail outlets. But while

cities are undoubtedly at an advantage in terms of diversity, this may not always be matched by tolerance. Florida (2002: 256) cross-referenced the 'Gay Index', which measures the total gay population in US cities as a proxy measure for liberalism and tolerance, with levels of innovation and high-tech industry. He found a very high correlation between gay population (i.e. tolerance) and concentrations of high-tech industry and innovation. These findings generated significant interest, as 'soft' cultural factors such as tolerance and diversity were suddenly argued to be critical in affecting the economic fortunes of a city.

Some of the demands of the knowledge economy are more direct. Florida argues that cities with a more educated population will gradually become more prosperous over time, while those with less educated populations will fall further behind. Creating a skilled population that is able to work within a knowledge-based sector requires education initiatives at school, university and adult levels. This involves encouraging more people to stay in education for longer and retraining unemployed industrial workers. Within the knowledge economy, higher education institutions like universities and research institutes act as centres for education and innovation. Harder questions related to education involve how to encourage entrepreneurship and business start-ups amongst the population of a city.

Three points merit further attention. First, the attributes identified by Florida are not only very different from those demanded by manufacturing industry, but are almost *antithetical*. Cities like Sheffield, which have suffered from deindustrialisation, are typified by a large pool of unskilled labour and a deteriorating urban environment that may be visually unappealing and socially undesirable. The image of British cities, particularly the inner cities, in the 1980s was incredibly bad – these were not places that people would move to out of choice. This was obviously a major problem when trying to attract footloose knowledge-intensive industries. Because cities require a complete face-lift in order to make them attractive destinations, it is hard to disentangle purely economic measures from more general regeneration measures to encourage cultural amenities and improve the environment and image of cities. Other desirable characteristics are less easily created, such as the presence of countryside and attractive villages nearby in which potential managers may live (Duffy, 1995).

Secondly, the attraction of a city will vary for different types of business. These different dimensions of competitiveness mean that contrasting cities will be competing in different markets. So, for example, London courts international financial business and thus competes with New York and Tokyo, while Cambridge seeks to attract high-tech ICT industries and thus lines up against the likes of Reading and Oxford. The major regenerating regional cities of the UK (such as Manchester, Glasgow and Leeds) are competing against one another primarily for business within the domestic market, while simultaneously trying to establish themselves as European and global players. The group of global cities constitute an exclusive club, but the potential rewards of breaking into this group means that cities expend vast efforts attempting to do so. While the new economy tends to be represented as a homogeneous and sweeping phenomenon, the place of cities within the global context is necessarily more differentiated than the term would suggest, responding to different economic opportunities and niches. This allows space for policies to be tailored to the unique characteristics of individual cities. The examples in this chapter, and Chapter 6 on design and culture, show how regenerating cities attempt to establish place-specific identities to enhance their competitiveness.

Thirdly, Florida's notion of diversity has been criticised for failing to describe the distribution of creative economies. For example, when he tested his indices of diversity in the UK, Manchester emerged as the most creative city, followed by Leicester. As Montgomery (2005) has noted, while Manchester is indeed a centre for creativity, it is outstripped by London's creative economy on every count – from number of employees and companies to overall economic output. Similarly, Leicester scores highly on account of its ethnic diversity, but is far from being a hotbed of innovation and creativity. Florida's three Ts of talent, tolerance and technology should not be seen as a one-size-fits-all solution, but as part of a more complex suite of factors that come together to allow a city to regain its economic prosperity.

While Florida's broad analysis of the growing economic relevance of creativity is generally accepted, his emphasis on the need for cities to cultivate alternative, high-density, inner city villages to attract them has been challenged. Some scholars have re-analysed his data to suggest that education levels correlate more accurately with the presence of creative firms than either the gay or bohemian population (Glaeser et al., 2004). Such people often prefer to live in leafy suburbs or rural villages rather than edgy inner city enclaves. Similarly, Florida systematically avoids discussing the negative effects of focusing urban policy purely on attracting the creative classes, such as the marginalisation of existing populations through gentrification, and the fact that because the creative classes are generally hyper-mobile they may simply leave (Long, 2010). But despite considerable criticism, Florida's messages have had an enormous effect on urban planners in the USA and the UK, who have taken on board the idea that the primary role of cities is to attract the creative classes by accommodating very specific kinds of lifestyles.

Urban regeneration to the rescue

If the problems facing UK cities are related to their general economic decline over the course of the twentieth century, then the goal of regeneration is to enable cities to compete within the new economy. Cities are vital to the prosperity of the UK as a whole, which explains in part the political priority afforded to their regeneration. In 2004, London contributed 17.9% of the UK's overall GDP, while housing 12.4% of the national population. Similarly, a government paper (HM Treasury, 2001) highlighted the strong links between the economic performance of cities and their regions – for example, Manchester generates 42% of the GDP of the north west region. Jane Jacobs (1985) argues that as engines for regional innovation and growth, cities are more important economic units of study than nations, heralding the emergence of the 'city-region' as a focus of concern.

Economic considerations underpin the entire urban regeneration agenda, to the extent that the social and environmental dimensions of regeneration are often justified as a necessary step in encouraging economic regeneration. When we look at the goals of the Urban White Paper concerning the creation of high-quality built environments, the underlying aim is to attract *people* back into the city. People who work, consume, and run businesses that generate jobs and wealth. Policy-makers are also realising the importance of cities as centres of innovation and enterprise within regional economies. Regeneration thus deploys local economic policies and initiatives to unleash forces of local enterprise and innovation within the city. The remainder of the chapter considers how regeneration has been funded, its economic successes and failures, and the impacts of the financial crisis.

Key points

i) In the twentieth century, UK cities were hit by the negative consequences of deindustrialisation, including chronic de-population and widespread dereliction.

ii) The overriding goal of urban regeneration is to revive economic growth by attracting investment and people back into cities.

iii) Within the context of **globalisation**, this involves courting the so-called New Economy, which is typified by knowledge-intensive industries like the service and ICT sectors.

iv) This process often takes the form of competition between cities.

Funding economic regeneration

At the most basic level, the challenge facing post-industrial cities has been to deal with the problems of inner city dereliction caused by people, shops and factories leaving. In classic urban land rent models, property values are assumed to increase with proximity to the city centre (Alonso, 1970), but by the 1980s widespread dereliction had led to a reversal of this relationship in many cities. Cheaper rent has the effect of attracting low-density land uses, such as car sales, to move in to more central locations, progressively dispersing the city centre. Lower densities of land use and population in the city centre make it impossible to maintain an efficient urban infrastructure and, without core services and facilities, the city centre gradually dies. The financial demands of addressing these physical, social and economic problems have been considerable.

Central government involvement was essential in the face of these challenges, and the Urban White Paper of 1977, *Policy for the Inner Cities*, kick-started urban regeneration, increasing government funding from £30m to £125m per year (Noon et al., 2000). Land-use planning is probably the most important form of local regulatory intervention in the economy, as it has the power to alter the physical landscape of cities. After their election in 1979, Margaret Thatcher's Conservative government focused on property-led regeneration as the means to re-establish higher rents in city centres. Urban Development Corporations were set up in 1980 to encourage the redevelopment of land in depressed urban areas. A key activity involved assembling land packages from diverse private owners, and improving infrastructure to attract subsequent private investment. It was intended that government funding would be supplemented by subsequent profits from land sales as an area became more desirable (known as the multiplier effect), but these returns were decimated by the property market crash of the late 1980s.

Early regeneration tended to be coordinated at the national level and enacted by local level organisations, which were created to function independently from city councils. This partly reflected the inherent mistrust of public institutions held by Thatcher's right-wing government, but also represented the recognition that there were serious institutional constraints on urban economic growth. City leaders tended to be more concerned with the services provided to residents, such as refuse collection and council tax, than with responding to global economic trends. In order to achieve comprehensive change, redevelopment efforts were focused on specific areas, an approach sometimes termed Area Based Initiatives (ABI). The logic was that limited funds would be more effective if they were concentrated in relatively small areas, rather than being spread thinly across entire cities. This would then cause a 'trickle-down' effect, as benefits accruing in the regenerated areas spread out to the areas surrounding it.

While achieving successes in some areas (for example, London Docklands attracted £2bn of funding in 1989) the property-led regeneration policies of the Conservative government have been criticised for:

- Failing to address social and environmental problems;
- Being driven from the top down and implemented by government quangos that failed to respond to local community needs; and
- Using public money to subsidise infrastructure for private developers. (Imrie and Thomas, 1993)

An early evaluation of the economic impacts of urban regeneration between 1983 and 1991 suggested that increased expenditure in an area led to some reduction in unemployment and the retention of 25–34-year-olds, but out of 57 areas studied, only 18 had positive effects, and 21 had poor outcomes (Robson et al., 1994). The report argued that in many schemes the focus on private property investment had alienated local communities and failed to utilise the skills and commitment of local people. Projects, it was suggested, needed to be more focused on local needs and inclusion through adopting a partnership approach. The failure of private developers to rejuvenate city centres indicated the need for a more comprehensive approach to regeneration, capable of generating better value for money for the public purse.

New Localism and the Regional Development Agencies

The 1990s saw a major shift in regeneration funding, away from grants and quangos towards integrated regeneration projects that were controlled by local councils. The first of these approaches was City Challenge, introduced in 1991. City Challenge was intended to be different in terms of its values, organisation, scope and delivery, and it is worth considering its main tenets as they set the tone for subsequent urban regeneration funding policy:

- *It adopted a comprehensive and strategic approach* that sought to address physical regeneration alongside economic and social problems.
- *It was limited to a five-year period* with each City Challenge adopting the same timescale with the same level of grant allocated in equal annual instalments.
- *It was competitive*, allocating £37.5m each to 31 Urban Programme authorities over five years on the basis of two competitions.
- *Bids were put together by cross-sectoral partnerships* of public, private and voluntary bodies.
- *It emphasised local implementation*, allowing local authorities to select areas and draw up plans to allow sensitivity to the demands of local circumstances.
- *Flagship developments were strategically targeted at specific areas* in order to kick-start further development.

City Challenge ushered in an era of '**New Localism**' within UK urban regeneration (not to be confused with ideas of 'localism' introduced by the Coalition government after 2010), whereby regeneration projects became driven by individual cities, but in a highly managerial, competitive and corporatist manner (Stewart, 1994). Successful bids had to identify measurable outputs and draw up delivery plans with their partners in order to compete with rival bids. While the competition format bred success within some local authorities, it penalized others that were unable either to develop comprehensive plans or demonstrate an ability to deliver them. For example, Bristol failed to secure City Challenge funding in either funding round (Malpass, 1994). Similarly, the logic of making local authorities compete against one another for funding has prevented cooperation between adjacent areas in setting regeneration strategies (Harrison, 2011). Although the neoliberal agenda of competitiveness has been criticised for being divisive, the logic of competitive bidding for funds has persisted as a defining feature of regeneration funding.

The ABI approach to regeneration was extended in 1994 with the introduction of the Single Regeneration Budget (SRB). Government evaluations of urban regeneration funding found that certain policies overlapped, and that this was hindering efficiency and cost-effectiveness. The SRB brought together a number of programmes from several government departments, simplifying and streamlining the assistance available for regeneration into one funding stream, but a review of the first three years of SRB highlighted problems with governance and resource allocation (Hall and Nevin, 1999). As with City Challenge, the competitive allocation of resources created winners and losers. If anything, SRB exacerbated this problem, as partnerships had to meet their stated criteria or else run the risk of receiving no resources. For example, over the first three rounds of SRB funding, Leicester attracted £12m while Newcastle received £109m, despite the similarity between the two cities in terms of size and levels of socio-economic deprivation. The amount of money made available under the Conservative government through SRB also fell by some 33% between 1994 and 1997, further tightening the focus on economic regeneration at the expense of social and environmental issues.

Politicians talk about a 'Europe of the regions' and, on the back of the successes of Scottish and Welsh devolution, the New Labour government made a concerted effort to create politically active regions in England. In 1997 the newly created Government Offices for the Regions were given the role of administering the SRB. Responsibility was subsequently transferred to the Regional Development Agencies (RDAs) when SRB was replaced by the Single Programme ('Single Pot') funding scheme in 2001. Administering the funds regionally was intended to make the process more flexible and responsive.

Under the Regional Development Agencies Act 1998, each Agency had a statutory purpose to further economic development and regeneration, promote business efficiency, investment, competitiveness and employment, enhance development and application of skills relevant to employment, and to contribute to sustainable development. The RDAs were expected to take a proactive role in establishing regional competitiveness by encouraging inward investment and working with regional partners, and they played a leading role in identifying and funding urban regeneration projects. Their goals mirrored the economic aims of the Single Pot Bidding Guidance to improve the employment prospects, education and skills of local people, and support and promote growth in local economies and businesses, but only provided for environmental and social considerations through their final acknowledgement of sustainable development.

City Challenge and SRB represented a commitment to increasing local participation in urban regeneration, and the further devolution of the Single Pot administration to the Regional Development Agencies represented a continuation of this trend. But while the Regional Development Agencies were publicly accountable, they were not publicly elected. When the Regional Development Agencies were given control of Single Pot funding it was envisaged that the newly established and democratically elected Regional Assemblies would provide a supervisory function over how the money was allocated. With the exception of London, the regional assemblies failed to become established as democratic entities (largely due to a lack of public interest), and Single Pot funding was almost solely controlled by the Regional Development Agencies. The specific economic brief of the Regional Development Agencies lent the regeneration funding process a pronounced economic bias.

The demise of central funding

Since coming to power in 2010, the Coalition government has pursued a different form of localism that aims to empower residents, local businesses and local authorities to drive regeneration projects. Rather than directing development through large centrally controlled funding streams, the Coalition sees the role of government as strategic, providing a system of local rewards and incentives in order to drive economic growth in specific areas. The most important impact of this policy shift has been the abolition of RDAs, which ceased all activities in March 2012. The Department for Communities and Local Government agreed to honour £1.3bn of existing Homes and Communities Agency and Regional Development Agency contracts but, beyond this commitment, the regional funding of regeneration that dominated since 2001 has ceased (CLG, 2011d).

RDAs can be seen as a casualty of the broader right-wing abhorrence for bureaucracy, although some of the stories of waste that have emerged certainly do them no favours (Yorkshire Forward spent £20,000 sending staff to the Dubai Film Festival in 2006, ten of whom flew business class (Taxpayers' Alliance, 2008)). Similarly, it is hard to assess their efficacy. For example, the relative contribution of the regions outside of the south east to the national economy actually declined after the establishment of the RDAs, although it is extremely difficult to disentangle cause from effect as regional growth reflects wider global economic cycles. What is not in doubt is that in real terms their closure has led to a massive reduction in the amount of funding available for regeneration.

In their place, the government has asked local authorities to form Local Enterprise Partnerships (LEPs) with business leaders, which are intended 'to create the right conditions for growth and enterprise' (CLG, 2011d: 14). LEPs are expected to comprise a board made up of at least 50% business leaders, and be chaired by a business leader. The specific roles of LEPs identified in the Local Growth White Paper include the alignment of planning and infrastructure investment with business needs, supporting enterprise and innovation, and attracting inward investment (BIS, 2010). Although intended to take their geographical boundaries from economically coherent areas at the sub-national scale, in practice regional political networks have tended to form the basis for LEPs. Only three out of 37 LEPs have geographical areas that cut across the pre-existing regions, reflecting the preference of local authorities to work with familiar partners and the haste with which they had to reorganise in order to begin bidding for money. While LEPs continue the New Labour preference for localism, they constitute a more networked form of urban governance that requires cooperation rather than competition between local authorities. As a result there are considerable overlaps in the membership of different LEPs. For example, the Greater Birmingham partnership has seven out of its nine local authorities included in other LEPs. Whether this shift towards cooperative working will facilitate more strategic regeneration, or whether projects founder upon the complexities of negotiating amongst multiple stakeholders remains to be seen. What is certain is that LEPs must deliver results in order to keep their business partners at the table (Harrison, 2011).

Two sources of funding for LEPs warrant mention. Early activity has involved coordinating bids to the newly established Regional Growth Fund (RGF), which has £2.4bn to allocate to projects and programmes across England between 2011 and 2015. Symbolising the shift to a business driven agenda, the fund is administered by BIS rather than CLG, and focuses on projects that aim to lever private investment into deprived areas to create economic growth and employment. Up to July 2011, in the first two rounds of funding, 956 bids were received amounting to requests for a total of £6.08bn (BIS, 2011a; BIS, 2011b). To put this figure into perspective, the RDAs handed out approximately £2.6b in 2006–07 alone, compared to the RGF's entire fund of £2.4bn over four years.

The Coalition government has also dusted off a familiar policy from the past – enterprise zones. Announced in the 2011 budget, LEPs were encouraged to put forward specific areas within their remit to form enterprise zones that would benefit from relaxed planning restrictions and financial incentives for businesses, such as tax breaks. Twenty-two enterprise zones have subsequently been approved, focusing on sites of strategic importance to the key city-regions. Examples include Manchester airport put forward by Manchester LEP; Nottingham Boots Campus put forward by Derby, Derbyshire, Nottingham and Nottinghamshire; and Darlaston put forward by the Black Country (CLG, 2012a).

Rather than replace the massive budgets of the RDAs with other forms of government funding, more innovative forms of financing are being made available to local authorities to allow them to plan regeneration in a strategic way. The most important of these is undoubtedly Tax Increment Financing (TIF). TIF allows local authorities to borrow against predicted increases in business rates and tax income from proposed developments to fund key infrastructure and capital costs associated with it. This funding mechanism has been used in the US for decades, as a way to facilitate private investment through providing infrastructure at an early stage. Although TIF is already available in Scotland, it has become tied up in a wider local authority funding review in England and is scheduled to be available by 2013.

The Community Infrastructure Levy (CIL) represents another strategic fund-raising tool that allows local authorities to set a mandatory charge on new developments to raise funds to spend on the provision of infrastructure to support growth. CIL was a New Labour innovation intended to replace S106 agreements, which were specific contributions negotiated with individual developers. For example, a large housing estate might be granted planning permission on the condition that they sign S106 agreements to fund intersections with existing roads, construct natural habitat and play areas for children. CIL was introduced to make this process more strategic, addressing concerns that S106 agreements were hard to coordinate and enforce. Rather than specify contributions, a blanket rate of tax is simply paid in proportion to the estimated added value of the development. Local authorities can then use this money to support services and infrastructure in a more coordinated manner.

Rather than funding specific developments, the Coalition government has adopted a model whereby local authorities are financially incentivised to meet central government targets. The New Homes Bonus, which commenced in April 2011, match funds the council tax raised from net new homes (i.e. those that increase the number of houses in the area after taking account of those that are lost) or empty homes brought back into use for six years or more. There is also an additional amount if these constitute affordable homes. Along similar lines, the Health Premium rewards local authorities for progress made against proposed public health targets.

The national funding landscape for regeneration has changed dramatically under the Coalition government, reverting from the comprehensive area-based Single Pot funding to a range of splintered funding sources. The Coalition government has also moved away from central funding towards more innovative financial mechanisms at the local level. Local authorities must work with communities and business leaders to produce comprehensive plans that **leverage** funding from a variety of sources. This is a resource-intensive process, requiring time and skill that will likely create financial winners and losers amongst LEPs.

European funds

Although European funding is primarily allocated at the regional level, it has played a major role in urban regeneration because many depressed regions of the UK contain extensive metropolitan areas. The original European Economic Community stressed the need to reduce inequalities between the regions of its various members, setting up the European Regional Development Fund (ERDF) in 1975 to provide investment in socially and economically challenged areas of Europe. The ERDF finances:

- direct aid to investments in companies (in particular SMEs) to create sustainable jobs;
- infrastructures linked notably to research and innovation, telecommunications, environment, energy and transport;

- financial instruments (capital risk funds, local development funds, etc.) to support regional and local development and to foster cooperation between towns and regions; and
- technical assistance measures.

While the fund initially targeted predominantly agricultural areas such as Greece and Ireland, deindustrialising regions in the more developed nations began to receive funds in the 1980s. For example, Birmingham received £260m between 1985 and 1994 (Duffy, 1995), which was then matched again by national and local government funding. Through the ERDF, £5bn has been invested in the regeneration of over 300 English communities since 1975. Currently, the Structural and Cohesion Funds are divided into three separate funds: the ERDF, the European Social Fund (ESF) and the Cohesion Fund. These are used to meet the three objectives of cohesion and regional policy: convergence, regional competitiveness and employment, and European territorial cooperation.

The EU budget for these funds runs on a six-year cycle, and approximately £3.5bn of funding was made available to the English regions between 2000 and 2006, with roughly the same amount going to Wales, Scotland and Northern Ireland collectively. In the 2007–13 round of the ERDF, England received £3.2bn. The money is split into convergence (previously Objective 1) and regional competitiveness (previously Objective 2) funding. Convergence funding promotes the development and structural adjustment of highly specific areas whose economies are lagging behind those of their neighbours. Regional competitiveness funding aims to assist regions whose economies are facing structural difficulties, whether they are industrial, rural or urban. The amount given to each region differs according to need, which is generally determined by their productivity relative to the EU average. Thus North West England received £511m of Objective 2 funding, while South East England received only £23m. Grants tend to go to projects like the Eden Project in Cornwall (£12.8 million), King's Dock redevelopment in Liverpool (£48 million) and the East Midlands Media Investment Fund (£6 million) that would not have been possible without it (CLG, 2012b).

Between 2000 and 2006, three English regions qualified to receive convergence (previously Objective 1) funding: the South West (Cornwall £190m), Yorkshire and Humberside (South Yorkshire £497m) and the North West (Merseyside £565m). West Wales and the Valleys, Northern Ireland, and the Highlands and Islands of Scotland also received considerable Objective 1 funding. From 2007–13 the only region that qualifies for special convergence assistance is Cornwall and the Scilly Isles, although the previous Objective 1 regions of Merseyside and South Yorkshire have received some transition funding. The UK has continued to receive substantial Structural Funds, amounting to just under £6bn for the period 2007–13, although this is less than the previous period 2000–06, as funds are being diverted to the various Eastern European countries that have joined the EU.

EU legislation also constrains UK government funding for regional development, only allowing direct state aid to be given to areas that qualify for Assisted Area status. These areas are defined by employment rate, adult skills, incapacity benefit claimants and manufacturing share of employment. Regional aid consists of aid for investment granted to large companies or, in certain limited circumstances, operating aid that is targeted at specific regions to redress regional disparities. Figure 4.1 shows the coverage of status for the UK for the period 2007–12. Aid to promote the economic development of areas where the standard of living is abnormally low or where there is serious under-employment is covered under Article 87(3)(a) of the EC treaty on state aid rules, while aid to facilitate the development of certain economic activities or certain economic areas, where such aid does not adversely affect trading conditions to an extent contrary to the common interest, is covered under Article 87(3)(c). As can be seen in Figure 4.1, the distribution of 87(3)(a) status covers rural areas that are relatively depopulated, but the 87(3)(c) status clearly focuses on post-industrial urban areas of the Midlands, Northern Ireland, the north east and the north west of England and Scotland.

Other funding sources

Three other funding sources are worth considering briefly: private investment (including Private Finance Initiatives); tax breaks; and the National Lottery.

As discussed above, Area Based Initiatives use public funding to lever in private investment. However, private developers are not primarily interested in funding urban regeneration projects to alleviate poverty or create jobs for the local population. As private companies they are driven by the need to make a profit, either for their owners or, if publicly floated on the stock exchange, for their shareholders. A project must be economically feasible to attract private sector investment.

Many urban regeneration projects tend to be characterised by higher levels of risk than regular development projects. For example, the risk of developing a greenfield site in a desirable area of the south east is far lower than that of undertaking a brown-field development in a regionally disadvantaged town in the north east. The potential costs and investment of time required to remediate brownfield sites can be high, added to which there is no guarantee that there will be sufficient demand for the premises when they are finished. Furthermore, the scale of many urban regeneration projects means that they can take years to complete, making them vulnerable to swings in the highly cyclic construction and property sectors. As Adair et al. (2003: 1075) state, 'the rules of the market inevitably encourage developers to go to the least difficult sites'.

The Urban Task Force report (1999) recognised that large-scale regeneration could not be financed by short-term debt or the public sector alone, and suggested the use of limited-life partnerships between the public sector and private developers in order to share the risks and long-term capital rewards. An example of a limited-life partnership is the Birmingham Alliance, set up by developers Hammerson, Henderson and Land Securities, to redevelop the city centre. The need to mitigate risk also drives the preference of developers to take on large land packages, as regen-erating a more comprehensive area gives them more control over the process, creates

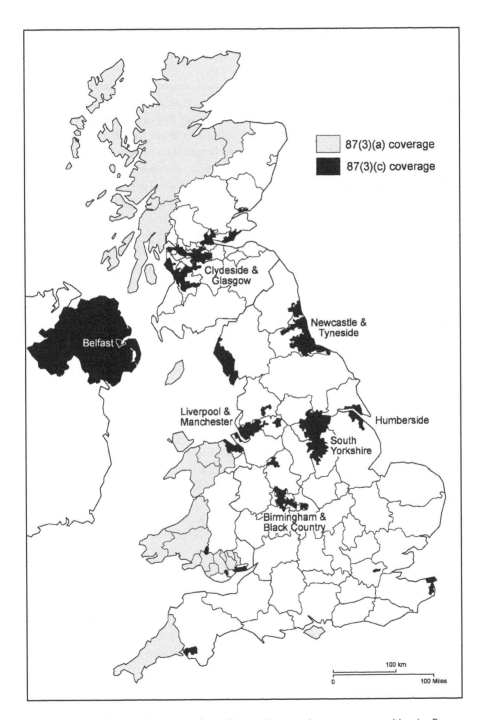

Figure 4.1 Map of Assisted Areas in Great Britain showing the areas approved by the European Union to receive regional aid from the government 2007–2012. The designation of these areas indicates which regions have abnormally low standards of living. Drawn by Kevin Burkhill.

economies of scale and allows them to benefit from the multiplier effect, whereby a successful development can increase the potential profitability of yet-to-be-developed surrounding sites.

The higher risks associated with urban regeneration projects have tended to deter institutional investors. Although they constitute a major source of private investment money in the UK they are highly risk averse. In order to offset this level of risk, companies funding regeneration cut deals that will allow them to achieve above-average returns in return for financing projects. Where financial backing is required for a large project, commonly a development company will be set up and the financial backers will transfer funds by purchasing equity in the company. Typically the development company will be responsible for insuring against the risk of non-completion. A limited number of institutional funds have been set up specifically for regeneration investments, such as the Igloo Fund within Aviva Investors, although they tend to be more involved with secondary development and leasing than actual construction.

Private Finance Initiative (PFI) is a partnership mechanism piloted by the UK to attract private investment in capital and infrastructure developments. First legislated for in 1992, PFI involves forming a partnership between a public and private organisation in order to fund a new asset that would normally be provided by the state. PFI generally involves the private sector designing, building and/or operating an asset, and the public supposedly gaining from better facilities and more efficient management. This has included schools, roads, hospitals, prisons and social housing schemes, which sometimes form part of an ABI regeneration scheme. In principle, PFI not only secures private funds to deliver public services, but shifts risk from the public sector into the private sector. Overall control lies with the private sector, with the role of the public agencies being to secure social benefits. Improvements to infrastructure can attract further investment into run-down areas, and open up new sites for development. PFI represents a way to use private sector finance to deliver public services, and 920 projects had been undertaken up to 2010 (Partnerships UK, 2011).

PFI can be freestanding, whereby the private sector constructs and runs an asset, recouping its costs by selling the service back to the public sector. It can also involve the private sector simply gaining revenue through the running of the asset, or can take the form of a joint venture, whereby the private and public sectors contribute money to either a capital build or service delivery programme. In cases of exceptional cost, PFI **bonds** can be issued to raise funds. PFI also forges longer-term involvement of the private sector in development projects, which can increase the emphasis placed upon environmental considerations, such as the costs of running buildings over their entire life rather than simply the short-term costs of construction (a point that is returned to in the next chapter).

PFI has been widely criticised in some quarters, as public assets (such as, for example, buildings and land associated with hospitals) are sold to private companies, who then lease them back to the public sector for a fee. While the PFI arrangement removes the capital build costs associated with large education and health facilities from the balance sheets of public sector organisations, it saddles them with long-running debts and/or expensive service agreements. In some cases these arrangements have seemed highly favourable to private business while compromising the public asset base; most notably it has been notoriously hard to pin down exactly how much risk the private sector actually bears in reality (Raco and Flint, 2012).

A slightly different form of funding involves the use of tax-based incentives to encourage development in areas where it is needed most. The Urban White Paper (DETR, 2000) highlighted the potential to use the tax system to influence property markets, both in terms of development, investment, ownership, letting and dwelling. Tax-based incentives include tax relief measures to make inner city projects more appealing, such as capital allowances, capital gains tax relief on eventual sale, limited rate-free periods and **remediation** relief. Increased capital allowances and capital gains tax relief in particular are intended to free up more cash to fund further land and property projects. Reduced stamp duty and remediation relief make it more attractive for developers to purchase old industrial property and where necessary to clean it up for use, and reduced business rates provide an incentive to attract tenants.

Finally, the National Lottery allocates 28p, out of every pound gambled, to 'good causes'. These cover a range of areas, from the arts and sport to heritage and communities. The funding is split amongst 14 organisations, including some with a specific focus (for example, the Arts Councils for England, Wales and Northern Ireland), and other more general funds (for example, the Millennium Commission, the Big Lottery Fund and the Heritage Lottery Fund). Lottery funding tends to be used to help build flagship regeneration projects such as the Lowry Centre in Salford (an arts and heritage complex, see Figure 4.2), Millennium Tower in Portsmouth (visitor attraction) and the Gateshead Millennium Bridge, which was the first opening bridge to be built across the Tyne for 100 years.

Key points

i) ABIs constitute the dominant approach to regeneration, concentrating funding in specific areas in order to create trickle-down effects in surrounding areas.

ii) Regeneration initiatives have shifted in emphasis from being purely property-led to seeking the integration of social and environmental factors, often through partnerships between different public and private organisations.

iii) Funding is competitive and primarily administered at the local level through the LEPs.

iv) A range of other funding sources exists, including the European Union, private finance initiatives and lottery funding.

v) Regeneration mechanisms are designed to mitigate the tendency of private developers to be risk averse, and to offer large-scale development opportunities.

Figure 4.2 The Lowry Centre, Salford, which opened in 2000, is an example of a flagship arts capital project which was heavily supported with National Lottery funds distributed through three different agencies: the Arts Council of England, the Millennium Commission and the Heritage Lottery Fund.

Regenerating cities in practice

It is possible to identify Area Based Initiatives in most major cities in the UK. Projects range from the refurbishment of a single derelict building to the regeneration of entire neighbourhoods. It is worth considering a few key examples to demonstrate the different types of project that have been used to regenerate previously run-down urban areas. This section will also explore how cities balance the need to compete to attract generally similar kinds of industry, people and functions, while also incorporating their own unique identities and legacies into regeneration schemes.

Individual regeneration projects: Manchester Printworks

The regeneration of Manchester's city centre was given a unique kick-start in 1996 by a 3,300lb IRA bomb, which destroyed much of the central shopping area. The devastation prompted a £750 million investment spree in the city, replacing a somewhat outmoded retail core with a host of fashionable developments – today a Harvey Nichols retail outlet stands on the site of the IRA bomb blast.

The Manchester Printworks building had been the headquarters of a number of national newspapers, occupying a prime city centre location on Corporation Street, but had stood derelict after the demise of Robert Maxwell's newspaper empire in the early 1990s. Refurbished at a cost of £150 million, the Printworks was marketed as Europe's first urban leisure and entertainment complex, covering approximately 32,500m^2 of floor space and housing 35 themed bars, 14 food outlets, a health complex, and the second largest Imax screen in the country (Figure 4.3).

The cost of refurbishing old industrial buildings is generally high, and this is the main reason that they tend to remain derelict. The internal layout of floors and walls had to be completely redesigned in order to accommodate retail and leisure developments, although the original layout of the Printworks makes it a unique space for this kind of development. Basic infrastructure such as electricity wiring and water supply needed to be re-installed. Analogues of the Printworks can be found in almost every city, such as Met Quarter in Liverpool and the Mailbox in Birmingham.

Despite these costs, it is desirable to retain these buildings as elements of industrial heritage, as local communities associate them with a city's former pride. They are also valuable as unique buildings that can be retained amongst otherwise generic

Figure 4.3   Manchester Printworks is a mix of generic restaurant and entertainment chains brought together, unusually, in a unique building. This combination has lent some character to a development which might otherwise be rather bland.

developments, enhancing the identity of a city and its ability to attract potential visitors and businesses. The Printworks development is also indicative of the importance of leisure uses to urban regeneration. Throughout the 1990s, Manchester City Council vigorously embraced this approach to regeneration (Robson, 2002), promoting a very positive vision of the city based around leisure, from the Commonwealth Games and its internationally renowned football teams to the 'Madchester' music scene that centred on the Hacienda nightclub and bands such as the Happy Mondays. In 2001 it was estimated that around seven restaurants and bars were opening each week in Manchester, not an inconsiderable amount in a city of half a million residents. The opening of Manchester Printworks in 2000 marked the final phase in the rebuilding of Manchester's retail centre after the bombing.

Major regeneration areas: Laganside in Belfast

Waterfront developments have become a dominant theme of urban regeneration in the UK (see Chapter 6). As industrial ports have shut down, waterfront areas have become a focus of dereliction, but offer clear design and marketing opportunities associated with waterside locations. One of the largest regeneration projects in Northern Ireland focused on the Lagan River that runs through Belfast. Belfast was little more than a village before the industrial revolution, which transformed it into one of the world's major ports. Over the course of the 1970s and 1980s, the area around the Lagan had deteriorated due to the decline of the dockyards, and the area suffered all the classic symptoms of urban decline. Socially, high levels of unemployment led to de-population and deprivation, while physically the area was dominated by derelict buildings and low-quality housing. Even the Lagan itself had become an environmental liability, heavily polluted and exposing foul smelling sandbanks at low tide.

As the map in Figure 4.4 shows, the Lagan cuts straight through the centre of Belfast, and the scale of the blighted area (140 hectares) associated with its decline acted to severely retard the redevelopment of the inner city. While the economic potential of a central area is obvious, the task of regenerating such an extensive and environmentally degraded area required large-scale action. With this in mind, the city drew up the Laganside Concept Plan in 1987 to outline options for rehabilitating the River Lagan and developing the adjacent areas. In 1989 the Laganside Urban Development Corporation was formed in order to begin the social and economic regeneration of the Laganside area. Their remit was extended to include the Cathedral Quarter nearer the city centre, bringing the total Laganside area to 200 hectares.

The Laganside Corporation used government money to encourage private investment in business and leisure, identifying key developments and working with private partners to deliver them. So, for example, the Laganside Corporation contributed £6m of funding to the construction of the Belfast Hilton Hotel and an undisclosed amount to the development of the McCausland Hotel. Flagship cultural projects such as the Belfast Odyssey Millennium project and associated facilities at Belfast Harbour were funded using approximately £90m of government money.

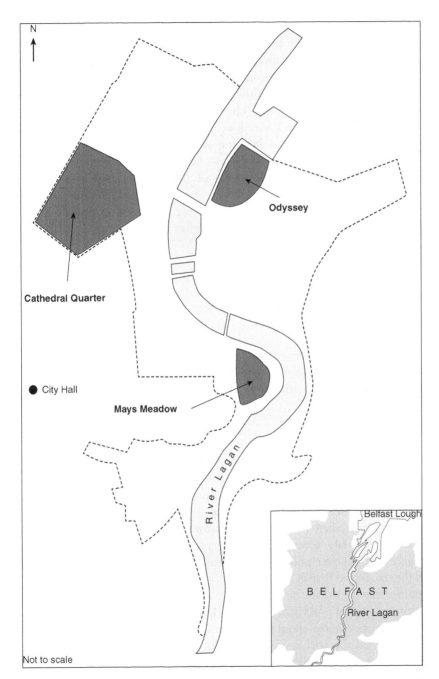

N

Odyssey

Cathedral Quarter

● City Hall

Mays Meadow

River Lagan

Belfast Lough

B E L F A S T
River Lagan

Not to scale

Figure 4.4 Laganside has been one of the longest running urban regeneration projects in the UK. The map shows the River Lagan, which cuts through the centre of the city of Belfast, and the large areas of regeneration that have taken place around it. The revitalisation of Belfast has, to a large extent, depended upon the regeneration of this central river corridor. Drawn by Kevin Burkhill.

The Odyssey was tagged as Northern Ireland's 'Millennium Project' with almost half of the funding coming from the Millennium Commission, 11% from the Laganside Corporation, 18.5% from the Department of Culture, Arts and Leisure, 18.5% from the Sheridan Group and 3.3% from the Sports Council. In addition to the Odyssey project, a range of cultural venues has been developed, including the Waterfront Hall, and Lanyon Place. The redeveloped areas have attempted to mix land uses. For example, at May's Meadow, 140 apartments have been built including 48 housing units provided by a housing association for tenants who qualify for social housing in the same development as a bar, restaurant complex, call centre, the Hilton Hotel and the local headquarters of the international accountancy firm PriceWaterhouseCoopers.

Laganside has been one of the longest running regeneration projects in the UK. Between its inception in 1989 and completion in 2007 it secured:

- £1bn of investment
- 14,700 jobs
- over 213,000m² of office space
- over 83,000m² completed retail/leisure space
- over 700 completed housing units.

The Northern Ireland Department for Social Development subsequently took control of the Laganside area, with the development corporation considered to have achieved its regeneration remit.

Developer-driven regeneration: Gunwharf, Portsmouth

In some cases, major redevelopment projects are taken on by a single developer and it is worth examining an example of where this has taken place to understand the economic trade-offs made between local authorities and developers in practice. The Gunwharf development in Portsmouth was a major redevelopment of part of the derelict port, undertaken by Berkeley developers in the late 1990s (Cook, 2004). Established in the late seventeenth century as the Naval Ordnance Department, Gunwharf employed over a fifth of Portsmouth's workforce in 1931. Successive reductions in the size of the British navy, coupled with a concentration of destructive power in fewer armaments, led to the abandoning of the site in the mid-1980s. Portsmouth suffers from a series of problems, including de-population, low levels of education and household incomes below the national average. In the early 1990s, Portsmouth City Council identified the port as an area ripe for property-led regeneration, comprising the usual mix of retail, housing and leisure.

In 1995 the city council and Ministry of Defence announced that the Gunwharf site was to be put out to tender for private development. The Berkeley Group were awarded the contract as they were willing to part finance the proposed Millennium Tower, a landmark building to act as a focus for the port and mark the year 2000.

The other developers refused to agree to part finance the tower, considering it to be uneconomic. The development was not guaranteed to be financially successful, however, and Berkeley negotiated a series of modifications to the initial brief with the city council. They demanded to be allowed to build a designer shopping outlet in order to provide some form of economic 'insurance' in case the residential element of the development encountered problems. The City Council had been against any major retail outlet, fearing that it would take trade away from the other shopping centres in Portsmouth, but eventually agreed as they needed Berkeley to finance the broader regeneration of Gunwharf. Berkeley also claimed that the more upmarket outlet would be complementary to the city's other retail centres, appealing to local rivalry by claiming that it would elevate Portsmouth's retail GDP above that of their close neighbour and rival Southampton.

The 165-metre Millennium Tower was one of only 18 landmark projects to receive Lottery funding and initially Berkeley were going to top up the £30m of lottery money with a further £9m. Controversially they reduced their contribution to £3m in 1998, as they believed that the tower would not attract as many visitors as the council claimed. While the intricacies of how the Portsmouth Millennium Tower was financed are too detailed to go into here, the point is that the developer was in a very strong position to dictate terms to the city. For similar reasons, Berkeley managed to refuse to include any social housing in the first phase of development, flying in the face of city policy. Private developers thus play a massive role in regeneration projects and can wield significant power within public-private partnerships, especially when a project is driven by a single developer.

Flagship projects and branding

From the account given so far, it can be concluded that the external forces acting upon UK cities are relatively generic. Their decline was due to the general waning competitiveness of the UK manufacturing industry and their salvation is to be found in reinvention through regeneration. The broad goals of regeneration are thus shared – cities need to enhance their appearance and liveability, improve their workforce and revamp their physical infrastructure. Within this general context, though, cities have begun to realise that, in order to 'stand out from the crowd' and attract a share of the global knowledge economy, it is necessary to establish a positive identity, by either building upon existing (perhaps neglected) heritage, or by establishing new attraction points.

Urban regeneration is critical to this process, and a range of strategies exists. For example, some cities have emphasised cultural attractions and industries, while others have sought to establish a reputation as world class sporting venues. Some cities have focused upon attracting tourists, while others have concentrated on becoming business or shopping destinations. Increasingly, companies and planners seek to 'brand' their developments as if they were a product, to create a favourable identity that will enable them to be sold to potential residents or businesses. While the idea of selling cities is not new (Ward, 1998), and is closely linked to the necessity of competing to attract people and business, branding is now standard practice for individual developments (for instance, the Park Central example in Chapter 3 involved extensive re-branding to change perceptions of an old council estate for marketing purposes). Increasingly the marketing logic of branding regeneration is being extended to strategic, city-wide partnerships. For example, 'Liverpool 1' (Figure 4.5) was launched as the brand for the £900m retail-led regeneration of Liverpool's city centre, unveiled in 2005. Liverpool One is an enormous scheme, covering six districts of the city, involving 30 individually designed buildings, 150,000m^2 of retail space, a 14-screen cinema, 21,000m^2 of

Figure 4.5 The Liverpool One brand logo was used to impart a clear identity to the regeneration of Liverpool's central shopping areas. The logo is typical of the current trend to brand redevelopments like products in order to attract potential investors, shoppers and residents.

restaurants, more than 450 new apartments, two hotels, offices, a revitalised 2-hectare park and new public transport interchange. The PR-friendly logo, selected after months of intensive marketing research, and catchphrase 'Love the City', is used to market the development to consumers and retailers through a variety of channels.

ABIs often seek to incorporate so-called 'flagship developments' that help establish an identity or brand. Often the facilities build upon local heritage, such as the BALTIC art gallery in Gateshead (these forms of culture-led regeneration are addressed in more detail in Chapter 6). At other times, flagship buildings are parachuted into the city, like the Cardiff Bay Visitor Centre ('The Tube'), an award-winning building by Will Alsop designed to look like a futuristic telescope looking out across the bay. The Laganside development was littered with flagship developments, such as the Odyssey Millennium project, while developments such as Manchester Printworks constitute stand-alone flagship buildings in their own right. In each case, these developments provide a symbolic and physical focus for an area's regeneration, and are often accompanied by a suite of less ambitious commercial developments around them. As with all ABI-led regeneration, the rationale for flagship projects is that a trickle-down effect will occur, whereby economic benefits will gradually spread to surrounding areas. Whether and how this process actually occurs in practice is highly contested, as the example of Portsmouth's Millennium Tower demonstrates. But despite the gloss and glitz of many regeneration projects, they have been criticised in some quarters for being superficial and failing to address underlying economic issues. The following example of Glasgow offers an insight into some of the issues surrounding economic regeneration.

Glasgow – critiquing economic regeneration

Glasgow was at one point the second city of the British Empire, acting as a hub for the massive concentration of ship-building and heavy industry in the Clydeside region. The decline of the empire coupled with deindustrialisation in the early twentieth century saw massive job losses and the politicisation of a highly unionised left-wing workforce. The population halved from its peak at 1.3m in 1930, and by the 1970s Glasgow was officially recognised as the most deprived city in Britain, associated with a rather undesirable public image of crime, slums and heavy drinking. In 1981 the Glasgow District Council established an Economic Development and Employment Committee charged with reversing the city's economic fortunes. The committee quickly focused on re-branding the city with the 'Glasgow's miles better' campaign in 1983, and established a series of arts and cultural projects. At around the same time they began to pursue private sector participation in the physical regeneration of the city centre, and set up Glasgow Action, a business-led quango whose goal was to make the city a more attractive place in which to work, live and play (MacLeod, 2002).

A series of high profile flagship regeneration projects were subsequently undertaken in key areas, including designer retail developments at Princes Square and the Italian Centre, café culture and gentrification within the Merchant City, and the transformation of Buchanan Street into a focal point for culture, shopping and leisure. On its own terms, the regeneration of Glasgow has undoubtedly been a success. Named European City of Culture in 1990 and British City of Architecture in 1999, Glasgow now attracts thousands of tourists and shoppers each year, and is a major conference location.

Despite the glitzy transformation of large parts of the city centre, doubts remain over the degree to which the city's inhabitants have benefited. For example, in 2011, over 25,000 people in the city were claiming unemployment benefits (Scottish Government, 2011), questioning the degree to which wealth has trickled down from the regenerated areas to the rest of the population. As Marxist geographer David Harvey has noted, flagship regeneration projects like convention centres and art galleries are enjoyed more by wealthy visitors than the locally disadvantaged populations who live there. Related to this, the regenerating city can be seen as a patchwork of spaces that have become detached from one another. ABIs have completely renovated and transformed parts of the city, whilst neighbouring areas remain physically derelict and socio-economically deprived, questioning the reality of trickle-down.

Gordon MacLeod (2002) notes that the spatial splintering of the city is accompanied by a social splintering, as certain types of people are excluded from the newly regenerated spaces. Again drawing on the Buchanan Street area of Glasgow, he describes how hostels in the area for the city's homeless have been cleared away as part of the re-fashioning of the space. Beggars, the homeless and street artists have no place in the newly imagined spaces of urban regeneration, which privilege economic consumption practices like shopping, eating out and leisure. Those elements of society who lack the money to be able to partake in these activities are excluded by private security forces, the police and CCTV. MacLeod argues that the most pernicious aspect of this process is the normalisation of this discourse through the popular press. Rather than arguing that the socio-economically marginal deserve help, the press tends to suggest that these unwanted elements of society are damaging the city's image and need to be removed or hidden from view. The economic success stories that are proudly proclaimed on regeneration project websites hide the story of who gains and who loses.

These problems are undoubtedly a side effect of the neoliberal logic that champions competition and markets to deliver change. It seems almost inevitable that welfare and wealth redistribution agendas will become marginalised in favour of private commercial wealth generation. But despite the rhetoric of Public Private Partnerships (PPP), the local state has often borne the main financial risks in delivering flagship regeneration projects, while private industry has reaped the rewards.

Evaluating ABIs

ABIs have constituted the main policy approach to urban regeneration over the last 30 years. Under the SRB, 1,027 bids were approved in the six competitive funding rounds between 1995 and 2001, equating to over £5.7bn in SRB support and £26bn of total expenditure across England (Rhodes et al., 2003). In examining the impact of delivery mechanisms over a two-decade period (1981–2000), Rhodes et al. (2005) estimate that the public sector spend on regeneration policy measures has been close to £10bn, which in turn attracted a £38bn spend by the private sector and other agencies. The estimated outputs of this investment have been nearly 18,000 hectares of reclaimed land, 22 million square metres of floor space, 350,000 net jobs and close to 195,000 new housing units.

On one level the impact of these schemes is obvious, as they have transformed the actual physical appearance of many urban areas. In economic terms the impacts are harder to measure. Most cities have numerous projects occurring simultaneously, so any positive economic benefits will be the result of multiple factors. Further, it is impossible to predict how a city's economy might have developed in the absence of a particular regeneration scheme (Noon et al., 2000). Rhodes et al. (2005) identify three analytical problems in assessing ABIs. Firstly, while the idea of focusing investment and resources on an area makes intuitive sense, the actual processes that are supposed to drive change are poorly understood. For example, it is assumed that the process of trickle-down will occur, but in practice there is a danger that ABIs merely displace investment from elsewhere in the city. Secondly, the tools used to evaluate ABIs have been poorly developed, partly due to the tendency of these initiatives to address a range of problems, from the provision of new infrastructure to job creation and crime prevention. Thirdly, and related to the diversity of problems addressed, there is a lack of data available to fully assess key goals against their outcomes. These problems have led some to argue that ABI regeneration has been largely superficial and has failed to address the underlying socio-economic problems of cities, merely displacing them.

Despite problems of quantification, there is little doubt that the ABI approach to urban regeneration has played a key role in reversing the economic decline of cities in the UK. Returning to Table 4.1, the population trends for the UK's main regenerating cities are either stabilising or have become positive. As the case studies above show, urban cores have been revitalised. By 2007, city-centre land was attracting high rents, business had been wooed back into the city and with it had come a skilled and more affluent workforce. But these trends have been threatened by a rapidly changing economic and political climate, which has brought the property boom to an abrupt end and prompted a swing to the political right with the accompanying tightening of public purse strings that such a shift inevitably entails. The next section turns to consider the underlying economic factors that drove regeneration between 1997 and 2007, and the implications of the subsequent financial crisis for regeneration activities.

Key points

i) Public funding is used to kick-start large-scale regeneration projects, providing infrastructure and stoking confidence which then attracts further investment.

ii) Flagship buildings are used to make powerful visual statements about regeneration projects that will put them on the map.

iii) Branding and image are increasingly central to regeneration partnerships, and are used to market schemes to developers, business and the public.

iv) While hard to measure in quantifiable terms, urban regeneration has generally been judged an economic success, although social critiques of the neoliberal approach highlight the uneven distribution of benefits.

The financial crisis and its impact on regeneration funding

Regeneration and the property boom

The regeneration policies of New Labour brought prosperity to many inner cities, as house-builders flocked to construct apartment blocks and move shopping centres back into city centres. Indeed, at the height of the boom many cities were reporting that 15–20% of their entire central areas were under regeneration (Punter, 2010b). The main drivers for what will surely come to be seen as an exceptional period of redevelopment activity were government policies to encourage high-density city-centre living, and the availability of cheap credit for these homes to be bought.

Between 1997 and 2007, apartment construction in the UK trebled, driving the average density of new residential developments from 25 to 44 dwellings per hectare. At its peak in 2008/09, apartments accounted for 50% of annual housing unit creation, falling back to 35% in 2010/11 (CLG, 2012c). Requirements for a proportion of new developments to be affordable housing drove densities higher, as developers sought to offset these perceived losses by cramming more units into the same space. Much of the pre-2008 demand for these properties came from buy-to-let investors, who were attracted by the rapid gains in property prices, the increasing rental yields of suddenly desirable city pads and the availability of relatively cheap credit with which to purchase properties. As Figure 4.6 shows, average house prices in the UK almost trebled from just under £80,000 to just over £220,000 between

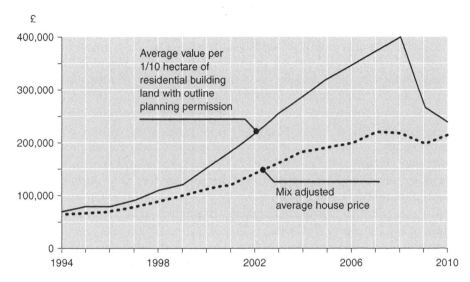

Figure 4.6 Average UK house and land prices 1994–2010.

Source: CLG (2012d)

1997 and 2007. Perhaps more starkly, land prices more than quadrupled over the same period, driven further by the increasing densities of new developments. In 1997, the average price per hectare of residential building land with outline planning permission was £921,000, rising to just over £4m in 2008, before falling back to £2.3m in 2010 (CLG, 2012d).

Interestingly, outside of London and key regional urban centres such as Edinburgh, Bristol, Leeds and Manchester which attracted service sector industries into new build offices, the majority of regeneration consisted of converting unwanted industrial buildings or office stock into apartments, and occasionally hotels. In their report on the competitiveness of English cities, Simmie et al. (2006) conclude that the presence of a strong knowledge economy, combined with high levels of economic productivity, are the best indicators of overall success. While economic success is concentrated in London and the urban areas to the west, south and north of London, Manchester, Derby and Newcastle also demonstrated strong economic growth. But while urban competitiveness depends on cities being able to offer a high quality of life in order to attract a skilled workforce, Simmie et al. found that economic success in cities like Derby and Manchester was still accompanied by high proportions of socio-economically deprived populations. Regeneration beyond the city centre tended to be concentrated in very specific places in the form of government-funded estate regeneration programmes, or the regeneration of former industrial or institutional sites (Punter, 2010a).

The financial crisis

The financial crisis that engulfed Western economies from 2008 onwards originated in the sub-prime mortgage market in the USA, where rapidly rising house prices had been fuelled by lending large amounts of money to relatively poor home-buyers. As interest rates crept up from a historic low of 1% in 2003 to over 5% in 2006, many home-owners defaulted on their mortgage repayments causing a wave of repossessions. Falling house prices plunged many home-owners into dreaded 'negative equity', whereby the value of their property was actually less than the amount they borrowed to purchase it. As home-owners defaulted in the face of falling house prices and high interest rates, banks were forced to write off increasingly large amounts of debt. This problem was exacerbated by the tendency of banks to lend to so-called 'sub-prime' individuals with either shaky credit ratings or low earnings in the run-up to the crisis.

Bad debt spread like a contagion from the USA through the global financial system because banks around the world had purchased financial securities that were actually comprised of sub-prime mortgage debt. Supposed to provide guaranteed returns to investors based on mortgage repayments, these securities effectively became worthless as the situation in the US housing market deteriorated. The British housing market was similarly afflicted by declining house prices and rising defaults on loan repayments. The exposure of many banks and mortgage companies to bad debt was sufficient to drive them out of business, prompting government bailouts on both sides of the Atlantic. Huge amounts of cash were injected into banks like Northern Rock and Royal Bank of Scotland in the UK, and mortgage lenders like Fanny Mae and Fanny Mac in the US, in return for shares in the companies (resulting in nationalisation in a few extreme cases).

The sub-prime mortgage crisis became a full-blown financial crisis as banks became either unable or unwilling to lend money. The closure of lines of credit to potential home-buyers and businesses exacerbated a global economic slow-down, while the inability of banks to lend even to each other paralysed the international credit system. Governments were forced to step into the breach to inject liquidity, or credit, into the system, in some cases simply printing money and drip feeding it into the economy through so-called quantitative easing. The financial implications for governments have been disastrous, as they themselves had to raise cash to bail banks out by issuing bonds for investors to purchase, which are a form of debt that must be paid back at interest over a number of years. The bad debts run up by irresponsible lending on the part of banks and mortgage companies have simply been turned into national debts that have a longer pay-off period.

The current crisis is perhaps different from the recessions of the 1970s and 1990s, in that central banks now have the power to keep interest rates low in order to stimulate growth through borrowing and spending (they reached a staggering 15%

in 1989). It is also arguable that underlying economic production is stronger now than in either previous period. That said, the current international financial system is so interlinked that coordinated reform is very difficult, and Western economies are hit by the double whammy of higher taxes and lower spending while they try to bear the cost of servicing high levels of debt.

The financial crisis threatens to undo many of the achievements of regeneration in the UK, and its specific implications are two-fold. Firstly, it is now considerably more difficult to borrow money to either fund developments or purchase property than it was pre-2008. Secondly, governments themselves are cutting back on spending in order to reduce levels of national debt, with the result that public funding for regeneration has been severely curtailed. A government report published in 2009 on the implications of the credit crunch for regeneration in the UK (Parkinson et al., 2009) found that commercial property in regeneration areas has actually been hit harder than that lying outside regeneration areas, with returns on properties inside falling over 6% in 2007, compared to falls of 3.4% across the UK on average. In terms of housing, the unavailability of credit has made it hard for would-be home-buyers to secure mortgages, and difficult for specialist mortgage lenders to secure funds to lend, with overall lending falling 43% between the first half of 2007 and 2008. As a result, home-building has also decreased sharply, with Berkeley Homes recording a 50% fall in sales between the onset of the crisis in 2007 and 2008. Within this overall picture, regeneration areas have been hit hardest, as many potential home-buyers in these areas are considered higher risk by lenders, due to their poorer socio-economic status.

Because the properties that increased most in value during the housing boom tended to be flats and apartments in the centres of northern cities, it is these same developments that have fallen furthest since the bubble burst. Housing Renewal Pathfinder schemes stalled due to the difficulty of attracting private developers to projects that would be reliant on selling properties to sub-prime house-buyers, and the publicly funded Pathfinders were themselves subsequently scrapped in the so-called 'bonfire of the quangos' (see Chapter 2). Activities in major growth areas like the Thames Gateway have been seriously impeded by the drying up of private investment, raising questions about the ability of the current regeneration agenda to deliver sustainable communities in the absence of economic growth (Raco, 2012). It is simply becoming harder to meet regeneration goals due to the dwindling number of development projects. For example, targets for a percentage of total housing to be social housing yield fewer homes when the overall number of homes being built is down. The lower margins of return available to investors have made them less likely to pursue developments with social goals, or additional costs associated with brownfield remediation. Conversely, London has been insulated most from the effects of the financial crisis by the continued wealth generation activities of the financial services and the appeal of commercial and residential property to global investors, who are using it as a safe haven against instability in other asset classes.

These geographical and economic trends run the risk of producing the kinds of socially homogeneous and spatially uneven development that the last 15 years of regeneration policy have sought to avoid.

Turning to the different types of development, apartments and volume house-building have been hit hardest, as demand at the lower end of the housing market has been decimated by the unwillingness of financial institutions to lend to first-time buyers. Public development schemes like hospital- and school-building or commercial developments with lower residential components have tended to continue, assuming greater importance to the sector as private developments have dried up. In 2008, public sector contracts amounted to £12 billion, of which 32% was for educational facilities, 24% for housing, 17% for infrastructure and 8% for health (Rydin, 2010). That said, as the PFI programme of school- and hospital-building committed to by the New Labour government winds up, there will be little public building to replace it under the austerity plans of the Conservative and Liberal Coalition government that took power in 2010, aside from the odd strategic infrastructure scheme. Indeed, it was in response to the 2009 Parkinson Report that the outgoing Labour government brought forward £775m of funding for the Homes and Communities Association and its KickStart scheme into its final budget, to help private developers and RPs complete stalled housing developments (discussed in the case study below). The Parkinson Report identified the RDAs as key to keeping the wheels of development turning, but these were subsequently abolished by the Coalition government. Huge cut-backs in public sector funding and support for regeneration mean that the knowledge-base and skills that have built up over the last 15 years have been significantly eroded (Carpenter, 2009).

Case Study: Kickstart and the Homes and Communities Agency

The Homes and Communities Agency (HCA) was born into the property crash of 2007–08 as an amalgamation of English Partnerships and the Housing Corporation. English Partnerships was the property development arm of urban regeneration, while the Housing Corporation dealt with funding affordable housing. Despite ingrained differences between the institutional cultures of the two agencies, there was a clear logic to bringing them together in terms of achieving the holistic goals of urban regeneration. Upon its creation, a key role of the HCA was to manage the National Affordable Housing Programme, which pumped some £8.4bn into social housing between 2008 and 2011 (HCA, 2012b). Government spending on housing has traditionally been one of the most effective forms of fiscal stimulus, and the New Labour government poured funds into the programme as part of their effort to prop up the ailing national economy.

The HCA also managed the Kickstart programme, which was created to help complete stalled housing developments and get new developments off the ground in disadvantaged areas. Kickstart worked by investing in private developments for a share of equity in the development, to be paid back once the development was sold (HCA, 2012a). By its very nature, however, as a stimulus fund for developments that have effectively become 'uneconomical' in market terms, very little money was recouped as selling prices were often too low to trigger repayment clauses. The HCA has also been criticised for using public money to help what have often been fairly conventional housing developments with few social or environmental credentials, and was the focus of a sustained campaign by the journal *Building Design* about the number of schemes with dismal scores on the Building for Life quality scale (Hurst, 2010). This controversy can be interpreted as a reflection of the tension between the goals of the Kickstart programme to stimulate house-building more widely, and the core remit of the HCA which is to provide quality social housing.

Under the Coalition government, funding for Kickstart and the Affordable Housing Programme was slashed. For example, the HCA budget for 2009–10 was £3.7bn, which compares rather unfavourably to its *total* budget of £4.5bn for the four-year period 2011–15 (HCA, 2012b). That said, the HCA now controls the considerable land investments of the former Regional Development Agencies as well as those inherited from English Partnerships. As a result it looks set to play a key role in supporting LEPs in the core city-regions, although the lack of regional ring-fencing will undoubtedly mean a return to a more competitive funding regime that pits local authorities against one another.

The outlook

Although the economic picture seems bleak, some authors have pointed to potential benefits associated with the financial crisis, even if they are relatively small. The long property boom that fuelled regeneration until 2008 and high levels of private investment are unlikely to return in the foreseeable future. This means that cities themselves will need to be far more proactive in driving regeneration and identifying different types of development (All Party Urban Development Group, 2009). Indeed, sociologist Anthony Giddens (2009), originator of New Labour's Third Way, has argued that 'the state is back' after years of deregulation and market dominance.

At a practical level, local governments with money have been able to attain cheaper land for future projects. But the credit crunch has also made it clear that the emphasis on high-density housing in city centres went too far at the expense of other types of residential development, and the current hiatus provides respite from a slew of poorly designed developments and space to reflect upon policies. New forms of regeneration might be stimulated by the green economy, which aims to direct public spending towards sustainable development, especially renewable energy infrastructure (New Economics Foundation, 2008). Policy-makers and urban planners seem to equate future economic growth with an ideology of enterprise and are fixated on attracting high-tech and other knowledge-intensive industries (Armstrong, 2001: 524). But opportunities to conduct regeneration in different ways are emerging at the grass-roots level, as community-led projects assume greater importance (Evans et al., 2009). The discourse of the Big Society and the provisions for Neighbourhood Planning in the Localism Act, 2011, lend legislative support to this potential direction for regeneration.

To summarise, the success of urban regeneration in the late 1990s and 2000s was based upon a growing national economy, cheap credit and high levels of public spending (Parkinson et al., 2006). None of these conditions is currently present, and neither do they look likely to return until at least the middle of the decade. While this opens up opportunities for different types of regeneration activity, with potentially greater involvement of communities and local governments, the overall level of regeneration can be expected to remain subdued for the foreseeable future. Within this context, the second major strand of UK economic policy, which attempts to generate organic economic growth within cities by encouraging entrepreneurship, has assumed greater importance.

Key points

i) Urban regeneration in the UK rode the wave of a property boom between 1997 and 2007.

ii) The current financial crisis and the bursting of the property bubble have severely reduced levels of regeneration, as developments are unable to secure funding.

iii) The crisis is hitting hardest in areas that either have been or are about to be regenerated, as these developments carry greater risk for developers.

iv) The hiatus in regeneration activity has opened up opportunities for alternative models of development, but the general outlook is challenging.

The entrepreneurial city

The knowledge economy and national policy

Economic policies to unleash the latent or internal potential of cities focus on improving the knowledge base, encouraging enterprise, providing education and training, and empowering local businesses. The UK government embraced the idea of the knowledge-based economy in the White Paper, *Our Competitive Future: Building the Knowledge-Driven Economy* (DTI, 1998). In it they argue that all businesses will have 'to marshal their knowledge and skills to satisfy customers, exploit market opportunities and meet society's aspirations for a better environment' (ibid.: 6). Two ways in which UK policy has attempted to harness high-value, knowledge-based industries are encouraging links between universities and industry, and cluster policy. The UK announced a ten-year science and innovation investment strategy in 2004 designed to help the UK exploit the commercial opportunities offered by new technologies such as micro and nanotechnologies (MNT). The potential economic value to the UK is considerable, with the creation of high-value jobs and industries. Many cities are seeking to develop and attract these types of new technologies through expanding the higher education sector, and encouraging knowledge transfer between universities and high-tech industry. The international model for this approach to economic regeneration is well known: located on the outskirts of San Francisco, Stanford University played a vital role in educating the internet entrepreneurs who went on to make Silicon Valley one of the most economically successful regions on the planet.

One of the key policy responses to encourage this sort of economic development has been cluster policy. Based upon the work of Porter (1990), the former DTI (2004) defined clusters as 'concentrations of competing, collaborating and interdependent companies and institutions which are connected by a system of market and non-market links'. The idea underpinning clusters is that similar industries will locate in close proximity to one another in order to facilitate various linkages, for example through the exchange of ideas, goods and workers. The DTI identified three 'critical success factors', which clearly resonate with the wider tenets of the knowledge economy: the presence of functioning networks and partnerships; a strong innovation base with supporting R&D activities where appropriate; and the existence of a strong skills base. The now defunct RDAs followed the DTI in adopting strong policies to encourage clustering, earmarking business parks as 'biotech-parks', or attempting to create high-tech corridors (essentially linear clusters) along key transport conduits.

While clearly influential in policy, the logic of clusters has been criticised. Perhaps of key importance to urban economies is the question of whether it is possible to generate new clusters of industry, given the need for a range of 'soft' networks and the lifestyle demands of the creative classes. A second key question involves the types of industry that are being courted. While every city covets a biotech cluster, few divert funds to support existing but less 'trendy' clusters, associated, for example, with logistics (transport) and manufacturing industry.

Enterprise

Increasingly, policy-makers are interested in how businesses start up and grow. Small and Medium-sized Enterprises (SMEs) have been important drivers of economic growth. Over the last 20 years these businesses have created two thirds of all new jobs, more than two thirds of the innovation in the economy and have accounted for two thirds of the differences in economic growth rates among industrialised nations (Walburn, 2005). Immigration has also had a startling impact on entrepreneurial activity. Almost a third of all high-tech firms started in Silicon Valley between 1995 and 1998 were run by Chinese- or Indian-born engineers. In 1998 these businesses had more than 58,000 employees and sales of close to $17bn (Saxenian, 1999). Jane Jacobs (1985) has argued that cities host innovation, as they are the only places capable of substituting goods and services that they import for things that they produce themselves. While the argument is fairly complex, it involves the realisation that only cities can generate a critical mass of supply chains and consumer demand for products and services. It is surely no coincidence that London lies in the south east, which has been the UK's most economically prosperous region in the post-war period. This region has produced approximately 33% more significant innovations than other English regions over the same period. It is also one of only ten 'islands of innovation' in Europe, defined as accounting for 20% of the national research and design budget, having a strong presence of both research institutions and enterprises. The key needs of this sector were access to skilled workers, proximity to international airports and general standard of living factors such as quality of housing and schools (Simmie et al., 2002).

Three government papers frame enterprise and innovation policy and show a clear development in government thinking that seeks to link knowledge and enterprise as the basis for global competitiveness. The DTI's Science and Innovation White Paper (2000) set a framework for the government's role as the key investor in the science base and facilitator of collaboration between universities and business. The White Paper on Enterprise, Skills and Innovation (DTI, 2001) linked the importance of science and innovation to regional (and national) economic growth, with the need to raise skills as a key issue. A number of initiatives were announced to invest in innovation and new technologies, including e-business and the need to foster an environment for enterprise. Building upon these themes, *Competing in a Global Economy: The Innovation Challenge* (DTI, 2003a) situated the importance of knowledge and invention within the global context, stating that:

> The creativity and inventiveness of our people is our country's greatest asset and has always underpinned the UK's economic success. But in an increasingly global world, our ability to invent, design and manufacture the goods and services that people want is more vital to our future prosperity than ever. (DTI, 2003: 5)

Creating the conditions for enterprise is notoriously hard, involving a suite of educational, financial and other support services and schemes. New facilities are often located within central regeneration schemes, such as the Moorgates Croft

Business centre in Rotherham. Common barriers to entrepreneurship have been identified as:

- the involvement of too many agencies and institutions;
- changing names and remits of institutions and lack of policy coherence;
- discontinuity of funding; and
- problems of access to finance.

These problems are often a consequence of the fact that public programmes in the UK are time-limited, designed to start up new businesses, or to demonstrate a commercial opportunity to a recalcitrant private sector. Programmes tend to collapse as soon as public funding ceases, damaging the credibility of the sector more generally. One emerging solution to these problems involves Community Finance Initiatives, which involve a form of charitable lending to enterprises that would be considered too high risk to be able to access traditional bank loans (Bryson and Buttle, 2005). While regeneration that focuses on bringing in investment from outside can be measured in terms of tonnes of concrete, jobs created or private funds, it is harder to measure the outputs of schemes designed to unleash local enterprise. This explains the current government's penchant for figures tracking numbers of business start-ups and the fortunes of SMEs, as the number of these businesses provides an indicator of the health of local enterprise.

Education and training

Early urban policy focused upon the need to create jobs and opportunity. For example, the Department of Employment White Papers, *Employment: The Challenge for the Nation* (1985a), and *Lifting the Burden* (1985b) emphasised the importance of creating jobs and a skilled labour force capable of doing them. The papers set out a decidedly neoliberal agenda of enterprise and competitiveness for labour policy, which was subsequently backed up by the Employment Department Group White Paper, *People, Jobs and Opportunity* (Department of Employment, 1992). In order to address the needs of the labour market, Training and Enterprise Councils (TECs) were set up in 1990 in order to channel public money into re-skilling and entrepreneurial programmes. The TECs were partnership-driven, but strongly influenced by the needs of private industry, advancing the neoliberal agenda of 'improved competitiveness, for individuals and businesses' (Hart and Johnston, 2000: 136).

These policies were criticised for prioritising private economic development at the expense of other important factors, such as health, environmental quality and the needs of community groups. When the Labour government took power in 1997 they retained the neoliberal approach to employment policy, but married it to a concern for including those groups in society who were excluded from mainstream economic activity.

In 2001, the Learning and Skills Council (LSC) was set up under the Learning and Skills Act 2000 in order to further the social inclusion agenda and help socio-economically disadvantaged groups who were relatively unskilled and dependent on benefits. The LSC was a non-departmental public body that replaced the former Further Education Funding Council and the 72 TECs. In 2006–07, they had a budget of £10.4bn to cover adult education outside of the University sector, making them the largest and most well-funded quango in the UK. Resonating with the goals of the national strategies on innovation and competitiveness, the LSC aimed to:

- raise participation and achievement by young people;
- increase adult demand for learning;
- raise skills levels for national competitiveness;
- improve the quality of education and training delivery;
- equalise opportunities through better access to learning; and
- improve the effectiveness and efficiency of the sector.

As might be expected, their remit was driven by the needs of industry, running the National Skills Academies that responded to employer needs to deliver the skills required by each major sector of the economy. The main criticism of the LSC was that because it dealt with formal educational courses and awards, it often failed to capture the skills that have been (or need to be) learnt 'on the job'. As discussed above with reference to enterprise, formal efforts to support economic growth struggle to be responsive and comprehensive enough to meet the rapidly changing demands of businesses.

In addition to strategic failings, the LSC was plagued by what the Public Accounts Committee described as 'catastrophic mismanagement' of its college building programme. The rebuilding programme that was supposed to renovate over half of England's colleges resulted in £2.7bn of debt, with 144 building contracts being terminated or breached, incurring financial penalties. Over 20 colleges have been left with a legacy of debt that accounts for more than 40% of their annual income. In the face of these chronic failures, the LSC was shut down in March 2008.

The rejection of centralised, top-down initiatives and quangos became a formal priority under the Coalition government, which has sought to make policy more responsive to local economic needs, through, for example, the creation of LEPs. In addition to partnering local authorities with local business leaders, the main thrust of the White Paper on Local Growth (BIS, 2010) was to redistribute power in order to encourage economic growth at the local level. In terms of entrepreneurialism, LEPs are the flagship vehicle through which locally driven training and skills provision is to be delivered. The Paper states:

[Local Economic] Partnerships will want to work closely with universities, further education colleges and other key economic stakeholders. This includes social and community enterprises, which play an important role in creating local economic growth through providing jobs and training, delivering services and helping create community wealth in some of the most deprived parts of the country. (BIS, 2010: 14)

In short, LEPs are encouraged to identify local training needs and work with Further Education (post-compulsory, pre-degree level) and Higher Education (degree level) partners to deliver them. The identification of training needs by LEPs is supported by the Skills Funding Agency, which invests £4 billion per year of public spending in colleges and training organisations to fund training for adults in England. Funding is allocated to colleges and other skills and training organisations who have discretion over expenditure to meet the needs of local businesses and communities.

The European Union also committed itself to a ten-year strategy of reform for Europe's product, capital and labour markets. The aim, agreed by Heads of State and Government in Lisbon in 2000, was to create a Europe by 2010 comprising 'the most competitive and dynamic knowledge-based economy in the world, capable of sustainable economic growth with more and better jobs and greater social cohesion' (DTI, 2003c: vii). In response to the Lisbon Agenda, European regional funding is now clearly focused on stimulating growth and jobs at regional and local level. For instance, 75% of the Regional Competitiveness and Employment objective funding is earmarked for the Lisbon Agenda in the UK. As part of the ERDF, the European Social Fund (ESF) is a key source of funds to extend employment opportunities and develop a skilled and adaptable workforce. The Department for Work and Pensions (DWP) has overall responsibility for ESF funds in England. From 1 April 2010, the Skills Funding Agency took over the ESF Co-financing Organisation responsibilities of the former Learning and Skills Council.

Regional grants are based upon employment and skills needs, and are matched with a similar amount of national funding. The 2007–13 England ESF programme is investing £5 billion over seven years of which £2.5 billion is from the ESF and £2.5 billion is national funding. Between 2007 and 2013, the north east has been allocated £196m, London £403m, and the West Midlands £305m. According to the DWP, 225,000 unemployed or inactive participants had been helped into work by 2011 (DWP, 2011).

The quality of jobs created is critical, though. As noted by Simmie et al. (2006), the presence of a strong knowledge economy, combined with high levels of economic productivity, are the best indicators of overall success, and these factors are generally linked, as productivity depends on the kinds of jobs that are created. This means that an increase in the proportion of low-paid, low-skilled jobs in a city may actually reduce the overall productivity of the workforce.

Many commentators have noted that while the rhetoric of enterprise and training pervades job policy, the types of jobs created by urban regeneration are often menial in nature, or what have been termed 'McJobs'. For example, the leisure industry offers among the lowest paid, least well trained and least secure employment, but often makes up the bulk of jobs created by new regeneration schemes. Furthermore, these jobs are disproportionately taken up by the poorer, ethnic minority and female populations of the inner city. David Harvey (1989) has argued that rather than spending millions of pounds in public money on flagship buildings that have no real purpose, this money could be better diverted into training and education schemes for disadvantaged communities to enable them to obtain better jobs.

Key points

i) Enterprise and innovation are seen as key drivers of economic growth in cities.

ii) This has led to an emphasis on education and training, in order to create skilled workforces that can work in the New Economy.

iii) Policies seek to establish clusters of knowledge-intensive industries, to encourage entrepreneurial start-ups and to empower local businesses.

iv) LEPs are being asked to play a key role in coordinating the delivery of training to meet business needs at the local level.

Conclusions

This chapter has focused upon the key mechanisms of urban regeneration that have been used to revive the economic fortunes of cities in the UK. For the most part, this has involved regenerating old industrial manufacturing cities that have suffered from dereliction, de-population, deskilling and deprivation to be attractive to the service sector industry. This task is not easy – as Richard Florida (2002) notes, the economically successful cities of today have to compete to attract a globally mobile 'creative class' of workers. Cities such as Glasgow and Manchester have undertaken major physical regeneration programmes, focusing on the wholesale redevelopment of specific areas of the city. ABIs have generally featured flagship regeneration projects designed to 'put the city on the map' as an attractive and culturally vibrant place, focusing on central areas that have been abandoned by manufacturing industry. Projects generally seek to maximise pre-existing assets like historic buildings and waterfronts, and draw upon a range of different funding sources to generate a mix of retail, leisure, business and residential uses, often organised around flagship developments to promote trickle-down. In addition to the ABI approach that hopes to attract industry to the city, regeneration has focused on unleashing the economic potential of its own inhabitants. These policies have focused on: improving the knowledge base; encouraging entrepreneurialism, education and training; and empowering local businesses.

On balance, it is hard to argue against the assertion that the UK's cities are in far better economic shape now than they were 20 years ago, although there are caveats to this conclusion. As with most evaluations, it is hard to know what would have happened to urban economies in the absence of regeneration policies, or given different policy goals. While the importance of a generally benign global economic environment in the decade to 2008 cannot be overstated, it is worth noting that in the context of different urban policies in the late 1980s even an economic boom failed to lift the UK's cities out of their decline.

These successes are not unproblematic, however. The agenda for urban regeneration has been dominated by neoliberal policies that emphasise the role of the private sector in generating wealth at the expense of welfare and social support. This has undoubtedly created tensions between economic policies and wider social and environmental goals. The mono-logic of 'global economic forces' tends to marginalise certain groups in society who do not or cannot fit into the skilled worker/consumer blueprint for which today's city is designed. Furthermore, questions have been raised over the extent to which all cities can play the same game. For example, the number of young professionals able to purchase city centre apartments and the amount of consumer spending power to support new retail outlets and leisure facilities are not infinite. The rhetoric of place marketing and flagship regeneration schemes belies the increasingly generic appearance of many of the UK's cities. Many cities cannot realistically aspire to achieve the knowledge base and environmental quality of a city such as San Francisco, or even Cambridge, in the near future. As Deas and Giordano note (2002), there is no inevitability about economic regeneration – while Manchester has performed well from a very weak asset base, its neighbour Liverpool has received far more funding and yet not achieved anywhere near the same level of economic success.

The current financial crisis will make these disparities greater. The contraction of credit has made private finance exceptionally hard to secure for developments, while the abolition of the RDAs has sharply reduced the availability of public funding for regeneration. The negative effects of an era of financial austerity will undoubtedly be felt most acutely in socio-economically disadvantaged areas, which are more economically dependent on public funding and regeneration. The devolution of power to LEPs is potentially liberating, but in the absence of funding to match the ambitions, their ability to secure money for projects remains to be seen. In this context, cities may well have to differentiate their regeneration models and goals more sharply from one another in order to succeed.

Social cohesion is vital in making a place safe and tolerant of difference; education and inclusion of the disadvantaged is needed to create skilled workforces; and improved environmental quality is necessary to increase quality of life and attractiveness of cities to the creative classes. None of these things will happen if regeneration focuses solely on generating wealth for private companies and individuals. While the ultimate goal of urban regeneration is to rejuvenate urban economies, the logic of private wealth accumulation needs to be reconciled with the need to include different social groups and improve the urban environment and infrastructure. Achieving this balance is the critical challenge facing urban regeneration in the UK, and the next two chapters consider the role that social, environmental and cultural factors play in this process.

Further reading

For those interested in the wider relations between cities and national economies, Jane Jacobs provides a good place to start, having established some of the most influential ideas about what makes urban economies special. Richard Florida's work on the Creative Classes is required reading for anyone intending to understand contemporary urban policy, while the edited collections by Begg and Oatley offer valuable commentaries on the competitive cities debate. In terms of ABI schemes, the review paper by Rhodes et al. provides an excellent overview of the schemes and insights into their successes and failings. Michael Parkinson, MBE, is perhaps the foremost government adviser on urban development in the UK. His 'State of the English Cities' Report for the Office of the Deputy Prime Minister in 2006 presents an authoritative analysis of cities in the UK towards the end of the long boom in property that drove regeneration, while his report of 2009 for CLG provides an insightful analysis of how the financial crisis has hit regeneration activity. Finally, Raco and Flint offer a critical reflection on the deeper implications of economic recession for the dominant model of urban regeneration based on assumptions of market-driven growth, which has characterised the approach of successive UK governments since the 1980s.

Begg, I. (2002) *Urban Competitiveness: Policies for Dynamic Cities* (Policy Press, Bristol).
Florida, R. (2002) *The Rise of the Creative Class: And How It's Transforming Work, Leisure, Community and Everyday Life* (Basic Books, New York).
Jacobs, J. (1985) *Cities and the Wealth of Nations* (Random House, Toronto).
Oatley, N. (ed.) (1998) *Cities, Economic Competition and Urban Policy* (Sage, London).
Parkinson, M., Ball, M. and Key, T. (2009) *The Credit Crunch and Regeneration: Impact and Implications* (CLG, London).
Parkinson, M. et al. (2006) *State of the English Cities* (ODPM, London).

Raco, M. and Flint, J. (eds) (2012) *The Future of Sustainable Cities: Critical Reflections* (Policy Press, Bristol).

Rhodes, J., Tyler, P. and Brennan, A. (2005) 'Assessing the effect of area based initiatives on local area outcomes: some thoughts based on the national evaluation of the Single Regeneration Budget in England', *Urban Studies*, 42(11): 1919–1946.

5 Sustainability

OVERVIEW

Sustainability is a central concept underpinning regeneration in the UK. This chapter explores the policy framework of sustainable regeneration, focusing on its social and environmental dimensions.

- *Sustainable development and regeneration*: explores what sustainability means and how it relates to urban regeneration.
- *The policy framework*: outlines the key policies that frame sustainable regeneration, including the UK sustainability strategies and English National Planning Policy Framework.
- *Social sustainability*: discusses the Sustainable Communities Plan and the challenges of social regeneration, focusing on housing, gentrification and studentification.
- *The brownfield development agenda*: examines the focus of urban regeneration on brownfield sites and how this relates to sustainability in terms of rejuvenating urban areas and preserving the countryside.
- *Climate change, cities and carbon*: outlines the emerging emphasis on addressing climate change through low carbon urban development.
- *Sustainable construction*: discusses how the construction industry can deliver more sustainable urban development, focusing on the importance of skills within the industry and mechanisms through which building practices can be steered.

Sustainable development and regeneration

Much ink has been spilt attempting to pin down the term 'sustainable development'. Originating in the World Commission on Environment and Development's (WCED) Brundtland Report, sustainable development was defined as development that 'meets the needs of the present without compromising the ability of future generations to meet their own needs' (1987: 43). The Brundtland definition is underpinned by the notion of equity, which means using resources fairly to meet the needs of both current and future populations. Since the Brundtland report, considerable effort has gone into refining and fleshing out the notoriously slippery concept of sustainable development. A common understanding of the term in policy is that it considers economic, social and environmental concerns, represented as a set of overlapping circles, where sustainable development occurs in the central area of overlap (Figure 5.1). This tripartite definition has been likened to a three-legged stool, whereby if one of the legs is neglected the stool will fall over. Another way in which the three elements of sustainability have been conceptualised is through the so-called 'triple bottom line', which extends the idea of an economic balance sheet to include social and environmental costs.

Roberts (2000) claims that the three pillars of regeneration are strategic vision, partnership and sustainability and, on the face of it, the goals of sustainable development

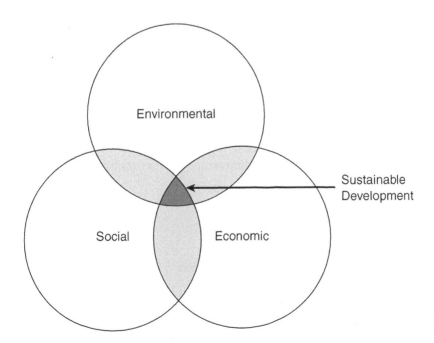

Figure 5.1   The three elements of sustainable development are often depicted as overlapping circles, with sustainability represented by the central area of overlap.

resonate directly with those of regeneration. Regeneration seeks to alleviate social, environmental and economic problems, through, for example, the re-use of derelict land and rejuvenation of impoverished housing stock (Couch and Denneman, 2000). Area Based Initiatives tend to address the needs of an area in a comprehensive manner over relatively long timescales, offering scope to address the three elements of sustainability in a joined-up way. Because they attract public attention and enjoy a high political profile, regeneration schemes often embrace the participatory approach of sustainable development in order to enhance the legitimacy of regeneration projects amongst local communities.

Since the Rio Earth Summit in 1992, UK planning policy has been framed by the principles of sustainable development. Sustainable development lies at the core of the regeneration agenda and is loaded with expectations of being a magic bullet for delivering 'better' cities. Despite the wholesale adoption of sustainability in government policy, however, there is a great deal of debate and tension over what a sustainable development looks like in practice. The definitions given above are far from rigid. For example, the Brundtland version does not specify what constitutes a 'need', or over what timescale the future should be considered. In terms of the tripartite definition of sustainable development, different weightings can be given to each of the three components leading to practical difficulties in balancing social or environmental gains and losses against economic impacts that can more easily be measured financially.

While the complexities surrounding the various meanings of sustainable development have generated a literature in their own right (Mebratu, 1998), the result has been a certain amount of ambiguity over what sustainable regeneration looks like in practice. It is worth noting that 'sustainable development' does not always mean the same thing as 'sustainability'. Although the terms are often used interchangeably, sustainable development is a mainstream formal policy discourse, while sustainability keys into a wider set of ethical ideas that emphasises social and environmental elements. The following chapter explores the role of urban regeneration in making cities more sustainable, especially in the face of climate change. It begins by outlining the key policies framing sustainable regeneration before moving on to consider the main social and environmental dimensions of regeneration.

The policy framework

From sustainability to carbon management

The UK government officially committed to the goals of sustainability at the United Nations Conference on Environment and Development Earth Summit held in Rio in 1992. In addition to signing a series of major treaties on climate change, biodiversity conservation, and principles on forests, it signed up to the Rio Declaration and Local Agenda 21, which set out the procedures through which sustainability should unfold. A key principle set out in these documents is that of *subsidiarity*, which holds that international policy priorities should be cascaded down through the national and regional tiers of government to the local level. It is this principle that lies behind the Rio tagline of 'think global, act local'. Sustainable development thus rests upon a decentralist philosophy that privileges action at the local level, advocating the inclusion of all stakeholder groups in decision-making to achieve legitimacy. It is not a 'one size fits all' policy, but recognises that decisions must be sensitive to the demands and opportunities of differing contexts. It is not about finding a perfect solution, but about achieving a balance that brings the most benefit to the most people.

The holistic approach of sustainability fits neatly with agendas of inclusiveness, multi-agency partnerships and the shift from government to governance that have been pursued with great enthusiasm since the election of the New Labour government in 1997 (see Chapter 3). Building on an earlier government paper, *Sustainable Development: UK Strategy* (DoE, 1994), the New Labour government published two strategies for sustainable development, *A Better Quality of Life: Strategy for Sustainable Development for the UK* (DETR, 1999) and *Securing the Future: UK Government Sustainable Development Strategy* (ODPM, 2005d). Four key elements ran through these documents: social cohesion and inclusion, protection and enhancement of the natural environment, prudent use of natural resources, and sustainable economic growth. In 2000 the general goals enshrined in the strategies for sustainable development were developed into a more specific vision for regeneration, in the Urban White Paper, *Our Towns and Cities: The Future*, which aimed to:

> ...bring together economic, social and environmental measures in a coherent approach to enable people and places to achieve their economic potential; bring social justice and equality of opportunity; and create places where people want to live and work. These issues are interdependent and cannot be looked at in isolation. For instance, there are close links between housing, health and education. That is why moving towards more mixed and sustainable communities is important to many of our plans for improving the quality of urban life. (DETR, 2000: 8)

As Table 5.1 shows, the Urban White Paper emphasised the holistic elements of sustainability and the need to incorporate environmental considerations into all aspects of design. While Table 5.1 categorises the elements of sustainable regeneration as environmental, economic and social, it is clear that in practice each goal addresses more than one element of sustainability. For example, rejuvenating housing stock simultaneously improves the economic base of an area, benefits the inhabitants socially by providing a better quality of life, and enhances environmental quality. Similarly, each element of sustainability is addressed by more than one regeneration goal. For example, 'prudent use of natural resources', emphasised in the UK strategy, is addressed by the re-use of derelict land (protecting the countryside), energy efficient buildings (reducing consumption of energy) and mixed-use, high-density

Table 5.1   Key elements of sustainable regeneration.

Element of sustainability	Goal	Reason
Environmental	Re-use derelict land for high-density development.	Protect countryside and decrease car use.
	Improve environmental quality.	Enhance quality of life and attract investment.
	Use energy efficient buildings.	Decrease ecological footprint of urban areas.
Economic	Rejuvenate housing stock.	Revitalise city centres.
	Attract development and create jobs.	Improve local economy.
Social	Mixed-use developments (combination of retail, residential and business).	Decrease car use (live, work and play in same area).
	Mixed communities (in terms of age, ethnicity, family structure and income).	Increase social integration.
	Inclusive decision-making.	Respond to local needs and increase social capacity

developments (reducing car use). The Urban White Paper made strong statements identifying 'sustainable' communities with those that are socially 'mixed', and this formed the defining feature for regeneration that was aiming to be socially sustainable. The paper also formalised the brownfield agenda, setting specific targets for 60% of new developments to be built on previously used land by 2008.

The Sustainable Development Commission was created in 2000 to act as an independent advisor on sustainable development issues and help hardwire sustainable development into the activities of government. As with many New Labour quangos it was abolished by the Coalition government that took power in 2010, but it would be a mistake to see its demise solely as a result of political circumstance. Between its inception in 2000 and its abolition in 2011, the challenges of sustainable development had narrowed to a more specific set of concerns surrounding the centrality of the economy to environmental issues, with climate change emerging as the defining issue. As such, the Coalition government came to power claiming to prioritise a shift from our current fossil-fuel-based economy to a so-called 'green economy', capable of generating economic wealth while rapidly reducing greenhouse gas emissions. The 'green economy' is a political compromise between the two coalition partners, marrying the economic development imperatives of the Conservative party to the rather greener agenda of the Liberal Democrats. The Department for Energy and Climate Change has set out a target to reduce carbon emissions by 80% by 2050, calling for a large-scale 'transition' to a low carbon economy. DEFRA's Natural Environment White Paper, sets out a framework for valuing environmental assets in financial terms to enable their worth to be considered more accurately in decision-making (DEFRA, 2011). The question of how many jobs will be created by shifting to low carbon technologies is critical in justifying decisions to direct investment towards greener projects, but it has become something of a political football. Its advocates emphasise that new jobs will be created that are sustainable in every sense, while its detractors point to the jobs that will be lost by forcing polluting industries either to relocate or go out of business.

In light of the growing emphasis on reducing carbon emissions, the sustainability of the built environment has become a persistent concern across academic, professional and policy arenas (Cities Alliance and UNEP, 2007; Strategic Forum for Construction, 2008). Buildings account for approximately 40% of total energy use worldwide (Cole, 2005), and improving the energy efficiency of building stock represents a critical part of the plan to achieve the UK's carbon emissions reduction targets. As a result, technical compliance with energy efficient building regulations has become an increasingly significant aspect of urban design and development in the UK (Guy, 2006). The Department for Communities and Local Government, for example, 'is committed to ensuring that the planning system, building regulations, the building control system and Energy Performance Certificate regimes support our ambitions for a low-carbon and eco-friendly economy' (DEFRA, 2011: 5). In terms of regeneration, the low carbon agenda has highlighted the importance of making sure that buildings are energy efficient, whether they are newly built or existing buildings that are retrofitted with energy efficient technology.

While the idea of a green (or low carbon) economy is not new – the erstwhile Department of Trade and Industry published a White Paper on the Low Carbon Economy (DTI, 2003b) calling on local and regional authorities to develop demonstration and pilot projects to reduce carbon emissions and boost the national economy – the emphasis is on measuring carbon emissions and setting targets for reductions. That said, it would be a mistake to see the low carbon agenda as somehow separate from or antithetical to the priorities of sustainable development. Sustainable development still frames policy in the UK, including urban regeneration, and as the most recent government strategy emphasises, tackling climate change requires an integrated approach to development and planning at all scales.

Planning and sustainability

The planning system is the core mechanism through which sustainable development is delivered. As Sue Owens points out, 'planning and sustainability share two fundamental perspectives – the temporal and the spatial. Both are concerned with future impacts on and of particular localities' (Owens, 1994: 440). For more than two decades, planning has been shaped by a set of planning policies that guide local planning authorities on issues ranging from flood control and housing to greenbelts and geology. Sustainability formed the guiding 'vision' of UK planning policy (Davoudi,

2000), with Planning Policy Statement 1 'Delivering Sustainable Development' forming an over-arching framework for all the other planning policy statements (ODPM, 2005b).

Planning Policy Statement 1, which framed planning policy under New Labour, identified five areas in which planning could deliver the goals of the UK strategy for sustainable development:

- Making suitable land available for development in line with economic, social and environmental objectives to improve people's quality of life.
- Contributing to sustainable economic development.
- Protecting and enhancing the natural and historic environment, the quality and character of the countryside, and existing communities.
- Ensuring high-quality development through good inclusive design, and the efficient use of resources.
- Ensuring that development supports existing communities and contributes to the creation of safe, sustainable, liveable and mixed communities with good access to jobs and key services. (ODPM, 2005b: 9–10)

These areas map onto the priorities for building design in the Sustainable and Secure Buildings Act, 2004, which aims to:

- further the conservation of fuel and power;
- prevent waste, undue consumption, misuse or contamination of water;
- further the protection or enhancement of the environment;
- facilitate sustainable development; and
- further the prevention or detection of crime;

The biggest task facing the planning system in implementing the principles of sustainable development has been the need to balance economic development against the protection of the environment and people's rights and interests. This tension was been thrown into sharp relief by the Barker Report (Barker, 2006), commissioned by the Treasury, which reviewed the efficiency of the planning system in the UK. The report highlighted the chronic undersupply of homes in the UK and suggested that proposed developments needed to be approved more quickly by streamlining the planning process. The Coalition government has enthusiastically taken up the challenge of simplifying the planning system, replacing the system of Planning Policy Statements (of which there were 25), with a single National Planning Policy Framework (NPPF). Although NPPF retains a commitment to sustainable development at its core, the balance has very firmly swung towards the development side of the equation. The Minister for Planning, Greg Clark, states in his foreword, '[t]he purpose of planning is to help achieve sustainable development' (CLG, 2012e: i), but the document casts the three dimensions of sustainable development in these terms:

- *An economic role* – contributing to building a strong, responsive and competitive economy, by ensuring that sufficient land of the right type is available in the right places and at the right time to support growth and innovation; and by identifying and coordinating development requirements, including the provision of infrastructure.
- *A social role* – supporting strong, vibrant and healthy communities, by providing the supply of housing required to meet the needs of present and future generations; and by creating a high-quality built environment, with accessible local services that reflect the community's needs and support its health, social and cultural well-being.
- *An environmental role* – contributing to protecting and enhancing our natural, built and historic environment; and, as part of this, helping to improve biodiversity, use natural resources prudently, minimise waste and pollution, and mitigate and adapt to climate change including moving to a low carbon economy. (CLG, 2012e: 2)

The key goals for the planning system are similar to those in the now defunct Planning Policy Statement 1 – to increase the supply of housing, provide land for development, and enhance the design of places. Similarly, the NPPF continues the emphasis of Planning Policy Statement 1 about working in partnership. The key difference between the two involves the degree of control exerted by the planning system. Rather than controlling development through top-down plan-making, the NPPF provides a framework for local authorities to balance their economic, social and environmental needs against one another and facilitate development more easily, with the intention that the planning system should not act as a brake on economic development, so long as that development is considered 'sustainable'.

Key points

i) Sustainable development frames UK planning policy and means achieving a balance between social, economic and environmental factors.

ii) Urban regeneration is ideally suited to deliver sustainability, as it offers the potential to address the problems of an area in a holistic, long-term way.

iii) Because sustainability cannot be delivered by the government alone, the planning framework for sustainability is partnership-driven.

Social sustainability

Sustainable communities

Urban regeneration between 2003 and 2010 was framed by New Labour's idea of *sustainable communities*, defined as 'places where people want to live and work now and in the future' (ODPM, 2003: 56). Then Deputy Prime Minister John Prescott launched the Sustainable Communities Plan (henceforth referred to as the SCP) in 2003, setting out a long-term programme of action for delivering sustainable communities in both urban and rural areas. The transformation of the ODPM into the department for *Communities* and Local Government (CLG) reflected this new emphasis, adopting the vision 'creating prosperous and cohesive communities, offering a safe, healthy and sustainable environment for all' as its over-arching mission statement.

The SCP translated the wider goals of sustainable urban development into actions for specific places (Raco, 2005). As with previous urban development agendas, the key element of the plan was to tackle housing quality and supply issues, but the SCP also prioritised the need to improve the quality of the **'public realm'** – the surrounding environment and community services that make an area more liveable. The SCP included a significant increase in resources for housing and major reforms to the planning system, with regeneration firmly positioned as the vehicle to create affordable housing in the south east and improve housing in the disadvantaged areas of the Midlands and northern England.

The SCP identified 12 dimensions of sustainable communities (see Box 5.1) that clearly follow the principles of social inclusiveness set out in the UK sustainability strategies, Planning Policy Statement 1, and the subsequent National Planning Policy Framework. From 2003, the government committed £22bn to infrastructure development projects as part of the SCP. Over five years, £6bn was invested in the Thames Gateway, while £1.2bn was invested in areas of low-quality housing in the north of England and the Midlands. The main regeneration mechanism to improve run-down housing stock was the Housing Market Renewal Pathfinders, and CLG estimates that they refurbished over 13,000 homes in this way from 2003 until they were scrapped in 2011.

The SCP attracted criticism on the grounds that it was little different from the urban development corporations of the 1990s, rejuvenating physical infrastructure but neglecting social sustainability in any broader sense. Further criticism focused on its market-distorting effects, highlighted by the first Barker Report (Barker, 2004) reviewing housing supply in the UK, recommending that more housing land be allocated in areas of high demand. Driven by the Treasury, it was more concerned with the need to reduce house prices in the south east than with the regeneration of disadvantaged areas in the Midlands and the north, leading to funding being directed away from deprived regions towards the over-heated south east, particularly the Thames Gateway.

The New Labour government attempted to redress the overriding focus on the physical renewal of housing in the original SCP with the publication of a five-year plan for sustainable communities (ODPM, 2005e). Stating that 'people live in neighbourhoods, not just in houses' (p. 2), Deputy Prime Minister John Prescott prefigured the report's key recommendation that more power over how areas are planned should be devolved to the local level. The second Barker Report set the Treasury in opposition to government policy once again, with many of the recommendations to streamline the planning system revolving around reducing the opportunities for local communities to contest major planning decisions.

BOX 5.1 PRINCIPLES OF SUSTAINABLE COMMUNITIES SET OUT IN THE SUSTAINABLE COMMUNITIES PLAN

- A flourishing local economy to provide jobs and wealth.
- Strong leadership to respond positively to change.
- Effective engagement and participation by local people, groups and businesses, especially in the planning, design and long-term stewardship of their community, and an active voluntary and community sector.
- A safe and healthy local environment with well-designed public and green space.
- Sufficient size, scale and density, and the right layout to support basic amenities in the neighbourhood and minimise use of resources (including land).
- Good public transport and other transport infrastructure both within the community and linking it to urban, rural and regional centres.
- Buildings – both individually and collectively – that can meet different needs over time, and that minimise the use of resources.
- A well-integrated mix of decent homes of different types and tenures to support a range of household sizes, ages and incomes.
- Good quality local public services, including education and training opportunities, health care and community facilities, especially for leisure.
- A diverse, vibrant and creative local culture, encouraging pride in the community and cohesion within it.
- A 'sense of place'.
- The right links with the wider regional, national and international community.

Turning to social issues, it has also been noted that while the SCP was clearly based upon the broader policy principles of sustainable development, it represented a very specific view of the role of communities in sustainable regeneration. Raco

(2005) identified a dual discourse within the SCP. Firstly, he argues that sustainable citizenship was equated to lessened dependence on the state, whereby communities are essentially being encouraged to engage in forms of self-governing and self-help with an emphasis upon training, entrepreneurialism and community stewardship. Secondly, the plan equates sustainable citizenship with the ownership of property. In Thatcherite tone, the SCP states, 'owning a home gives people a bigger stake in their community, as well as promoting self-reliance' (ODPM, 2003: 37). This emphasis upon self-help and independence has more in common with neoliberal policies that emphasise the restriction of aid to those that demonstrate the capacity to help themselves than the principles of equity upon which sustainable development is based. The further retrenchment of the state and dismemberment of the remaining social welfare systems under the Coalition government has reinforced these tendencies, with the so-called Big Society idea explicitly pushing an agenda of self-help onto citizens and communities.

A further issue within the Sustainable Communities framework involves how the problem of housing was framed. In the south east, the problem involves the inability of so-called 'key workers' (school teachers, nurses, firemen, etc.) to afford housing. In the Midlands and northern England, the problem involves economically self-sufficient households fleeing inner city areas for suburban or rural locations. While poor households have suffered from problems of unaffordable housing and inner city blight for a number of years, in each case the solution was to use regeneration to attract middle-class households into disadvantaged areas in order to improve them. Both of these issues raise the question of who is included and excluded from the idea of the sustainable community – an issue explored in the case study below.

Case Study: Salford Quays

Located 4km to the west of Manchester and employing 3,000 people at their height, Salford's docks were built in 1894 to service the Manchester Ship Canal. The industry gradually declined from the post-war period until 1982 when the docks were closed down. The derelict docks covered a substantial area (150 hectares of land and 75 hectares of water) and left a considerable legacy of pollution (the shipping canal was so polluted it actually caught fire in the 1970s). The closure of the docks compounded the problems of what was already a depressed area of Salford, typified by relatively high levels of unemployment and poverty.

Salford City Council purchased the land in 1983, realising that it represented an opportunity to rapidly transform a major eyesore into a focal point for development. A development plan was established, which branded the area as 'Salford Quays'. The plan aimed to place equal emphasis upon work, leisure and residential land uses, as well as to provide infrastructure such as roads and key services. The regeneration scheme separated the actual docks from the shipping canal by demolishing the warehouses and pushing the rubble in to the quays to block them off. The resulting pools were then aerated using massive pumps to prevent stratification and stagnation, and a series of artificial habitats were created to prevent algal growth. The cleanliness of the water was demonstrated very publicly in 2002 when the Quays were used for the swimming leg of the triathlon event as part of the Manchester Commonwealth Games.

The regeneration partnership placed great emphasis on design quality and infrastructure provision, and, 20 years on, Salford Quays is widely regarded as a model of success, turning a large derelict area into a thriving mixed-use development with over 150 businesses, 2,000 dwellings and 18,500m^2 of office space (Figure 5.2). In perhaps its crowning glory, Salford successfully bid to secure the relocation of the BBC to Media City in the Quays in 2006, involving 1,500 staff and costing some £400m.

Despite these economic and environmental successes, the social credentials of the regeneration scheme are less clear. Work by Raco and Henderson (2005) has highlighted a series of tensions in terms of how successful the development has been in creating a sustainable community. These can be categorised as internal, external and strategic problems. Internally, there has been a lack of attention paid to the needs of the residential community that moved into Salford Quays. Commercial and residential development was prioritised at the expense of developing community services and spaces. This is perhaps understandable, as private finance provides the life-blood of

Figure 5.2 Attractive waterfront flats at Salford Quays, which sit opposite the Lowry centre (Figure 4.2). This enclave of wealthy professionals sits close to areas of relative deprivation, raising questions about its social sustainability.

regeneration projects, but it has resulted in a situation where the projected quality of services available to the community has been compromised. The lack of clear strategic thinking in terms of what the resultant community might look like and how it would function has resulted in a fairly one-dimensional population of young professionals.

The lack of focus on local public services, including education and training, health care and community leisure facilities, means that, like many urban regeneration projects, there is little provision for other types of potential residents, such as young families. Services like public transport need to be installed at the beginning of a development. If they are neglected or added as an afterthought then the residents will have already made other arrangements, in this case to drive. Similarly, a young family will not move in to a development and 'wait' a number of years for a nursery to be built. This is a widely known problem in many regenerated city centres, as young professionals are forced to leave when they start families due to the lack of inner city schools.

Externally, the Salford Quays community is relatively isolated from its neighbouring areas, representing an island of owner-occupied housing within a sea of predominantly publicly owned housing. Advocates of trickle-down theory would argue that the Quays will serve to raise the expectations and opportunities of the surrounding less-advantaged population, but in practice the residents in the surrounding areas feel very little attachment to the development as a whole, as the people who have moved into Salford Quays tend to be wealthier and mix very little with them.

This absence of trickle-down benefits from regeneration projects to the surrounding areas is a widely noted phenomenon, often starkly visible as new developments directly adjoin run-down council estates (Healey, 1997). For example, regeneration often focuses on waterside locations that afford desirable views, but in the process of doing so tends to create 'canyons' of wealthy regenerated areas along rivers and canals that conceal derelict and deprived areas behind them. The resulting social tensions are expressed most acutely in terms of muggings and thefts, and the high levels of security and surveillance that are built into new residential schemes to counter them. Indeed, many new developments boast of their security credentials in terms of guards, CCTV and physical features such as fences and defensive planting in their marketing literature (see Atkinson and Helms, 2007, for a comprehensive review of security and urban regeneration). Issues of social segregation were not unforeseen at Salford Quays, but the various training and employment schemes put in place in order to help the redundant industrial workforce in the surrounding areas to access job opportunities in the nascent service sector have not proved sufficient to integrate the communities.

Strategically, these challenges question the ability of regeneration projects to deliver sustainable communities. The rejuvenation of specific areas such as Salford Quays set within larger areas of inner city decline attracts a new type of household into an area that has already been upgraded for them, constituting a form of purposeful gentrification (see, for example, Cameron, 2003; or Smith, 1996, for the classic analysis of gentrification in the city). While this process may re-invigorate the local housing market, it can also have the effect of excluding poorer inhabitants from being able to buy property in their own area. This is clearly a problem given the emphasis of the Sustainable Communities Plan upon ownership of property as the bedrock of sustainable citizenship.

Indeed, the kinds of owners that were encouraged by the dominant development logic of one- and two-bed flats was limited to young professionals and buy-to-let investors targeting young professionals. Contra the Sustainable Communities Plan, this did not often result in a well-integrated mix of homes of different types and tenures capable of supporting a range of household sizes, ages and incomes. Furthermore, because young professionals have to be highly mobile, both nationally and internationally, in order to chase career opportunities, they are essentially migrant populations. This is almost antithetical to the qualities of 'a diverse, vibrant and creative local culture, encouraging pride in the community and cohesion within it' that the SCP preaches. Indeed, the government's focus on building high-density flats has exacerbated the chronic shortage of family homes in many parts of the UK.

These difficulties highlight the tension between physical regeneration as the transformation of the built environment and social regeneration as a community transformation. The first tends to involve attracting new people to an area, which can exclude pre-existing residents. The second is by definition inclusive of the pre-existing population. This tension is partly related to the flagship status of regeneration projects, which means that their success is judged largely in terms of making derelict areas economically successful. Politicians and investors demand 'quick wins' – highly visible transformations that distance regeneration projects from the pre-existing problems of an area and/or demonstrate profitability. As an economic planner in the Midlands told one of the authors while surveying the view of the city centre from the window of his 18th-storey office, he can tell how well he is doing in his job by the number of cranes visible. Physical transformation is often accompanied by symbolic transformation, and the re-labelling of regeneration areas reflects a conscious move to dissociate an area from its past.

While not on the same scale as the *tabula rasa* (clean slate) approach to regeneration that characterised the wholesale slum clearance programmes of the 1950s and 1960s, the logic of 'build it and they will come' works economically by attracting a new population into an area (Jones, 2008). Whether this form of economic regeneration actually creates sustainable communities is highly contestable as the property-led approach of the SCP does not in and of itself deliver 'sustainable communities'. This begs the question of whose responsibility it is to ensure social integration, given that the majority of resources tend to be poured into physical regeneration. The issue of social mixing (or a lack thereof) has also become prevalent in relation to the problem of studentification, discussed in the next section.

Universities, studentification and regeneration

Higher education in the UK is big business, and universities have long been key actors in real estate development, expanding campuses and constructing student accommodation. Within the context of higher education's rapid expansion in the UK, universities have contributed to the ongoing regeneration of cities (Smith, 2009). Although the New Labour government fell short of their aspiration for 50% of 18-year-olds to attend university, their policies stimulated a massive increase in the student population. The number of students starting a degree rose from 329,000 in 1998 to 457,000 in 2008 (Curtis, 2009), while the overall number of students in higher education in the UK rose from 1.6m in 1995 to just under 2.5m in 2008, a level around which it has remained since (HESA, 2010). As Smith (2009: 1796) notes, despite the huge increase in student numbers there has been no national policy for the development of student accommodation. As a result, private sector provision has grown in a largely ad hoc manner to accommodate demand, creating a series of implications for the social sustainability of the places in which they are based.

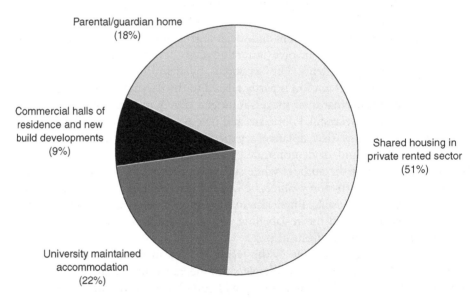

Figure 5.3 Occupancy patterns of UK students in 2008. Note the high proportion living in private sector rented properties.

Source: Munro et al. (2009)

Figure 5.3 shows that over half of students across the UK in 2008 occupied shared housing in the private rented sector, while less than a quarter of students resided in traditional university-maintained accommodation. The demand for private sector housing from students has led to a rise in the conversion of properties into Houses in Multiple Occupancy (HMOs), defined by the Housing Act, 2004, as households comprising more than two people who are not relations. The distribution of student HMOs is highly varied. Nationally only 1.1% of wards record more than one in 20 properties occupied by students, but within these figures 55 neighbourhoods display a majority of student occupation. Almost 10% of the population of major cities like Leeds, Manchester and Bristol is made up of students (Munro et al., 2009), but concentrations vary dramatically within parts of these cities. For example, rates of student occupation are around 80% in Edgbaston and Selly Oak in Birmingham, and approximately 76% in Fallowfield and Hulme in Manchester.

The influx of students into HMOs has led to some areas becoming *studentified*. While relations between students and the cities in which they live have been notoriously strained (as long ago as 1298 a clash between Oxford students and local residents resulted in four deaths and a set of long-running disputes!), growing numbers of students in more recent years have had more direct impacts on the cities in which they live, shaping development patterns and creating new urban lifestyles. So-called studentification denotes an 'influx of students within privately-rented accommodation in particular neighbourhoods' (Smith, 2002: 6), including the changes associated with areas in which students are concentrated. Negative aspects of studentification include noise, disturbance and late hours, which are linked to the tendency of student lifestyles to blur distinctions between day and night, work and play, and weekdays and weekends. The transience of students also leads to a perception that students rarely invest in a neighbourhood or community, as the following quote from the *Guardian* newspaper exemplifies:

> Transient populations of students with no long-term interest in the area turn up for eight months of the year, party hard, dump their rubbish to fester on the streets, crowd residential roads with their cars and make a noise late into the night … Come the summer … they disappear, leaving 'ghost' streets behind them. Many families have sold up – to private landlords – and fled to quieter parts of town. (Tickle, 2007: 10)

As Chatterton (2010: 512) argues, student life is now established as a 'marketable urban lifestyle brand' which creates distinctive urban monocultures of bars and fast food outlets at the expense of local services. As such, studentification has become something of a derogatory phrase used to mark an apparent social problem whereby communities are driven out of residential areas.

A number of local authorities have therefore attempted to mitigate the influx of students into residential areas. Measures have ranged from banning cars in Loughborough and Durham to running community engagement sessions to improve relations between students and residents in Manchester. In some cases, city councils have introduced legislation to limit the licensing of HMOs. Ironically, such attempts to de-concentrate student accommodation in residential areas have stimulated the emergence of gated high-rise student accommodation in city centres, creating even more exclusive enclaves (Hubbard, 2009). In tandem with the wider range of accommodation choices opened up by the favourable credit arrangements available to students, and the influx of overseas students who prioritise security and comfort, this has created a demand for privately managed city centre apartments with single accommodation. The case study of the Student Castle development discussed below is indicative of the scale and characteristics of these types of development, which are an increasingly familiar sight across the UK. While Figure 5.3 indicates that less than 10% of students were living in commercial halls of residence and new build developments in 2008, this number is increasing rapidly. Although there are a growing number of developers focusing on constructing high-density student accommodation, Downing, Unite, and Opal are the main private providers in the UK. Interestingly, all grew from regional cities like Bristol and Manchester, spotting the growing market need. Many enter into Private Finance Initiative (PFI) contracts whereby 'universities lease back accommodation from the private sector over long periods' (Chatterton, 2010: 510).

The benefits of hosting a large student population are rarely discussed, but the boost to the local economy comes not just in the form of fast food and drink receipts. The growth in student numbers has driven substantial regeneration in many cities, and the importance of universities in urban development has become even greater in the recessionary period after 2008, when traditional forms of private development have dried up. Beyond the need for new accommodation, universities have engaged in massive campus development schemes. For example, the University of Manchester is currently completing what it claims is the largest capital investment programme ever undertaken by a higher education institution in the UK. This includes constructing over 10 new buildings and large-scale improvements to the public realm at a projected cost of £600m, some of which are contributing to the Oxford Road Corridor regeneration scheme discussed later in this chapter.

Case Study: Student Castle, Newcastle

Student Castle is a development and management company that creates bespoke high-rise accommodation for students in the form of city centre apartments. Their Newcastle development opened in 2011, Manchester and Cardiff in 2012, while developments in Bristol and London are planned for 2013. Their developments are purpose built in or near city centres, and they have ambitious expansion plans backed by the CEO of Carphone Warehouse/Talk Talk Group. The Newcastle development, pictured in Figure 5.4, is a large block of self-contained studio and one-bed apartments located on the edge of the city centre, with high-speed broadband and Sky 3D piped directly into every room. The Student Castle website states that they have '...changed the perception of traditional private student accommodation by meeting 21st Century student aspiration, namely ultra fast new

Figure 5.4 Student Castle development in Newcastle. This kind of luxury student accommodation is increasingly common, mimicking the high-density developments built for young professionals across UK city centres.

generation broadband, bigger beds, TV and media packages, low utility bills and flexible letting terms' (Student Castle, 2012). Their slick, interactive website is aimed as much at the parents who pay the increasing bill for higher education in the UK as it is at students.

In the context of studentified areas that are dominated by HMOs, city councils see these new developments as a means to disperse students across cities, but others argue that these developments simply increase segregation between students and other residents, creating new enclaves and new problems. As Hubbard (2009: 1921) points out, 'if one accepts the need for revitalized public spaces and mixed-use environments that promote social contact, tolerance, and political engagement, then purpose-built student accommodation seemingly poses as many questions as it answers'. More broadly, developments like Student Castle's highlight a wider trend, namely the 'increasing blurring between student and post-student lifestyles' that is taking place as students inhabit a similar world to that which they hope for once they graduate, replete with the trappings of a young professional lifestyle (Smith and Holt, 2007: 156). In this sense, the social problems caused by studentification are increasingly hard to distinguish from those associated with the more widespread process of gentrification that characterises most city centre urban regeneration projects.

Key points

i) The Sustainable Communities Plan emphasised the role of regeneration in providing quality affordable housing stock, skills and amenities for disadvantaged populations.

ii) While sustainable communities are supposed to be economically viable, mixed and have a sense of ownership over the place in which they live, regeneration schemes tend to attract to an area relatively homogeneous populations, such as young professionals, and there can be difficulties integrating new and pre-existing populations.

iii) There is a tension between the emphasis of regeneration on physical transformation and economic development, and the social goals of creating sustainable communities.

The brownfield development agenda

The defining environmental characteristic of urban regeneration in the UK has been its emphasis on the re-use of derelict or contaminated urban land for development in order to protect the countryside and rejuvenate urban areas. The primary development pressure upon land in the UK has been the need for new housing, but since the spread of suburbia in the inter-war period, housing has been seen as the primary cause of urban sprawl. Given rising demand, policy has focused on building a higher proportion of houses in urban areas, especially on brownfield sites. The idea of developing brownfield land is eminently sensible (Parliamentary Office of Science and Technology, 1998). Many urban areas have a legacy of derelict and contaminated sites as manufacturing industry in the UK has declined, and derelict land is often perceived as an eyesore that is associated with social and physical decay. People may be afraid to walk past or through areas characterised by so-called 'blight'. Although unused, these spaces are often in close proximity to city centres with the potential to fetch significant economic rents. Further, city centres already have the infrastructure to support developments, and filling in these 'gaps' in the urban landscape, rather than developing on the outskirts, creates more efficient, compact cities that encourage lower car use.

For these reasons, the Urban White Paper of 2000 proposed that 60% of new housing should be located on brownfield land by 2008, prioritising the remediation and use of contaminated land for house-building and urban development. Between the publication of the White Paper in 2000 and the credit crunch of 2008 the regeneration agenda in the UK was synonymous with the redevelopment of brownfield land. Figure 5.5 shows the percentage of total new residences built in rural and urban areas between 1985 and 2003. The graph clearly shows that the amount of housing development in urban areas grew from under 50% in 1985 to over 65% in 2003, and that within the urban category it is vacant and derelict land that has accounted for this increase (Karadimitriou, 2005). Some of the tenets of sustainable regeneration have been adopted enthusiastically. For example, higher density developments have proven popular as more units on a site allow developers to make more money, and the density of new dwellings built increased substantially from 26 to 40 dwellings per hectare between 1996 and 2006 (CLG, 2007a).

At the same time, the Urban White Paper recognised that locating increasingly dense developments in cities could potentially exacerbate environmental, social and economic problems, unless attention was paid to the provision of quality public spaces. *Planning Policy Guidance 17: Planning for Open Space Sport and Recreation* (ODPM, 2002b) identified four emerging themes relating to open space policy:

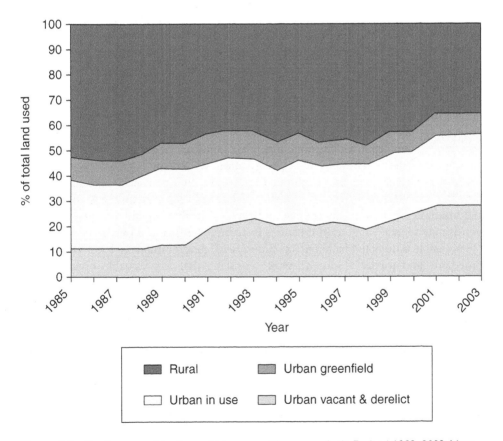

Figure 5.5 Previous use of land on which new residences are built, England 1983–2003. Note the increase in the proportion of previously used urban land to build houses.

Source: Karadimitriou (2005)

- an increasing emphasis on the wide range of roles played by open space in enhancing the liveability of towns and cities;
- the importance of taking a holistic view of planning for green space in towns and cities, whether parks, river valleys, linear walkways or incidental open spaces;
- the importance of incorporating sustainable development principles which, for example, would increase the emphasis in favour of retaining and creating small accessible open spaces in towns and cities for use by local residents; and
- a greater emphasis on the improved management of open space and greenspace networks.

The open space agenda is seen as critical in supporting the kind of urban renaissance that the Urban White Paper called for:

> local networks of high quality and well managed and maintained open spaces, sports and recreational facilities help create urban environments that are attractive, clean and safe. Green spaces in urban areas perform vital functions as areas for nature conservation and biodiversity and by acting as 'green lungs' can assist in meeting objectives to improve air quality. (ODPM, 2002b)

In the same year, an ODPM report (ODPM, 2002a) titled *Living Places: Cleaner, Safer, Greener* linked the open space agenda to the problem of environmental exclusion, whereby poor local environmental quality is related to areas and households experiencing multiple deprivation, and is a significant factor in maintaining social exclusion and perpetuating cycles of deprivation. Within the current era of austerity a lack of public finances has heightened interest in the open space agenda, which is viewed as providing a series of potential social benefits for very little cost. In addition to community cohesion, the mental and physical health benefits of open space are increasingly seen as long-term measures to reduce the financial burden on the NHS.

The environmental challenge of brownfield development is thus twofold: to remediate land for development, while ensuring that any valuable open space is either retained and enhanced in proposed developments or replaced elsewhere. Over time the problems of reclaiming brownfield sites have grown, due to the simple fact that the preferential development of uncontaminated sites has left an increasing proportion of contaminated sites relative to overall brownfield stock. The debate is complicated further by the broad range of land included under the umbrella term 'brownfield'. Brownfield land is land that has been previously developed, defined in planning guidance as that which 'is or was occupied by a permanent structure (excluding agricultural or forestry uses)'. As a number of authors have noted, this includes vacant, derelict and contaminated land and could range from an overgrown railway siding to an old colliery site contaminated by heavy metals (e.g. Alker et al., 2000). Despite attempts to distinguish between different types of brownfield site in policy, terms like contaminated land and derelict sites are often used loosely and interchangeably in practice.

Some sites that are classified as brownfield are used informally by local residents for recreational activities, or have conservation value. The example of biodiversity nicely highlights this difficulty. Lord Rogers states in his introduction to the Urban White Paper that 'building more than 40% of new housing on greenfield sites … will … damage biodiversity' (DETR, 2000: introduction). The assumption that bio-diversity occurs on rural greenfield sites but not on urban brownfield sites is not supported by ecological science, which indicates that vast tracts of arable monocul-ture in the countryside support very little biodiversity, whereas urban areas are often highly biodiverse due to the variety of unmanaged habitats provided by brownfield sites (Shirley and Box, 1998) (Figure 5.6). Within the context of urban liveability, the amenity value of urban open space within easy reach of a massive population is vastly higher than that of a field of wheat in East Anglia. Brownfield development represents a key arena in which tensions within the notion of sustainability are worked out, and are explored in the Selly Oak case study below.

Focusing on redeveloping cities makes sense in so far as urban areas already have pre-existing infrastructure, but the imperative to conserve rural areas runs the risk of isolating cities from their surrounding region. The separation of rural and urban

Figure 5.6   A brownfield river corridor on the Vincent Drive site in Birmingham prior to redevelopment. The area adjacent to the river was made up of important wetland habitat, which supported a range of rare species such as the water vole. It was recognised as being ecologically valuable at both the regional and national levels, and indicates the sometimes surprising levels of biodiversity found on brownfield sites.

affairs can be traced back to the Town and Country Planning Act of 1947, which formed the bedrock for modern, comprehensive planning in Britain. The detailed history of this division falls outside the remit of this chapter, but it is salient to note that the division still underpins national policy, with the government White Papers on sustainability being split into urban and rural papers. This separation between urban and rural policy has been criticised for contradicting the holistic ethos of sustainability. Cities are highly connected to the regions in which they are located through flows of people (e.g. commuters) and materials (e.g. water, food). Separating their planning functions means that cities lose 'control of the areas where their growth would naturally go' (Gracey, 1973: 77). This tension underpins debates concerning urban and rural sustainability in the UK and informs current calls to establish 'city-regions' as political units.

Case Study: Selly Oak

The residential area of Selly Oak lies 4km south of Birmingham city centre and 6km from the city periphery. Birmingham City Council adopted a Local Action Plan for the area in 2001 to provide a framework for its sustainable development. The specific goals of the plan were to revitalise the shopping centre, attract quality investment to under-used sites, improve public transport and cycling provision, enhance the environment for residents, and enhance conditions for major land users. The goals reflect national priorities for sustainable development set out at the time, seeking to attract private investment in order to improve the quality of the area.

The development plans for the area hinged on the redevelopment of a brownfield site known as Vincent Drive. Vincent Drive occupied approximately 30 hectares of floodplain to the north and south of the Bourn Brook, and was the largest remaining semi-natural green space in south Birmingham (Figure 5.7). The northern half of the site was acquired by the Cadbury Trust (the landholding/charity arm of local philanthropist George Cadbury's chocolate empire) in the nineteenth century and sold to Birmingham City Council for £100,000 in 1926, for the development of the Queen Elizabeth Hospital. The southern half of the site, Battery Park, was home to a number of small industrial ventures that left behind substantial waste tips. By 1950 the site was distinguishable as a discrete green space, enclosed by Victorian terraced housing to the south and east, post-war housing to the west, and the Queen Elizabeth Hospital to the north.

The legacy of the old gardens, lack of management and varying drainage created an array of habitats on Vincent Drive. The remnant deer park land and pasture was over 1,000 years old, with no records existing of any ploughing having occurred. The Bourn Brook was characterised by well-developed woodland, with wetland habitat along its eastern stretch, and the linear features of remnant hedges were still identifiable. The Vincent Drive site was designated a Grade C Site of Importance for Nature Conservation (SINC) with parts of the site considered to be at the level of a Site of Special Scientific Interest.

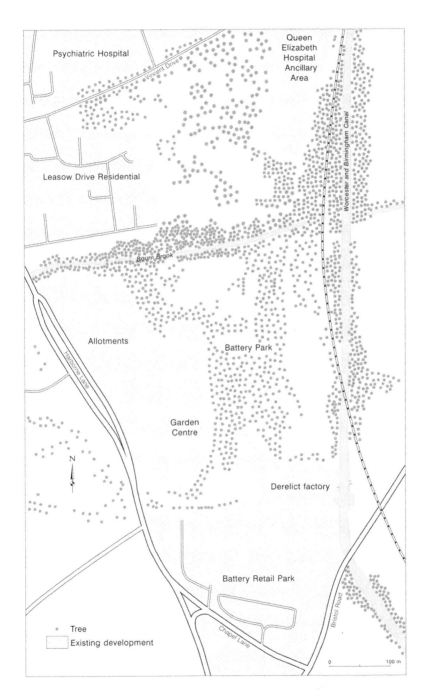

Figure 5.7 Land uses at the Vincent Drive site, Birmingham, prior to redevelopment. Note the very large area of semi-natural open space in the centre of the site, and the variety of land uses around the edges that have accumulated over time. Drawn by Kevin Burkhill.

As national policy shifted towards urban regeneration and brownfield development in the 1990s, a key task of the first Unitary Development Plan drawn up for the city in 1990 was to identify large sites for potential development within the city. Vincent Drive was earmarked for two major developments. Proposals from the Birmingham NHS Trust involved building a £300-million hospital on Vincent Drive, covering approximately two-fifths of the site and providing 1,009 beds. Although the planning proposal was only officially submitted in 1999, the Regional Health Authority had adopted a major hospital building programme for the city ten years earlier outlining the closure of some 20 hospitals and the centralisation of hospital services on four mega-hospital sites, as part of a regional health strategy. The developer stated that 'the proposals are a positive move towards sustainability in that the new hospital would be provided on a brownfield site' (Babtie, 2000: i). Sainsbury's supermarket chain agreed to finance a new link road traversing the floodplain, canal and railway, and alterations to major road junctions at either end in return for development rights over the southern half of the site. Their proposals for a large retail park involved the complete reclamation of Battery Park, including the decontamination of waste tips and soil patches, removal of the derelict buildings and levelling of the site.

A series of local groups contested the plans. The local Wildlife Trust highlighted the loss of valuable habitat, and questioned the decision to site a major development on a floodplain. Local resident groups protested that the extra traffic the scheme would generate would overload an already heavily congested local road network. Politicians questioned how a regional hospital and retail development, intended to serve the entire of the southern half of the city, were contributing to local sustainability as part of the local action plan. Local business groups protested that far from revitalising the local shopping centre, the new development would shift the retail centre of gravity away from the high street.

The final development proposals clearly attempt to juggle economic development and open-space provision in line with government policy. It was suggested that the loss of habitat could be offset by creating new habitats elsewhere, but the destruction of the area's largest natural resource is not offset by plans for similarly sized or equivalent replacement space in the locality. A key environmental element involved the enhancement of the Bourn Brook as a wildlife corridor, which would function as a recreational feature, with walkways, benches and landscaping (Birmingham City Council, 2002).

Vincent Drive highlights key tensions within the brownfield agenda (Evans, 2007). It is a highly diverse site, with areas of high ecological worth and areas of serious contamination. This makes it difficult to apply an overall judgement as to the development's environmental sustainability. In decontaminating the waste tips, the development is improving the environment, but in building on a large semi-natural habitat it is undoubtedly destroying an environmental asset. As some studies have suggested, this problem may be partly related to the lack of urban ecological know-how in the planning and development sector, which tends to have difficulty in representing these habitats in the decision-making system (Harrison and Davies, 2002). Comparing Figures 5.7 and 5.8 gives a clear indication

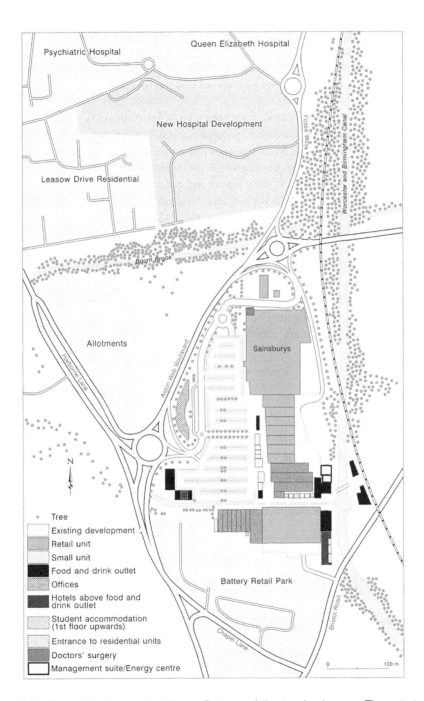

Figure 5.8 Planned land uses at the Vincent Drive site following development. The majority of the green space has been lost in the new development, with the retention of the river corridor the only major exception. Note the link road that opens up the middle of the site, paid for by Sainsbury's in return for development rights over the southern half. Drawn by Graham Bowden.

of the trade-off between development and enhancement of open space. The key environmental trade-off was achieved by the planning department requesting that the developers retain and enhance the habitat alongside the Bourn Brook, and improve public access to this area, in return for permission to develop the bulk of the site.

The outcome highlights the shift in policy away from speaking purely about environmental aspects such as biodiversity conservation and air quality, to focusing on a liveability agenda that prioritises the provision of publicly accessible, quality open space. The Selly Oak case also highlights the multiple understandings of what sustainability actually means. Planners, developers and residents all have different interpretations based upon different priorities. A regeneration scheme that is sustainable at the city scale may not be sustainable at the local scale, while what may enhance the economic vitality of an area may damage it environmentally. Quite often it is argued that economic interests override other factors, as powerful interests exploit the ambiguity of what sustainability actually means to prioritise their own interests. While a number of studies have argued that this is indeed the case, one of the strengths of sustainability as a rallying point for partnerships is precisely that it is flexible and open to interpretation (for example, Evans and Jones, 2008, have explored how common meanings of sustainability are established in regeneration schemes).

Key points

i)   Regeneration in the UK seeks to stimulate urban areas and preserve the countryside by re-using brownfield land for development.

ii) Tensions between the logic of high-density development and the provision of a quality environment that includes sufficient open/green space are often worked out at the development level.

Climate change, cities and carbon

Climate change and cities

Since the second Earth Summit held in Johannesburg in 2002, the language of sustainability has increasingly been overtaken by a more specific concern with climate change. According to their 2007 report, the Intergovernmental Panel on Climate Change (IPCC) are 90% confident that climate change is happening and that it is being caused by humans. In order to prevent the unpredictable and potentially catastrophic impacts associated with global warming of more than two degrees

Celsius, rapid reductions in greenhouse gas emissions are required (Pachauri and Reisinger, 2007).

Cities are central to this task. Globally cities account for 75% of the total energy used by humans and produce approximately 80% of greenhouse gas emissions (United Nations, 2007), making urban regeneration a key mechanism through which to address climate change. Private consultancy firm McKinsey and Company (2009) ranked different measures to reduce emissions in terms of their overall costs and benefits over a 20-year time period. Figure 5.9 shows the resulting cost curve for carbon abatement, with the potential size of each abatement measure on the horizontal axis in giga-tons of emissions ($GtCO_2e$) per year, and the net cost of each measure in pounds per ton of avoided greenhouse gas emissions on the vertical axis. The curve is based upon the maximum possible savings for each abatement measure in the 20 years up to 2030, if currently available technical solutions were to be pursued as aggressively as possible.

Interestingly, many of the most cost-effective measures (those lying below the x-axis) relate to buildings and building design, most notably insulation, air-conditioning and lighting. These measures relate not only to the creation of new buildings, but also to the retrofitting of existing building stock with more sustainable technologies. New cities are springing up at an alarming rate in the global south, with the total urban area in developing countries predicted to triple between 2000 and 2030, but most of the buildings in the UK are already built. While it can be debated whether repair and maintenance activities technically constitute 'regeneration' per se, it is worth noting that they account for just over half of the construction activity in the UK (UNECE, 2006). The background rate at which building stock is renewed sits at approximately 1% per year (Shaw et al., 2007), meaning that without intervention it will take 100 years to retrofit the UK's buildings with basic sustainable technologies. In a country like the UK, in which existing building stock vastly outweighs new developments, retrofitting existing buildings so that they are more energy efficient is an important area in which urban regeneration can address environmental challenges.

Fifty per cent of CO_2 emissions come from building and the process of construction, while the sustainability of resultant developments depends on the materials that they are built from and the running costs associated with them (Kotaji et al., 2003). The so-called 'embodied carbon' in construction materials, which is the amount of carbon that was emitted producing them, is often surprisingly high. Cement, a staple of new developments, is produced at very high temperatures using vast amounts of energy, emitting 0.83kg of carbon for every kg produced. Incredibly, it is estimated that 5% of all global carbon emissions result from its production. Using recycled materials also has a massive impact on the embodied carbon of a development. For example, producing 1kg of 'virgin' (i.e. new) steel emits 2.75kg of carbon, whereas recycling steel only emits 0.43kg (Hammond and Jones, 2008). The sustainable design of buildings should therefore try to use materials with as little embodied carbon as possible.

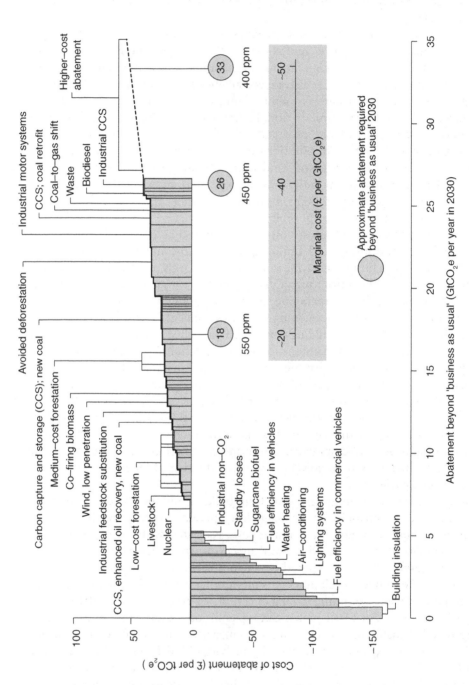

Figure 5.9 Potential carbon dioxide emission savings assuming currently available technical solutions are aggressively pursued.

Source: McKinsey and Company (2009)

As Rydin (2010) points out, though, the second part of the sustainable design jigsaw involves how a building functions once built. South-facing windows will reduce the amount of energy required to heat a building, while a south-facing sloped roof will create a suitable space for solar panels. Cement and concrete, while having high levels of embodied carbon, have a high thermal mass, meaning that they absorb large amounts of energy during the day, for example, and release it slowly at night when it is needed. While relatively unsustainable to produce, this makes them useful in the design of low carbon housing (Rydin, 2010).

Urban planning also has a vital role to play in reducing carbon emissions. For example, creating places that can be negotiated without the excessive use of cars is perhaps the most important factor in making day-to-day existence more sustainable. In the USA, '**smart growth**' planning has emerged directly to address the unplanned sprawl of cities based around the motor vehicle. Smart growth aims to limit the amount of space that cities can take up, forcing an intensification of land use and creating denser, more accessible urban landscapes (Danielsen et al., 1999). As concentrations of people, cities are hotspots for overall emissions but their per capita emissions are generally lower than those of non-urbanised populations (Dodman, 2009). Urban regeneration has a vital role to play in addressing climate change through implementing ecologically efficient design, sustainable building technologies and high-density planning principles.

In addition to mitigating (lowering) carbon emissions, cities will have to adapt to a changing climate. Even if all emissions ceased tomorrow, the amount of carbon dioxide already in the atmosphere would continue to cause considerable warming. A TCPA report on designing for climate adaptation identifies high temperatures, flood risk, water resources and water quality and ground conditions as key challenges that will face cities in the UK over the next 30 years (Shaw et al., 2007). The UK Climate Change Risk Assessment reinforced the government's view that flooding is the main future threat in the UK (HM Government, 2012).

Given this, cities are increasingly being planned in ways that will allow them to adapt to climate change (Hodson and Marvin, 2007). Recent research on climate change adaptation in urban environments emphasises the importance of green space in providing cooling from higher temperatures and absorbing rain to lower the risk of flash floods (Gill et al., 2007). A patchwork of gardens, parks and open spaces is seen as critical to the ability of cities to cope with climate change. The TCPA also identifies three urban design principles for climate change adaptation: inner courtyards that provide shaded open spaces to mitigate high temperatures; circular house forms to combat strong winds; and buildings on stilts to minimise flood damage (Shaw et al., 2007). As the TCPA report points out, adaptation measures that advocate high levels of green space need to be thought about carefully if they are not to conflict with the high-density design principles that underpin mitigation measures (Shaw et al., 2007). That said, it is important not to overstate the tension between mitigation and adaptation. For example, compact urban forms that do not rely on fossil fuels for transport

and energy will not only reduce emissions but be more resilient to infrastructure disruptions and potential shortages or spikes in the cost of oil and gas in
the future.

Case Study: Stratford City

The TCPA report discussed above uses the redevelopment of Stratford City in East
London as an example of an economic regeneration project that is committed to low
carbon development. Westfield Stratford City in East London is one of the largest urban
regeneration projects ever undertaken, aiming to deliver 1.9 million square feet of
retail and leisure space, 1.1 million square feet of office space, 18,000 permanent new
jobs, two new hotels, and new homes and public spaces (Stratford Renaissance
Partnership, 2012). The regeneration of Stratford City aims to make Stratford
London's third economic centre, seeking to benefit from the broader Olympic
legacy, with 70% of spectators passing through the development en route to the
Olympic Park (for more details on the Olympic regeneration, see Chapter 8).

The project's green credentials centre on adopting low carbon building technologies and upgrading public transport connections. The development promises
to use a series of eco-innovations, including green roofs, heat pumps, maximised
insulation and combined heat and power systems. Office developments in the area
incorporate passive systems and design solutions to produce buildings that are
relatively sustainable in terms of resource use and which provide comfortable
working and living environments. Westfield Stratford City has a highly efficient
combined Cooling and Heating Power Plant that provides 75% of its energy and
helps it to achieve carbon emissions 25% lower than the current benchmarks.
According to projections, this will rise to 50% by 2020 and 80% by 2050. The
sustainable supply and drainage systems seek to harvest, store and treat water on
site, cutting residential water consumption by 30% and commercial consumption
by 20%. In the context of an inner city location, the goal of reducing the need
for energy intensive air-conditioning is central. In order to counteract the urban
heat island effect and uncomfortably high summer temperatures, façade materials
were chosen to absorb less solar heat, plants are located in open areas to provide
shade, and open water features were installed to cool the air (Rydin, 2010). In
terms of public transport, the regeneration area is well located for London City
Airport, lies on the Crossrail line and is benefiting from a £50 million upgrade
to Stratford Station to make it capable of receiving international high speed rail
services.

Cities and the low carbon economy

As the case study above shows, lowering carbon emissions has become a mainstream consideration in urban regeneration projects. In tandem with the gradual

decentralisation of planning in the UK, the importance of cities in addressing the challenges of climate change has lent them greater political influence. The emergence of cities in the climate change arena represents the logic of subsidiarity, whereby the challenges of lowering carbon emissions are tackled at scales at which it is easier to legislate for, regulate and measure change. National commitments to reduce emissions are cascaded down to sub-national levels, like regions, cities, and ultimately individual developments, because it is assumed that these smaller scales can facilitate rapid, context-specific action (Bulkeley and Betsill, 2003).

Because they have coherent local governments, strong senses of identity and clear boundaries, cities represent ideal spatial units within which to lower carbon emissions (Bulkeley and Betsill, 2003; Rice, 2010), and many cities are now quantifying the carbon emissions of their activities as a basis for future planning and management (While et al., 2010). As noted in the previous chapter, cities tend to compete with one another in order to attract business and residents, and the propensity to compete now extends to environmental action as well. Nottingham, Leicester and Manchester have all stated a desire to become the greenest city in the UK, while the city of London has set more stringent city-wide emissions reduction targets than those required by government (Hodson and Marvin, 2007). Ambitious green targets can be seen as the latest spatial 'fix' for capitalist development, whereby cities seize upon sustainability and the low carbon agenda to address the negative externalities of congestion, industrial dereliction and lower quality of life and, in doing so, provide more attractive environments in which to invest (While et al., 2004).

The logic of low carbon development assumes that it is possible to decouple economic growth from emissions through technological innovation and joined-up thinking. Germany is often held up as an example of a country that has decoupled carbon emissions from economic growth by switching to more high-tech forms of manufacturing. Although there is an argument that the West have simply exported their polluting activities to elsewhere – recent studies have estimated that 25 per cent of China's emissions are generated producing goods for the West (Wang and Watson, 2007) – the logic of decoupling underpins many current urban growth strategies. Directly picking up this theme, the UK White Paper *Creating a Low Carbon Economy* (DTI, 2003b), calls on local authorities to develop projects that can reduce carbon emissions while generating economic growth. In response, local authorities have increasingly partnered with public and private property owners to seek regeneration opportunities that focus on stimulating the growth of green businesses and the deployment of renewable technologies. In many cities, low carbon development represents the latest model of urban regeneration, as demonstrated in the case study below.

Case Study: the Oxford Road Corridor

Manchester City Council has embraced an ambition to become a low carbon economy, setting targets to reduce carbon emissions by 41% by 2020, compared to

2005 levels (Manchester City Council, 2009). The city-region is designated as the only Low Carbon Economic Area in the UK focused on the built environment which encourages the deployment of new low carbon technology to reduce the region's carbon footprint. As home to the University of Manchester, Manchester Metropolitan University, the Central Manchester Hospitals NHS Foundation Trust, a science park, and several noted cultural institutions, the Oxford Road corridor is fundamental to achieving this goal. Accounting for 22% of Manchester's gross economic value, the Oxford Road Corridor covers 243 hectares stretching from St Peter's Square in the central business district to Whitworth Park on the southern edge of the University of Manchester (Corridor Manchester, 2010). Despite its economic might, the area suffers from a series of environmental problems relating to severe traffic congestion and the associated issues of air pollution and noise (Figure 5.10). Current regeneration plans seek to transform the corridor into a leading centre for low carbon innovation and industry through major investments in the physical landscape to make it more sustainable.

Established in 2008, the Corridor Manchester partnership seeks to maximise the benefits from an estimated £1.5 billion of capital investment that is committed or planned on the corridor by Manchester City Council, the universities, and the Hospital Trust over a five-year period (Corridor Manchester, 2010). Adhering to the

Figure 5.10 The Oxford Road is a key strategic bus route within Manchester, bringing severe problems of congestion, pollution and noise.

logic of partnership, pooling the resources of these three key stakeholders is intended to allow more strategic, integrated improvements to be made to the urban infrastructure. As stated in the partnership's plan:

> The Partnership's core objective is to maximise the economic potential of the area by harnessing the investment currently being made by key institutions (Universities, the Health Trust and the private sector); by stimulating future improvement and growth at key locations within the area; and by capturing economic benefit from this investment for disadvantaged local residents in the wards surrounding the area and in the city as a whole. (Manchester City South Partnership, 2008: 5)

In order to double the number of workers in this part of the city, the corridor will receive major upgrades to the transportation and communication networks, in addition to investment in high-tech business activities, cultural amenities and the public realm. Strategic capital investments focus on five integrated themes that are designed to create a low carbon urban area: transport; environment and infrastructure; research and innovation; employment, business and skills; and sense of place (Corridor Manchester, 2010). The centrepiece of the transportation plans involve replacing the existing system of largely unregulated diesel buses that cause noise and congestion, with a rapid transit bus system that will make transport along the corridor cleaner and more efficient. In addition to transportation upgrades, opportunities exist to develop sustainable energy technologies like combined heat and power, heat transfer, energy efficient retrofits, smart metering, and smart grids.

The City Council's implementation of the low carbon economy through the Oxford Road Corridor is typical of the latest iteration of urban boosterism (Harding et al., 2010), as cities compete to establish themselves as economic leaders in the burgeoning low carbon world. Such projects work on a larger scale than that of a single development or quarter, thinking strategically about how to create an environment conducive for business investment through major infrastructure interventions. Although the low carbon agenda frames the entire plan, it is very much positioned as an engine for future economic growth; indeed the corridor is presented as critical to the economic fortunes of Manchester, the North West and the UK as a whole (Corridor Manchester, 2010). In this sense, such schemes represent a commitment to sustainable transport and renewable energy that clearly plays into the current low carbon agenda. That said, in terms of what actually happens on the ground, these schemes adhere to a familiar model of Public Private Partnerships between local authorities and private developers, in which the core goal involves economic growth and job creation. It remains to be seen whether the low carbon agenda gets railroaded by the logic of economic development or whether it represents a genuinely different direction for urban development (While et al., 2010).

> ## Key points
>
> i) Cities are critical in addressing climate change, producing most carbon emissions and being potentially most severely affected by environmental change.
>
> ii) The materials from which buildings are made, their design, and the planning of regeneration schemes can all contribute to lowering carbon emissions.
>
> iii) The low carbon economic agenda is seen as a silver bullet capable of addressing the environmental and economic issues facing cities and increasingly frames urban regeneration schemes.

Sustainable construction

Development involves purchasing a site, conceiving a suitable project and obtaining planning permission. Once the planners have reached a decision and the overall design for a site has been agreed, the actual job of building a development falls to construction companies. As argued in the first section of this chapter, the state cannot deliver the goals of sustainability alone, and the construction industry plays an important role in determining how a development is built and what specification it is built to. While there is a wealth of information available about why we need to build more sustainable buildings in more sustainable ways and how to do so, evidence suggests that the uptake in the construction industry is limited. In order to understand why the construction industry has been slow to respond to the environmental challenges of sustainable regeneration, it is necessary to understand its policy-drivers and practical workings.

Sir John Egan's task force report on the industry, *Rethinking Construction*, set out the key challenges and opportunities facing the construction sector in the UK (Construction Task Force, 1998). The report focused on the need to improve the skill-base of the construction sector, and the need for the sector to work more closely in partnership with clients. The focus on the skill-base was not surprising given the challenges presented by the sustainability agenda, such as new technologies and integrated development, in the face of the progressive move away from a dependence on specialist labour on building sites. It was also reminiscent of similar issues concerning the shortage of skilled workers during the 1960s building boom.

Egan's call for transparent partnership between the construction industry and other organisations involved in the regeneration process was more innovative. Regeneration studies tend to focus on planners, architects, land agents and developers, forgetting that the construction industry is at the 'sharp-end' actually laying the bricks, pouring the concrete and so on. By getting the industry involved, Egan hoped to get away from the traditional 'tendering' system, whereby a building or development would be designed, put out to tender and contracted to the construction firm who promised to build it in the specified time for the least money. This form of competitive tendering often led constructors to assume a very short-term mentality, cutting corners in order to meet costs. Egan's emphasis on longer-term partnerships, engaging constructors at a far earlier stage in order to find the best method to deliver the product, would not only improve quality through the constructor having more of a stake in the development, but also efficiency through joined-up thinking.

After the Egan report, an organisation called Constructing Excellence was established to draw together government, the construction industry and major clients in order to identify and disseminate best practice. Constructing Excellence identified six areas in which the construction industry is central to the delivery of many of the government's policies for sustainable development:

- regeneration of housing, particularly to revitalise town centres;
- planning communities to reduce car use;
- protection of the countryside;
- minimising mineral extraction;
- using energy and water more efficiently; and
- the provision of training through schemes such as Welfare to Work and the New Deal.

The first four of these areas revolve around the development of brownfield land in urban areas.

Progress in the sector was reviewed in *The Construction Industry: Progress Towards More Sustainable Construction* report prepared by the Sustainable Construction Task Group (2003). The report concluded that while some companies have made significant progress, most have made no or limited numbers of steps towards more sustainable operations. A key issue concerned information overload and the confusing array of initiatives. This is partly due to lack of coordination at government level, where responsibility for construction is spread across many departments, and the failure of information to be focused on the business benefits of actions towards sustainability. The biggest barrier to establishing closer links between the construction industry and sustainability is probably the institutional separation between CLG, which deals with planning, and the then DTI (now BIS), which deals with the construction industry. Institutional separation is compounded by the divergence between the goals and associated language of integration associated with the public realm, and the technical language of the private sector (Moore and Rydin, 2008).

In terms of building practices, the construction industry has tended to be largely reactive and driven by legislation. Building Regulations set standards for the design and construction of buildings primarily to ensure the safety and health of people in or around those buildings, but also for energy conservation and access to buildings, and are an important driver of construction practices. The government also sets energy efficiency standards for new-build homes, measured using Standard Assessment Procedure (SAP) ratings. In terms of legislation, the landfill tax has arguably proven to be the most successful tool used to influence construction practice. The construction industry in the UK produced 91m tonnes of waste in 2003, of which 29m tonnes went to landfill. This accounted for 32% of all waste sent to landfill in the UK. A landfill tax was introduced in the UK on all waste in 1996, with the charges for disposal per ton escalating at a rate of £8 annually. The tax means that it costs approximately £40 per tonne to send material to landfill, in addition to the associated haulage costs, lending what is an environmental issue serious financial implications. In the case of material from contaminated land there are only a few waste sites in the country that can accept it, and only then with a slew of accompanying paperwork, further increasing the costs of disposal. It has thus become a priority within the industry to find ways to reduce the amount of waste that is removed from sites. This can involve mixing contaminated soil with uncontaminated soil on larger sites in order to bring the average levels of contamination below the legal thresholds. Rubble from demolished buildings is sorted in order to recover steel, and concrete is crushed and graded for aggregate. Part of the revenue generated by the landfill tax is channelled into environmental conservation projects and forms a major funding source for many environmental NGOs in the UK.

Interestingly, the government has tended to encourage sustainable construction more than legislate for it, preferring demonstration projects like BedZED in south London to legal regulations. The Beddington Zero (Fossil) Energy Development (BedZED) is a mixed-use scheme of 82 homes and 3,000m² of commercial space in south London developed by the Peabody Trust housing association (Figure 5.11). The scheme is famous for making use of environmental building technologies to reduce energy and water uses, and for providing flexible accommodation that doubles up as work and living space. The BedZED model has become quite influential and has been applied to designs for settlements as far afield as China. The reliance on exemplars rather than legislation may in part be a response to the construction lobby, which is generally averse to any tightening of building regulations on cost grounds. While it can be criticised for failing to force builders to become more sustainable, it has led to an interesting situation whereby sustainability in the construction sector is often equated with innovation (Moore and Rydin, 2008), and more responsibility is placed upon local authorities to negotiate the kinds of developments that they want.

It was in this context that the Building Research Establishment (BRE) developed the EcoHomes standard to more easily assess the environmental friendliness of developments. Developments were scored on areas such as energy, transport, pollution, materials, water, land use and ecology, and health and well-being, aggregating them to give a scheme an overall rating from 1 (pass) to 4 (excellent) to be used as a marketing tool to attract buyers. These standards were critical in making developments more environmentally sustainable by reducing resource use and waste, but also played an important part in promoting social sustainability. For example, more efficient heating helps combat fuel poverty and improves human health. Housing associations were required to at least pass the EcoHomes standards if their schemes were to qualify for government subsidy.

Figure 5.11 BedZED, the Beddington Zero Energy Development, is an architecturally striking scheme with echoes of the Victorian terraced street. It sets the benchmark for environmentally friendly urban development.

EcoHomes was subsequently superseded by the Code for Sustainable Homes, introduced in England and Wales in 2006 in an attempt by the government to make it simpler for local authorities to request specific levels of sustainability for different developments. The Code defines six levels of achievement across nine areas of environmental performance, including carbon emissions, water use, materials, surface water runoff, waste, pollution, health, management, and ecology, whereby level 6 equates to a zero-carbon home. Rather than have to be conversant with the technical details of each area, local authorities can simply specify a level which they require a development to conform to. Rather than dictating how a developer must meet the target, this system allows them freedom to adopt the most efficient and appropriate solutions (Rydin, 2010).

While the Code has been widely used by local authorities, evidence suggests that enforcement of agreements and their subsequent monitoring have hampered its ability to deliver results (ibid.). Difficulties in implementation have been compounded by an ongoing debate over what zero-carbon actually means in practice. For example, only on-site renewable energy was allowed to count towards the zero-carbon rating, ruling out community developments that share a wind farm or hydro-power source. This also had the effect of making zero-carbon housing ten times more expensive to deliver in high-density urban brownfield developments (£6,000–13,000 per dwelling) than in rural developments (£800 per dwelling) (ibid.), working against stated policy to encourage development in cities. These discrepancies have hampered the effectiveness of government measures to promote sustainable buildings by offering subsidies to build more sustainable homes, such as New Labour's promise to exempt low carbon homes from Stamp Duty until 2012, and represent the manifest difficulties of pinning down exactly what sustainability is in practice.

The most effective way to promote the merits of sustainable building technologies is not on account of their environmental credentials, but because they are cost effective in the longer term. The Royal Institute of Chartered Surveyors (2005) collaborative report *Green Value: Green Buildings, Growing Assets* drew upon Canadian expertise to suggest that eco-friendly buildings have economic advantages that developers are not taking advantage of. So, for example, green buildings have marketing potential to domestic and commercial customers, they are associated with better health and have lower running costs. Working along similar lines, the Egan report promoted the Lifecycle Cost Analysis approach, which judges a technology on its construction *and* running costs. So for example, installing better insulation will cost more during construction, but may prove cheaper if lower heating costs are taken into account over the life of the building. This approach complements Egan's emphasis upon partnership and longer-term engagement between construction companies and their products. Developers who wish to immediately sell a development will not benefit from this approach, whereas developers who have a long-term stake in the building's profitability will benefit from maximising rental value through attracting and keeping tenants more easily. Given that two-thirds of the new build construction in the UK is non-residential, including retail premises, industrial and office buildings and public buildings like schools and hospitals (UNECE, 2006), the issue of long-term running costs is highly pertinent.

Traditional accounting practices have undermined this approach by separating capital costs (initial costs of construction) from operating costs (heating, water, lighting, etc.). However, new modes of owner-occupation like Private Finance Initiatives (see Chapter 4) have encouraged the use of environmentally friendly technologies, as the PFI company might not only meet the construction costs, but also absorb the running costs for upwards of 25 years. The government report on sustainable construction (DTI, 2006) emphasised the need to standardise techniques such as lifecycle analysis within the industry, a conclusion which echoes Guy and Shoves' (2000) analysis of the barriers to constructing energy efficient buildings. Increasingly, lifecycle analysis tools like WRATE (Waste and Resources Assessment Tool for the Environment), developed by the Environment Agency, and REAP (Resource and Energy Analysis Programme), developed by the Stockholm Environment Institute, are using carbon accounting to determine the most sustainable building options. This involves calculating the embodied carbon in the materials used, the carbon cost of construction itself, and the running costs of the building over its lifetime (Rydin, 2010).

Other studies have indicated that the industry tends to over-estimate the costs of environmentally friendly technologies. Bartlett and Howard (2000) have argued that quantity surveyors, who examine how much building plans will cost given certain materials and technologies, tend to over-estimate the costs of installing energy efficient technologies by between 5% and 15%. They argue that if technologies are integrated into the design and construction process at every stage then they should add no more than 1% of the overall cost of the building. Often these savings are invisible, because costs incurred in one area will produce savings in another. For example, while energy efficient windows will cost more, they will save money in other areas, for instance through less powerful heating equipment being required. Bartlett and Howard's study resonates with the Egan recommendations, highlighting the lack of expertise within the industry in this area and the failure of designers to work collaboratively with different teams of construction engineers. The fragmentation of the construction industry into so many different parts (tens and sometimes even hundreds of companies can be involved in bringing a development to fruition) exacerbates the problem, making it hard to ensure that the gains of installing sustainable technology influence decision-making (Rydin, 2010).

Key points

i) Construction has a massive impact on the sustainability of regeneration projects, in terms of the construction process and technologies used, but rarely goes beyond legal and financial requirements.

ii) The Egan agenda pushed for a more highly skilled construction industry that works with developers and designers rather than simply providing the cheapest tender.

iii) Lifecycle analysis tools are increasingly being used to show how environmentally efficient buildings are cheaper to build and run over long periods of time.

Conclusions

Sustainable development provides the major policy framework for urban regeneration, and there is no doubt that the integrated nature of urban regeneration makes it an ideal vehicle to deliver the holistic goals of sustainability. The long-term, large-scale approach of regeneration facilitates a strategic dimension of planning to incorporate social and environmental issues into development schemes that may not exist in piecemeal developments. This is a vital part of the challenge to make cities attractive places in which to live, and can be seen as a key element of the wider regeneration agenda. In many ways, the idea of sustainable regeneration can be seen as the means by which the government is attempting to ensure that a balance is struck between the purely financial benefits of new developments for the private sector, and longer-lasting benefits to local communities.

That said, there are a number of challenges involved with balancing economic, environmental and social factors. One of the most important arenas in which these tensions are expressed is through debates surrounding house-building. Housing provision and economic development lies at the core of government policy, but, as the National Planning Policy Framework suggests, may come at the expense of environmental and social considerations. Greenbelt regulations may be relaxed in order to achieve the new higher national targets for house-building, and local authorities are being asked to presume in favour of proposed developments.

While unshackling the constraints on development may hamper the ability of local authorities and residents to prevent regeneration projects that are perceived to be undesirable, from happening, advances in building techniques and technologies might make them more environmentally sustainable in practice. Given further impetus by the climate change agenda, considerable efforts are underway to make construction more sustainable in the UK, with a system of codes, tools, subsidies and taxes being used to change the way construction occurs. That said, there are still a number of issues with translating the principles of sustainability into practical building guidelines. Undoubtedly the notion of 'sustainability' does not offer a perfect pre-determined solution, but is still in the process of being worked through in policy. Despite these difficulties it seems set to form the major approach to urban regeneration for the foreseeable future, and is returned to throughout the remainder of this book.

Further reading

It is hard to place boundaries around a topic like sustainable regeneration because it cuts across so many different fields of inquiry. Girardet provides a thought-provoking consideration of the broader context of sustainability and urban regeneration, while Owens and Cowell provide a thorough overview of the general challenges sustainability poses to the UK planning system. Gibbs provides an interesting discussion of the role communities can play in achieving more sustainable urban development, while Raco and Henderson expand upon the issues surrounding brownfield planning and sustainable regeneration. Shaw et al. explore how urban design and planning should take account of climate change, while Rydin gives an excellent account of the role sustainable construction plays in urban development.

Gibbs, D. (2002) 'Urban development and civil society: The role of communities in sustainable cities', *European Urban and Regional Studies*, 9: 350–351.
Girardet, H. (2006) *Creating Sustainable Cities* (Green Books, Totnes).
Owens, S. and Cowell, R. (2002) *Land and Limits: Interpreting Sustainable Development within the Planning System* (Routledge, London).
Raco, M. and Henderson, S. (2006) 'Sustainable planning and the brownfield development process in the United Kingdom', *Local Environment*, 11(5): 499–513.
Rydin, Y. (2010) *Governing for Sustainable Urban Development* (Earthscan, London).
Shaw, R., Colley, M. and Connell, R. (2007) *Climate Change Adaptation by Design: A Guide for Sustainable Communities* (TCPA, London).

6 Design and Cultural Regeneration

OVERVIEW

This chapter examines the increasing emphasis on producing high-quality urban design and the value of promoting culture to foster regeneration.

- *The urban design agenda*: explores how notions of 'good' urban design have infiltrated urban regeneration policy, including an examination of masterplanning and design coding as well as the influence of new urbanism.

- *Cultural regeneration*: explores the broader notion of culture-led development through case studies of waterfront redevelopment, the re-use of historic buildings, cultural anchors and signature buildings, cultural quarters, sub-cultural quarters, Liverpool as the European Capital of Culture 2008 and sports-led regeneration.

Introduction

The meaning of the word culture is somewhat ambiguous. Individuals and communities can be labelled as belonging to a particular cultural category and the term can also be used to signify the products of those individuals and communities, whether these be material objects or performances. Hence culture allows us to think about symbolism and the image of cities as well as a mindset that drives decision-making in particular directions. In urban regeneration the term 'culture' tends to be used rather uncritically and is applied to a whole range of issues, from design and architecture through artistic works and sporting events, to a more general sense of creativity and the knowledge economy.

During the New Labour years (1997–2010) there was a new emphasis on the importance of 'high-quality' design in improving urban environments. Unfortunately 'design' also has a somewhat ambiguous meaning, combining notions of both aesthetic and functional quality – the way things look and the way that they work. Assessments of aesthetics and even function are somewhat subjective, making 'design' difficult to measure and audit. Design quality is frequently linked to the broader idea of cultural regeneration, with aesthetic and functional design at the heart of 'good' urban regeneration. An obvious manifestation of this is where new flagship cultural resources – whether this be an art gallery or a football stadium – are seen as having anchoring qualities for regeneration programmes, with an architecturally impressive new building attracting private investment to a previously unfashionable area. It must be noted, however, that securing an iconic building for a site does not guarantee that the cultural resource within it will be a success, nor that other regeneration activity will follow in its wake.

Notions of cultural regeneration are often seen as a key strategy in making cities economically competitive. This brings us back to Richard Florida's argument, discussed in Chapter 4, about the need to attract members of the 'creative class' working in the knowledge economy. Flagship buildings and cultural resources are a part of this, but also the idea of fostering cultural clusters or cultural quarters, where creative people can work in close proximity and develop the kinds of 'soft' personal networks seen as crucial for innovation in the knowledge economy. This raises questions about *which* kinds of culture are incubated within these cultural quarters and whether policies to encourage economically 'valuable' cultural clustering risks shutting out more marginal/experimental cultures.

The urban design agenda

Urban design has been around as long as settlements themselves, from the simple defensive ditch and the Greek agora, to the medieval burgage system and the Edinburgh New Town. It was not until the nineteenth century that architecture emerged as a specific discipline, separate from engineering and construction. The idea of the professional planner regulating changes to the built environment developed even later, not becoming formalised until the early twentieth century. Urban design as a distinct concept is a still more recent arrival, which seeks to create a synthesis between the architecture and planning disciplines, looking at the aesthetics and functioning of towns and cities at a variety of spatial scales. The idea of urban design developed in part because of a frustration about the lack of integration between individual buildings and the townscape as a whole.

It tends to be taken as read in policy discourse that good urban design is a prerequisite for good urban regeneration. David Bell and Mark Jayne (2003), however, have taken issue with the notion that high-quality design really makes a significant difference to urban regeneration strategies. Indeed, they argue that the meaning of 'design-led' regeneration is fundamentally ambiguous, in spite of attempts being made to assess the impact of design activity on redevelopment projects. The phrase is most clearly associated with things such as flagship buildings and improvements to the public realm (squares, fountains, landscaping, etc.), which are then tied into more traditional place-marketing strategies in order to attract economic activity to the area (see Chapter 4). The new cafés, restaurants and other service facilities that are attracted have become the signifiers of a post-industrial urban economy. In a sense, this is an attempt to build the kind of urban environment that will attract the 'creative classes' of designers, media people, policy-makers, ICT workers and so forth that are believed to drive the knowledge economy.

Urban design policy

The foundations of design-led regeneration policy were laid by the Urban Task Force report (1999). The report itself was a vision statement, rather than a policy document, and it should come as no surprise that, with internationally renowned architect Richard Rogers leading the task force, high-quality urban design was given a great deal of emphasis. Nonetheless, some of the ideas about design found their way into the subsequent Urban White Paper (DETR, 2000) which shaped the approach to development throughout the New Labour period. In part, the emphasis on good urban design can be seen as a reaction against the perceived failings of post-war urban design, with its concrete canyons and crime-ridden estates. This kind of discourse makes an implicit link between the environment and human behaviour in a way that many social scientists would be rather uncomfortable with. As an aside, it should also be noted that some of the features of the post-war period, for example the notorious 'rabbit warren' Radburn layout, were seen as best design practice at the time.

Six years on from the original Urban Task Force report, a follow-up document was produced, this time without being commissioned or supported by the government.

In the introduction, Rogers explicitly criticised the continuing poor quality in urban design:

> Few well-designed integrated urban projects stand out as international exemplars of sustainable communities, despite public investment in new housing. (Urban Task Force, 2005: 3)

Here an explicit link is made between high-quality design and the creation of a sustainable community. Commentators generally have lamented the quality of much urban design since the original Urban Task Force report, although where post-war design is often seen as monstrous, post-1999 design is merely bland and characterless. Whether the mere fact of living on a generic-looking housing estate inhibits people's ability to form a sustainable community (however defined) is moot, but there can be no doubt that few ordinary housing schemes built over the last decade have excited those with an interest in urban design.

The concept of **mixed development**, heavily promoted by the Urban Task Force report, has become somewhat of a shibboleth in contemporary urban design. It would be unfair to characterise the Urban Task Force report as completely ignoring suburban, family housing, but there is a palpable enthusiasm for a somewhat **metrocentric** model of living perhaps overly biased toward the needs of young, childless professional couples (suburban development will be discussed in the next chapter). The vision which gained such traction during the New Labour period was one of central cities filled with three- to five-storey apartment blocks, built on brownfield land, containing live/work spaces, where people walk to access their local shops and services.

This high-density, walkable-city model has gained increasing global popularity, underpinning North American ideas of 'smart growth', for example. By cutting down on travel time and CO_2 emissions, mixing places of business and residential accommodation is seen uncritically as a good thing – much as it was taken as read during the post-war reconstruction that it was a good thing to rigidly separate residential accommodation from places of work. Similarly there is an assumption of social mix, with such developments diluting concentrations of poverty, by providing a combination of private housing and socially rented accommodation. In practice, there is limited evidence that social mixing manufactured purely through built form and tenure mix actually generates connections between different communities or improves social cohesion (Smets, 2011).

The Commission for Architecture and the Built Environment (CABE) created under New Labour was weakened and merged into the Design Council as part of the Coalition government's 'bonfire of the quangos' (see Chapter 2). Nonetheless CABE's priorities shaped a generation of urban design in the UK:

- Character: a place with its own identity.
- Continuity and enclosure: a place where public and private spaces are clearly distinguished.

- Quality of the public realm: a place with attractive and successful outdoor areas.
- Ease of movement: a place that is easy to get to and move through.
- Legibility: a place that has a clear image and is easy to understand.
- Adaptability: a place that can change easily.
- Diversity: a place with variety and choice. (CABE, 2000: 15)

These are quite interesting in that they indicate the wide range of topic areas that were considered as underpinning urban design. There is also an implicit reaction to the perceived failures of modern architecture and planning as it was played out in post-war Britain. Questions around delineating public and private space, for example, were a major criticism of modernist planning. It was argued that many post-war developments created spaces where there was no sense of 'ownership' which thus went unregulated by the community. The architectural critic Jane Jacobs (1961) referred to this regulatory effect as the 'eyes on the street', an idea which was later formalised into the concept of defensible space (Newman, 1973). Contemporary urban design frowns upon spaces where public and private are not clearly divided, something reinforced through the advice given to designers by Police Architectural Liaison Officers, who widely employ the concept of defensible space.

   CABE's anti-modernist stance is also clearly seen in the notion of legibility, which developed out of the work of Kevin Lynch (1960), who criticised urban spaces where movement and function were not clear. One only has to think of the muddle of underpasses, changes in level and blind corners that typified post-war shopping precincts in the UK to understand this emphasis on legibility in contemporary urban design. In the rhetoric of legibility, the subtleties of Lynch's argument are sometimes lost, but there has been a renewed emphasis on lines of sight in master-planning (see below), attempting to render spaces more readily understandable to people entering them for the first time. Similarly, Lynch's idea of 'imageability' explores the characteristics of areas that are particularly vivid and distinct – as well as pleasurable – in people's mental maps of the city. This notion of visual clues which give a city coherence to the person moving around it clearly reacts against the blandness of many modernist city developments. Again, the general idea of image-ability has been embraced, in rhetoric at least, by those interested in contemporary urban design.

   CABE (2005b) responded enthusiastically to the reforms in the Planning and Compulsory Purchase Act, 2004, in replacing local and unitary development plans with smaller scale and more flexible local development frameworks (LDFs). Subsequent reforms to the planning system under the Localism Act, 2011 and the National Planning Policy Framework (CLG, 2012e) have reinforced the idea that 'design' is not simply a site-specific concern, but should be considered across a variety of scales in the wider urban environment. If done well, LDFs and Neighbourhood Plans can operate like a good redevelopment masterplan. There is, however, an unresolved tension in the Coalition government's rhetoric on planning between empowering local areas to determine their own future and ensuring that high standards of design are adhered to. Again, part of the problem is the fact that what comprises good 'design' can be somewhat ambiguous; thus, even in its new guise as Design Council CABE, hosting design workshops for local authority staff remains a core function for the organisation.

Masterplanning and design coding

Masterplanning is a term which is applied ambiguously and encompasses several different approaches to urban development from the design brief or framework (which implies a degree of flexibility) through to a plan or a code (which suggests a greater degree of prescription). The fundamental idea is that the masterplan should lay down an over-arching set of principles which inform the development of a large site. Masterplans thus become a means of coordinating the activities of multiple actors meaning that a larger area can be planned in a coherent way than would be possible with a single developer alone (Tiesdell and Macfarlane, 2007).

Masterplans are not a particularly new invention. Haussmann's nineteenth-century reconstruction of Paris, for example, saw an overall plan laid down by the state, with individual firms constructing buildings along the new boulevards, sticking to a set of design principles. In terms of what we now think of as regeneration, London Docklands was a pioneer of masterplanning with the Canary Wharf development in the late 1980s. A key criticism of Canary Wharf is that while the masterplan produced a coherent built environment, it did little to consider wider issues of social justice, leaving areas of severe deprivation right next door to the glittering towers of the finance houses.

Masterplans can cover areas of different scales and they are not always produced by a public body. Landowners and private developers frequently commission urban design specialists to produce masterplans. These help ensure that new developments will fit together in a coherent fashion, particularly where landownership is fragmented across a site. Pragmatically, masterplans can also help to convince planning authorities that permissions to build should be granted where they stick to the plan. Masterplanning can be quite expensive, particularly where a set of landowners come together to pool resources and create a larger development opportunity across property boundaries. There is also the risk that a privately produced masterplan will fail to convince planners, leading to delays as the plan is reworked, even before any proposals for actual construction come in for consideration. One of the functions of the Urban Regeneration Company (URC) model was precisely to take on the risks of putting together large-scale masterplans coordinating numerous landowning and other interests across both public and private sectors.

Bristol Harbourside is a good example of how masterplanning can influence the shape of a development. In common with many cities, Bristol experienced a boom in inner urban redevelopment from the late 1990s until the property bubble burst in 2008. The Harbourside project has its origins in a development plan produced by Drivers Jonas in 1993, commissioned by a consortium of land-owners and developers including the city council, British Rail, Lattice Properties, Crosby Homes and Crest Nicholson. By 1998 a revised development framework was adopted as an annexe to Bristol's local plan. While some schemes went ahead within the framework, Crest Nicholson's proposals for the Canon's Marsh site ran into significant local opposition. A rival masterplan for this portion of Harbourside was drawn up by a vocal campaign group. In the end, a new mas-terplan, drawing on some of the principles suggested by the campaigners, was produced by Edward Cullinan Architects and approved in 2001. The new mas-terplan saw much more coherent production of public spaces, including the Millennium Square, Millennium Promenade and Cathedral Walk, which signifi-cantly increased the legibility of the area (CABE, 2008). Ultimately higher-quality urban design should boost sales, though it should be noted that Harbourside was built during the period of intense property speculation both by UK and international investors when, frankly, virtually any development would have sold almost immediately regardless of quality. Indeed, some local developers noted that there were cases of international consortia buying whole blocks of unbuilt property without even seeing the plans (Boddy, 2007). In today's less fevered property market, however, quality urban design is becoming a more important factor for driving sales, which can only be to the benefit of our towns and cities (Box 6.1).

Design coding is a specific type of masterplanning which was introduced to the UK policy mainstream through a series of pilots championed by CABE from 2004–06. The idea of design coding is fundamentally inspired by new urbanism (see below) and designates a series of design specifications for a redevelopment area, with varying degrees of detail at different spatial scales. These specifications might include, for example, height of building, storey height, set backs from the street, overall street/frontage patterns, guidance on materials, textures and colours, sometimes even guidance on detailing of buildings and public realm infrastruc-ture. The overall intention of these codes is to make design quality auditable, such that where developers stick within the **design code** they should have an almost automatic right to develop on the site that has those guidelines attached to it. The presumption is that if developers stick to the code then good designs for the area should follow. Design codes are used widely and successfully on the continent, especially in Germany, although Richard Rogers has been somewhat scathing about the aesthetic results of design-code-led urban planning. This said, there is general agreement that good design codes can at least stop the worst architectural abuses and can inspire genuinely diverse and interesting architecture. A team led by the Bartlett School of Planning, which evaluated design coding, gave it favour-able reports and it was subsequently integrated into *Planning Policy Statement 3: Housing* (CLG, 2006a). Despite the presumption of permission to build that design coding brings, the requirement to produce codes was watered down under the Coalition government's replacement, pro-growth *National Planning Policy Framework* (CLG, 2012e). Codes remain quite a useful tool when putting together a Local Development Framework or Neighbourhood Plan, but the *National Planning Policy Framework* warns against being too prescriptive on the detailing of buildings in case this slows development.

BOX 6.1 POLNOON MASTERPLAN

Polnoon is a planned extension to the small village of Eaglesham, around 13km south of Glasgow. The site has become a demonstration project for the Scottish government to look at improvements to urban design. The Polnoon masterplan envisages adding an extra 121 homes to the south-east corner of the village using a compact layout mixing houses and flats. The road network has been designed to increase legibility and integrate the new area into the existing village. Extensive community consultation was undertaken, as well as studying the history of the area to inform the design. The masterplan was produced in collaboration with developers Mactaggart and Mickel Ltd, who had already secured planning permission for a more conventional project on the site, but were persuaded to revisit the designs in order to produce a higher-quality urban environment.

The masterplan is highly detailed, with a set of special housing designs produced just for this project and even going so far as to identify the paving colours for different parts of the development. Particular attention was paid to the visual transition into the new development from the conservation area which forms the core of the original eighteenth-century village. Historic trees were retained and the layout was designed, paying attention to the site's topography, putting the taller three-storey buildings in areas of lower relief so as not to dominate the skyline. The whole of Polnoon was designed to be pedestrian friendly, with cars moved out of public realm areas and speeds limited to 20mph. Even the tenure mix is specified in the masterplan.

The developers acknowledge that this project will be slightly less profitable than the original approved scheme, but are keen to be involved in a high-profile demonstration project. Until the housing market recovers from the 2008 slump, however, the developers cannot afford to begin work in realising the project, despite receiving renewed planning permission in 2009.

Source: Scottish Government (2009)

New urbanism

Proponents of design coding in the UK have been inspired by the work of the new urbanist movement. Although the term 'new urbanism' has had less exposure in the UK than the United States, many of its key tenets have been absorbed into UK policy, in particular the rhetoric of mixed development, diversity and compact walkable cities (Talen, 1999). In the US, new urbanism is frequently entangled with the debate over 'smart growth'. Where new urbanism as a movement was developed by architects and planners, smart growth was developed by environmentalists and policy planners. As a result the terms are not exactly interchangeable, although both talk about mixed uses and walkability. New urbanism stresses design elements, where smart growth is driven by considerations of economic development and environmental sustainability.

Some social scientists have been a little uncomfortable with the kinds of environmental determinist claims made by new urbanists that 'good' design can promote 'good' communities. Equally, however, new urbanist practitioners complain that social scientists do not engage with the practicalities of delivering urban regeneration on the ground and the importance of good design for achieving this. New urbanists, architecturally, have leanings towards the **neo-vernacular**, which means highly qualified architects self-consciously producing updated versions of the historic building styles that were developed locally by non-architects. The adherence to the neo-vernacular is not universal, however. Indeed, the idea of design coding was developed in the new urbanist settlement of Seaside in Florida, famously the location for Peter Weir's film *The Truman Show* (1998). The film did, however, carefully pick locations in the town where neo-vernacular design predominated to generate a particular vision of an idealised Americana. Less traditional designs were employed elsewhere in Seaside, with design coding used to set general parameters to give an overall coherence to the town, but with variation permitted within those parameters.

The most prominent example overtly applying new urbanist concepts in the UK is Poundbury in Dorset, which was designed by Luxembourg architect Léon Krier to a commission by HRH the Prince of Wales. Work began on Poundbury in 1989 and helped to cement some of the principles which are now in the policy mainstream, particularly mixing residential accommodation and workplaces, high-density walkable urban areas and, in theory at least, mixed demographic and community groups. Stylistically it's a 'myth-mash' of fake Georgian and fake Victorian (Figure 6.1) which is not to everyone's taste. The architectural critic Jonathan Glancey (2004), for example, was somewhat cutting about how the rhetoric has been played out, noting that the 'mixed uses' included an equine vet, a chocolate shop and other rather bourgeois services.

Poundbury does make the car subservient to the pedestrian, tucked away in separate car parks with many roads entirely traffic free. Though low-rise, it is a high-density development, with limited space around the houses. The socially rented and private housing is indistinguishable and intermixed, but as property prices have risen rapidly,

Figure 6.1 Poundbury divides opinion between those who like its village character and those who are uncomfortable with its fake historicity. Narrow winding streets lead to Brownsword Hall, which sits at the heart of the 1990s development and hosts local events.

it has become rather an expensive place to live. Poundbury's defenders would argue that the rise in property prices proves that the design works well and is successful because it delivers what people want from an urban settlement. While one may criticise the pastiche fake historicism on *aesthetic* grounds, in more general terms there is no doubt that the design principles have been influential. The same principles are now being applied to a follow-up project by the Prince with a planned extension to newly fashionable Newquay (nicknamed 'Surfbury' by some detractors), which received planning permission in 2010. Once again, design coding and the principles of walkable, mixed developments are at the fore; the difference is that where Poundbury was somewhat experimental, the ideas it pioneered are now mainstream.

Key points

i) Contemporary urban design is a synthesis of architecture and planning which examines the coherence of development at the area scale.

ii) The meaning of 'good' design is somewhat ambiguous, containing notions of both aesthetic and functional quality.

iii) There is a strong anti-modernist reaction in debates over contemporary design quality, with much of post-war urban design held up as worst practice.

iv) Masterplanning is an umbrella term which encompasses a number of approaches to bringing different actors together to develop an area in a coherent fashion. Statutory instruments such as Local Development Frameworks and Neighbourhood Plans essentially function as masterplans.

v) Design coding is a highly prescriptive version of masterplanning, which can define every aspect of the built environment in an area, from the width of the streets to the types of materials used and even the colours of buildings.

vi) Walkability, mixed development and design coherence have become major tenets of urban design policy, inspired by North American ideas of new urbanism and smart growth.

Cultural regeneration

Perhaps the most important factor driving the move towards regeneration through culture has been the development of the post-industrial economy described in Chapter 4. The key impacts of this have been twofold: firstly, very large formerly industrial areas within cities, having fallen into disuse, have provided major redevelopment opportunities; secondly, the change to a more knowledge/services-based economy has created a broader cultural change within society with different types of employment driving a demand for different types of work/leisure/residential spaces.

Waterfront redevelopment

The redevelopment of former industrial waterfronts is a classic example of how structural changes in the global economy have given rise to regeneration opportunities. Waterfront redevelopment has now become so common that it is almost the cliché of regeneration that where once men sweated in docks and shipyards, we now have middle-class professionals sipping cappuccinos in pavement cafés and living in converted loft apartments. The post-war move towards containerisation led to bigger ships needing deep-water port facilities which made many older docks in inner cities redundant. This created an opportunity to transform the image of cities, putting dockland areas to new uses and creating whole new quarters of the city. This has transformed the cultural identity of cities along with their physical appearance.

Waterfront redevelopment is not a particularly new phenomenon. In the late 1960s the city of Baltimore, with financial assistance from the United States

Federal government, began regenerating its Inner Harbor district. Pollution was cleaned up, historic buildings restored, parkland replaced dockland, and through the 1970s the area became the location for various cultural events. This culture-based regeneration continued with the Inner Harbor becoming home to the National Aquarium and Maryland Science Center alongside Harborplace, a large retail and leisure complex. An abandoned, polluted space was transformed into a highly attractive quarter right at the heart of the city, helping to drive the broader cultural transformation and economic redevelopment of the city centre.

The model developed in Baltimore has been copied across the post-industrial world; indeed it is so successful that in Amsterdam entirely new islands have been built in the River IJ (hence 'IJburg') to accommodate the demand for waterfront development. In the UK there have been two distinct phases of waterfront redevelopment, the first through the 1980s until the property crash of the early 1990s, the second from the late 1990s until the crash of 2008. It is important to note that when the UK's industrial waterfronts were in use, and indeed when they were derelict, it was actually quite difficult to get access to the waterfront. People could not simply walk into a dockyard to have a stroll by the river. Indeed, no one would have wanted to promenade along the waterfront given the high levels of pollution suffered by many of the UK's working rivers. Through the 1980s, the decline of British industry and new regulations on discharges combined with better sewage treatment meant that water quality began to improve dramatically such that, for example, by the early 1990s, salmon had returned to the once toxic River Mersey.

Waterfront regeneration has involved giving people access to the waterfronts where none existed before, to complement improvements in the marine environment. Improved water quality reinforces the innate attraction of waterfront sites, with the aesthetic appeal of reflections on the water, boats going by, leisure activities and so on. This in turn can attract commercial attention. The pioneers of waterfront development in the UK were not private developers, however, but urban development corporations. These Thatcherite instruments of central government intervention in acutely deprived areas had perhaps their most notable successes with Canary Wharf in London and the Albert Dock in Liverpool.

Canary Wharf is today a hugely wealthy office district built on what was, in the early 1980s, a largely abandoned area. Very little of the historic built fabric was retained in this project, with a focus very much on new high-rise offices and, subsequently, apartments. In terms of innovation, the work of the Merseyside Development Corporation in reviving the Albert Dock was perhaps more interesting. The architecturally valuable historic dock buildings could not be demolished and so were redeveloped. The ground storey was a mix of retail and cultural uses – including the Merseyside Maritime Museum and, later, the Tate Liverpool art gallery – with the upper storeys being a mix of offices and loft-style apartments (Figure 6.2). Granada Television also located offices and studio in the redeveloped site; indeed, as with the Salford Quays development discussed in the last chapter, media companies are often perceived as the ultimate seal of approval for a cultural regeneration. The mix of uses at the Albert Dock was highly innovative for the UK at the time, with some elements of the scheme quite high risk for a city with a depressed property market. Nonetheless the mixing of uses insulated the Albert Dock from the slump in the office property market in the early 1990s which saw the newly completed Canary Wharf partially empty and its owners filing for bankruptcy in 1992. After that early wobble, however, London Docklands has gone on to become a world hub for financial services.

On many levels one can depict these kinds of waterfront developments as win–win. Polluted waterscapes have been cleaned up, historic buildings given a new lease of life, economic activity created from derelict areas and cultural uses given a new home. As noted above, however, Docklands did little to tackle deprivation in neighbouring districts. Nonetheless, the dramatic visual impact of a whole new quarter of a city arising from derelict waterfront was exceedingly exciting both to politicians and developers so it is little wonder that this approach has proved so popular, with many examples of similar successful projects elsewhere.

The Albert Dock did not generate anything like the wealth of Canary Wharf and it is today looking just a little tired and worn around the edges. Nonetheless, the waterfront remains a tremendously iconic location attracting the Echo Arena and BT Convention Centre which have extended development to the neighbouring Kings Dock along with the usual mix of residential and retail uses which are so familiar in any development. The model that Liverpool helped to pioneer is now so mainstream that the Kings Waterfront project, though impressive in scale, does not seem particularly innovative, as a great many other interesting (and not so interesting) waterfront schemes have been carried out across the UK in the last 25 years. Gloucester, for example, which is not one of the 'usual suspects' in discussions of urban regeneration, has undertaken a major programme redeveloping its inner dock areas. The completion of the Gloucester and Sharpness canal in 1827 allowed Gloucester to become England's most significant inland port. As the docks fell out of use they lay derelict until the mid-1980s when the city council moved its main offices there in the first phase of a redevelopment scheme, although initially this only dealt with the interesting historic buildings closest to the city centre. A second wave of development in the early 2000s saw a series of new schemes for the docks, including a mix of conversion and new build residential flats.

The Gloucester Quays scheme received planning approval in 2004 as a partnership between British Waterways (who own the canals) and Peel Holdings, assisted by a newly established Urban Regeneration Company (URC), Gloucester Heritage. The £200m scheme was given the go-ahead in 2006 to

Figure 6.2   Jesse Hartley's 1840s Albert Dock is now Grade I listed – the highest level of protection for historic buildings in England. In the 1980s a process of redevelopment produced a mix of offices, shops and apartments as well as cultural uses. The Albert Dock represented Liverpool's first major foray into urban regeneration and the city's latest scheme, a new arena and conference centre, has been built alongside it.

redevelop 25 hectares of previously developed dockland. The few remaining historic buildings of interest were retained, but the rest of the site was completely cleared to make way for a 'designer outlet' shopping centre, large new supermarket and Gloucester College's new campus, all set around a cleaned-up canal and upgraded road infrastructure. The scheme produced very significant changes to the urban landscape of inner Gloucester, although it is unlikely that developers would adopt a similar retail-led project had the scheme been attempted in the post-2008 economic climate. Such projects can be accused of threatening existing high streets, meaning that they are not automatically win–win. Nonetheless, Gloucester Quays does demonstrate how a large semi-derelict area can be transformed into an attractive waterside destination. It must be said, however, that the newly built apartment developments are not particularly inspiring in terms of their architecture, even though some attempts have been made to fit them into the profile of the historic dock buildings.

Re-use of historic buildings

The dockside warehouses in Gloucester and Liverpool are good examples of a particular kind of historic building, which has been culturally validated through being listed for preservation and given a new lease of life through redevelopment. Cleaned up and recycled, such architecturally interesting buildings can lend character when sensitively integrated into a development programme. Indeed, English Heritage (2005) has promoted conservation-led regeneration as a model for protecting buildings and areas of specific historical interest. It is, however, considerably more expensive to reuse an old building than to create a new one from scratch, as the development process requires more ingenuity to fit new uses and new requirements for structural and environmental function into an existing superstructure. In addition, Value Added Tax is charged on building materials for refurbishment, but not for new build, giving an extra incentive not to retain older buildings.

One way around this problem is façadism. Essentially the front of the building is kept, such that it looks the same to a passer-by, but the remainder is demolished and a new building erected behind the façade. This can be particularly effective where properties appear in terraces, although can look a little strange where an original façade is used to form the lower storeys of a much taller new building (Figure 6.3). There is, however, a broader philosophical point about façadism in that while it may preserve the aesthetics of the streetscape, it is fundamentally dishonest in that the functional logic of the historic building is destroyed. John Pendlebury (1999; 2002) has examined these issues at length through a study of Newcastle's Grainger Town district (Figure 6.4).

Figure 6.3 Postmodern architecture often borrows from past styles, but in this case, part of Birmingham's Orion Building, a section of terracotta Victoriana has been literally built into the new development. There has, however, been relatively little attempt made to integrate the old façade into the design of the new building.

Speculative developer Richard Grainger was responsible for building a large portion of central Newcastle between the 1820s and 1840s, creating some rather wonderful streetscapes in the neo-classical style. While some of these buildings were destroyed as part of comprehensive redevelopments in the 1960s and 1970s, the inner core area around Grey Street and Grainger Street was made the subject of a conservation area. In the early 1990s, the Grainger Town district was identified by the local council for a major redevelopment programme. Between 1997 and 2003, the Grainger Town Partnership, a coalition of the city council, English Partnerships and English Heritage, led the regeneration of this area. The streetscape and façades were, by and large, retained in this process, but there was a tension between the demands of developers and their clients for large floorplate-type offices and the existing buildings which had smaller, less flexible spaces and in some cases were in a state of disrepair. A great many of these buildings were demolished, with the façades retained to front new, modern buildings with all the facilities demanded by contemporary businesses.

At the end of the project, the Grainger Town streetscapes are largely intact. Arguably, the cleaned and repaired façades in combination with a scheme of pedestrianisation have in fact significantly improved the aesthetics of the area. In many

Figure 6.4 Grainger Town in Newcastle retains the attractive streetscape of Richard Grainger's original development and combines it with a sensitive scheme of pedestrianisation. Some of the original urban fabric behind the façades has, however, been lost, which raises interesting questions about the trade-off between contemporary needs and historic value.

cases, however, the historic grain of the urban fabric has been lost, which raises questions about the kinds of culture which are valued in these schemes – in this case, aesthetics over substance perhaps. The counter argument is that the Grainger Town district was declining in the early 1990s and the intervention has seen a significant improvement in its fortunes. Again this highlights a critical point that regeneration schemes which overtly draw on notions of culture are not automatically win–win for the *existing* culture of an area; as with all regeneration, there are compromises to be made. Essentially there is a tension here between culture as physical artefacts and culture as a way of life that is difficult to resolve.

The treatment of historic buildings in redevelopment is very dependent on current fashion. During the post-war reconstruction there was a clear sense that Victorian architecture was of relatively limited value and could be sacrificed. Even the high-quality Georgian buildings produced by Richard Grainger in Newcastle were not immune to this destructive urge – while the 1960s city council retained the central area, other buildings were demolished, for example the Royal Arcade which was replaced by an urban motorway and roundabout (Pendlebury, 1999: 427). When lamenting the losses of the 1960s, it should be remembered that not many people were shedding tears at the time. In contemporary regeneration it is clear that some buildings are seen as more worthy than others of being given a new lease of life, rather than simply being replaced. There seems to be a blanket assumption that anything built in the 1960s is automatically of limited value and fit only for the wreckers' ball.

The listing of historic buildings for preservation is the main mechanism for protecting the highest quality examples of architecture from a particular period. This is not an uncontroversial process, particularly when it comes to twentieth-century buildings. Park Hill in Sheffield was one of the first council housing megastructures in the UK designed by two young architects Jack Lynn and Ivor Smith whose ideas can be broadly fitted into the 'new brutalist' movement associated with Alison and Peter Smithson. Park Hill was the first built example of the deck access model in the UK – the idea that the dynamics of the working-class street could be replicated in high-rise form through everybody's front door opening onto a wide gallery which ran the length of the building. When Park Hill was listed as Grade II★ in 1998 there was an outcry in Sheffield that this huge concrete 'monstrosity', which by that time had become quite a rundown estate, should be deemed worthy of preservation. Sheffield City Council found themselves reluctantly having to form a complex partnership arrangement to find a way of preserving the estate.

Urban Splash made its name in the 1990s pioneering the redevelopment of factories and warehouses into fashionable apartments in north-west England. The company has expanded its regeneration work and is now one of the most in-demand developers for large, complex sites, including Bristol's Lakeshore and Royal William Yard in Plymouth. In 2006 Urban Splash were chosen to lead the redevelopment of Park Hill, creating a fashionable inner city apartment development, reducing the number of socially rented units to one third of the total and bringing in a variety of 'hip' new businesses. Only the concrete frame of Park Hill was listed, so the developers removed the brick panels and other fittings from one part of the building, stripping back to a skeleton before refitting with larger windows and colourful metal panels (Figure 6.5). Following advice from English Heritage, repairs to the concrete were undertaken along the same principles used for medieval cathedrals. Thus the new concrete patches do not quite match the original, so that it is apparent to the careful observer where the repairs have taken place. Nonetheless, only one comparatively small section of this giant building has been regenerated in the first phase and the current financial climate suggests it is unlikely that the remainder will follow any time soon. The original development suffered partly because it became a sink estate for the poorest and most vulnerable tenants and partly because of severe centrally imposed restrictions on maintenance spending that left the area physically neglected for many years. With a much smaller number of social housing units managed by the well-funded Great Places Housing Group, the regenerated part of the estate has a greater chance of success this time around.

Figure 6.5 Regeneration of Ivor Smith and Jack Lynn's Park Hill megastructure. Urban Splash have undertaken a very sensitive reworking of this building, but only a small portion has been completed, leaving most of this giant block in its original, rather run-down condition.

Park Hill is not the only mid-twentieth-century building which has had its architectural and cultural value validated by a contemporary redevelopment. Denys Lasdun's 1957 Keeling House in Bethnal Green has been refashioned as exclusive apartments while Ernö Goldfinger's Trellick Tower, opened in 1972, has today become an icon of modernist chic run by a tenant management organisation. All of these buildings have, however, received listed status. There are, however, many good buildings of this period which, although not of the high quality required for listing, may in time be rehabilitated to fashionable status in the way that Victoriana has been. Indeed, Aidan While (2006) has discussed some of the tensions that arise where the urban renaissance agenda runs headlong into the remains of the modernist cityscape. There was a local outcry when a proposed redevelopment of Portsmouth's brutalist Tricorn shopping centre prompted consideration of it being listed. After an extensive lobbying campaign both by the pro- and anti-redevelopment sides, the proposed listing was rejected and the Tricorn demolished. Meanwhile, Coventry's 1950s Lower Precinct, the first retail precinct of this kind, although largely retained, has received a makeover not entirely sensitive to its original post-war form. At the time of writing, the inverted pyramid of Birmingham's Central Library is under a death sentence, to be demolished once the replacement building, designed by Dutch firm Mecanoo, is complete.

Aside from the handful of people with an interest in this particular kind of architecture, not many lament the destruction of the built fabric of modernist culture. Again, however, it is important to reiterate that fashions and tastes change over time and those things deemed of little value culturally today, may come back into vogue at a later date. This is not an argument for blanket preservation, but rather to note that where urban regeneration talks about fostering cultural values, these are highly subjective and tend to be driven by current tastes.

Cultural anchors and signature buildings

Just as post-war architecture has fallen out of favour and can therefore be ignored/ sacrificed in redevelopment, so other cultural markers are emphasised or effaced in the regeneration process depending on how they are currently valued. A key question therefore is to ask whose culture is being validated through a 'cultural' regeneration process.

This question of 'whose culture' is particularly important when considering schemes where a cultural facility is being used to anchor a larger regeneration programme. Cultural anchors are often argued to be a useful mechanism to give developers confidence to invest in parts of cities which are run down or unfashionable. The classic international example of using a signature building to drive regeneration activity was the 1997 Guggenheim Museum built in the declining industrial city of Bilbao in northern Spain to a design by Frank Gehry. There is a question of what the building actually says about Bilbao itself, the town and its existing cultures, being hidden behind an icon in a global architecture guidebook. The building has become a tourist attraction in its own right and arguably validated a particular kind of spectacular architecture in cultural anchor buildings. A similar 'alien spacecraft' quality can be seen in the Imperial War Museum of the north which sits amid the Salford Quays redevelopment, the Firstsite gallery in Colchester and at the Sage in Gateshead (Figure 6.6). The completion of the Sage in 2002 gave the north east an extremely high-quality concert hall, to act as home both for the Northern Symphonia and Folkworks. Folkworks, promoting traditional music and dance had been heavily involved in community and educational work since its foundation in 1988. This emphasis on community engagement continues with the educational facilities in the new building.

The eye-catching design of the Sage is clearly meant as a signature building; the bulbous metal slug was designed by the internationally renowned Foster and Partners and cost £70m. The Sage is part of a larger complex of cultural resources on the south bank of the Tyne, which includes the BALTIC, a major modern art gallery housed in a converted flour mill, and the Millennium Bridge which links the facilities to Newcastle on the other side of the river. Ironically, it was neighbouring Newcastle which perhaps benefited most from these developments, with a series of apartments, bars and restaurants on the northern bank of the Tyne benefiting from

Figure 6.6   The Sage, Gateshead, designed by Foster and Partners, provides a striking outlook to those sitting in the riverside cafés on the Newcastle side of the Tyne.

views of the new cultural facilities in the neighbouring town. Gateshead intended to capitalise on the public sector investment in the waterfront through promoting a large mixed-use scheme on the site between the BALTIC and the Sage (the Hawks Road/South Shore area). Kier properties were lined up as a preferred developer for the site in 2006. In 2008 the city issued a new development brief for the site, but little has happened since. Gateshead missed the window for developing this kind of scheme prior to the credit crunch, meaning that any subsequent development will be slower to arrive and generate less money for the local authority.

Simply securing a landmark iconic building housing a cultural resource, therefore, is no guarantee of regeneration success. The important lesson of such developments is that the cultural resource must itself be a success, working hard to draw visitors to an area and maintain its flow of income. There have been a number of high-profile flops, such as the National Centre for Popular Music in Sheffield and, perhaps even more dramatically, The Public, a community arts resource in West Bromwich (Figure 6.7). Designed by Will Alsop with an original budget of £38m, the cost went over £50m and, uniquely for a project of this kind, The Public went into receivership even before it opened. The building, a black box pierced with blob-like magenta openings, is certainly striking, but it was never really clear who the audience was and the development has not really generated critical mass, either artistically or in terms of leveraging further investment. While there are a number of redevelopment and regeneration projects currently being undertaken by Sandwell Council, proximity to The Public is not flagged as a major incentive to invest in the town. Although it is now functioning as an arts resource, it has not proved an effective catalyst and is somewhat of an embarrassment. In Bilbao, the Guggenheim was simply one element of a culture-based redevelopment strategy, but, as Sara Gonzàlez (2011) has argued, it is an excellent example of how regeneration models travel and mutate as policy-makers seek to replicate their impact. Dropping an inferior arts venue onto a small, deprived town like West Bromwich was never going to be enough to transform it into a Bilbao-style success story. Indeed, arguably a Tesco hypermarket recently built a short distance from The Public will have a much more dramatic impact on the lives of people in the town.

Cultural quarters

As discussed in Chapter 4, the idea of 'clustering' has generated some debate in terms of its impact on local economic development. When considering cultural regeneration it is taken as read in policy that clustering together cultural resources and the creative industries will have inherently beneficial effects. As a result, the idea

Figure 6.7 The Public, West Bromwich, is a lovely building to photograph, though looks somewhat less impressive when actually standing in front of it. A financial disaster, the scheme has yet to prove its value in attracting investment to this run-down part of the West Midlands.

of fostering cultural quarters is a key tenet of urban regeneration discourse (Montgomery, 2003). Culture is often defined quite broadly in this context, classically stretching from media companies and IT, through craft-based businesses, music, graphic design and arts organisations. Companies can range in size from the multinational IT provider to the micro-business of one person making and selling their own products. The idea of clustering is that by working in proximity to each other, creative people will be still more creative, with the clustering reinforcing innovation and economic development.

The classic counter argument against cultural clustering is that it generates a process of gentrification. It is quite common for artists of various kinds to 'occupy' run-down parts of cities, because they are inexpensive places to live and work. The presence of this artistic culture can help re-image that part of the city and make it fashionable enough to attract other people and businesses, which eventually makes the area too expensive for the artists that colonised it in the first place (Zukin, 1982). Where cultural clusters are given the official seal of approval, this gentrification process can be accelerated. Marginal and experimental artists and businesses will be squeezed out by higher rents, unless they fit into the tastes and strictures of work that attracts public subsidy. Again, therefore, notions of cultural quarters raises questions about the kinds of cultures that are valued in terms of regeneration.

The Cultural Industries Quarter (CIQ) in Sheffield builds on a pre-existing cluster of cultural users. Sheffield was hit particularly hard by deindustrialisation in the late 1970s and 1980s, with the collapse of the city's steel industry. The CIQ area, running east and south from the main railway station, had been in decline even before then, having been a location for small workshops involved in the metals trade. With assistance from the city council, a number of cultural businesses were brought into the area, including Red Tape Studios, joining existing cultural facilities such as the Leadmill live music venue which opened in 1980. The Workstation opened in 1993 with 460m^2 of space which is rented to media companies working in video, sound, design, etc. The idea was that it should act as something of a hothouse, encouraging collaboration and mutual support, providing flexible working space for the kinds of small and micro-businesses that flourish in this sector.

More high profile, but less successful was the National Centre for Popular Music which opened in 1999, housed in a dramatic signature building by Nigel Coates (Figure 6.8). Costing £15m with funds from the National Lottery it ran into financial difficulties within seven months and closed. The buildings have now become the student union for Sheffield Hallam University. By 2000 the city council had decided that the cultural quarter was not developing in a sufficiently coordinated fashion and produced the CIQ Action Plan which was adopted as supplementary planning guidance. A new body, the CIQ Agency, was established to coordinate the development of the quarter, with funding secured from round six of the single regeneration budget. Although the CIQ Agency still exists, by 2006 much of the area had already been redeveloped and the remit to foster the creative economy

Figure 6.8 Originally the National Centre for Popular Music, Sheffield, this collection of futuristic curling stones is now the students' union for Sheffield Hallam University and sits at the heart of the city's Cultural Industries Quarter.

within Sheffield was passed on to the Economic Development Company Creativesheffield, which was itself absorbed into Sheffield City Council in 2011.

Creativesheffield has four key priorities:

- Attracting and supporting inward investment to Sheffield.
- Supporting the growth of indigenous major strategic businesses and high-growth companies.
- Encouraging business innovation and technology transfer.
- Ensuring a portfolio of key infrastructure projects are delivered to support the city's economic growth objectives. (Creativesheffield, 2011)

The work undertaken within the CIQ area itself was quite interesting, particularly in attracting resource from the Heritage Lottery fund to convert and reuse 20 historic buildings, including the Grade II★ listed Butcher Works. This mid-nineteenth-century factory courtyard was sensitively restored using the original materials to make use of a significant heritage asset. Most of the building is now apartments, with a café and gallery on the ground floor. It also contains craft workshops associated with the Academy of Makers, giving some links not only to the creative economy agenda, but also to the city's rich history of manufacturing.

There were other attempts to do something more creative than simply building a large number of apartments for rent, despite the fact that these would have been highly profitable prior to 2008. The Cube was a demonstration project with ground-floor offices and apartments above which was promoted as giving entrepreneurs an opportunity to deeply embed themselves in the networking opportunities offered by the density of cultural businesses in the CIQ. It has, however, largely been converted to student accommodation, seemingly having failed to create the necessary buzz around the creative industries.

A few glitches aside, the CIQ was successful in giving Sheffield a new quarter around which to frame the broader regeneration of the city. The presence of the CIQ was a catalyst for producing an integrated transport hub at the adjacent bus and train stations, which gave a much more coherent welcome into the city, with more legible connections into the CIQ and the city core through public realm improvements. The CIQ is also adjacent to the Sheffield Digital Campus, a city centre business park for small and medium-sized firms working in the ICT sector. It is unlikely that the Digital Campus proposals would have held any real credibility without the presence of the CIQ to demonstrate an established market for creative businesses wanting to take floor space within the city core. There is also, however, a continuing dependence on the public sector to catalyse this kind of development, with the city council in 2009 taking control of the Electric Works, the first completed building in the Digital Campus. While it may feature the world's only helter-skelter inside an office block, as a business incubator the Electric Works is clearly still too high risk for a depressed office market to see as profitable.

The idea of promoting 'cultural industries' is clearly a key strategy among local authorities and Local Enterprise Partnerships, which returns us to the question about the kinds of cultures being promoted through these processes. New media, ICT, television and film appear to be the holy grail in terms of economic regeneration through the cultural industries, none of which necessarily reflects or develops the unique cultures of local areas. Where culture is only seen as a means to an economic end there is a danger that the somewhat ephemeral qualities of creativity, which cultural quarters seek to foster, will be lost because of an external conception of what are the 'right' kinds of cultures to encourage regeneration.

Sub-cultural quarters

There is a strange tension in the notion of a cultural quarter, because the idea of quarters suggests a space given over to a particular *sub*-culture, one part of the rich tapestry of cultural life in a city. Traditionally, quarters or districts were associated with ethnic groups – China town, the Irish quarter and so on. The idea of a generic *cultural* quarter is therefore a little strange, but perhaps reinforces the idea that culture in this context means mainstream, economically productive 'creative' industries.

Ethnically defined quarters have been the target of regeneration activity, but it is perhaps gay quarters that have become the most iconic of the sub-cultural clusters in contemporary urban regeneration. The sheer size of cities has tended to make them more 'gay friendly' and much more tolerant of diversity. Larger populations have also enabled critical mass to develop in certain areas, with specifically gay shops and services catering to the needs of a population clustering in part to offset the negative consequences of homophobia.

Given that gay couples are less likely to raise children, this produces a tendency toward reducing lifetime housing costs, freeing up resources for consumption. This in turn makes the 'city living' lifestyle more attractive, with proximity to specialist services of more importance than issues of child safety, open space and good schools that make suburban areas attractive. Alan Collins (2004) has examined the formation of gay villages and their role in urban regeneration. While many areas may have some of the precursor conditions for establishing a gay village, such as a large diverse population and a low-rent district where more specialist businesses can get established, Collins argues that it takes a kind of historical accident to transform these precursors into a fully fledged cluster. This might be, for example, a microeconomic decision such as opening a gay or gay-friendly bar in a particular district, which leads to cumulative processes attracting similar business where a market need is demonstrated, which in turn establishes the area as one where gay households want to locate.

While gay villages such as Newcastle's 'pink triangle' or London's Soho may begin to develop in this rather organic way, the economic potential of the pink pound has meant that policy-makers and developers have taken an interest in the gay market. Canal Street in Manchester is the archetype of a previously marginal space which has been heavily invested in and is now promoted by the city council as one of the city's major tourism/leisure attractions. In the late 1980s, the Canal Street area had nowhere near its current visibility or coherence, consisting of just three traditional gay bars with proximity to two major cottages – locations for casual semi-public sexual activity among gay men. This last point is important because it indicates that certain sub-cultural phenomena that a local authority would not want to be associated with can help to incubate the more politically acceptable manifestations of that sub-culture. The opening of Manto, in the early 1990s, gave Canal Street an architecturally designed, highly *visible* gay bar and started a trend for major investment. Pedestrianisation of the area followed, complementing a street café culture and expensive loft apartment development occurring by the mid- to late-1990s (Binnie and Skeggs, 2004). A previously marginal area thus became very fashionable and developed rapidly on the back of its association with a particular sub-culture.

Marketing Manchester, a public-private partnership, developed a specific marketing campaign in 1999 based on the city's gay friendliness. This campaign was helped significantly by a TV series broadcast the same year, *Queer as Folk*, which was filmed in Manchester. The image of Manchester as a gay idyll made the series a cult hit in the United States and helped in the city's broader international re-imaging process

(Hughes, 2003). The way that the Canal Street quarter has developed has not been uncontroversial, however. The area was one of the first in the city to develop the model of more continental-style late night café culture and as such was rather fashionable for a time. It also became popular with women as a location where hedonistic impulses could be indulged without the threat of an aggressive heterosexual male presence. Unfortunately this very fact attracted straight men into the area, resulting in somewhat of a backlash, with gay-only entry policies and tension within the community with the feeling that straight people were coming to voyeuristically observe gay behaviour as if visiting a zoo. Attempts by mainstream cultures to co-opt sub-cultural spaces have the potential, therefore, to produce significant tensions and can indeed threaten the very sub-cultural qualities that had made the area attractive in the first place.

Liverpool, European Capital of Culture 2008

The European City (later 'Capital') of Culture (ECoC) scheme began in 1985, and in 1990 Glasgow was the first UK city to be awarded the designation. While this raised some eyebrows, particularly among some cynical (particularly English) commentators, ECoC designation provided an opportunity for Glasgow to shift focus away from its image of being a deprived post-industrial city and to remind people of its rich cultural heritage. Among policy-makers, the Glasgow experience was deemed a huge success although, as discussed in Chapter 4, it was not uncontroversial and there are those who continue to argue that it did not really have that much of an effect in terms of social regeneration (Mooney, 2004). Regardless of the arguments on the success or otherwise of economic restructuring, in terms of city re-imaging Glasgow's reputation has been transformed post-1990 and it is little surprise that when it was again the UK's turn to host ECoC, there was fierce competition between cities for the 2008 designation. When the result was announced in 2003, it was Liverpool that came out on top.

In common with Glasgow, Liverpool today has a significant disparity between a revitalised, exciting, well resourced city centre regeneration catalysed by notions of 'culture', and truly diabolical poverty in its inner urban and suburban social housing estates. One of the stories that was told in the aftermath of Liverpool's victory in the ECoC competition, was that the significant public involvement in the bid process was the factor that tipped the scales. It has since been characterised as the 'people's bid'. Jones and Wilkes-Heeg (2004) argue that perhaps a more important underlying factor was the belief that Liverpool was the city most likely to 'do a Glasgow' by using the Capital of Culture label as the lynchpin of a broader regeneration process. Rival cities such as Oxford, Birmingham and Bristol, though hardly free from poverty, arguably would not benefit as greatly from the additional impetus generated by the Capital of Culture label in their ongoing regeneration programmes.

ECoC was just one in a line of explicitly culture-driven regeneration programmes in Liverpool that began in the mid-1980s with the Albert Dock. The Ropewalks area of the city, for example, just to the south of the CBD, was investigated as a possible area for a regeneration scheme through the 1990s. The coordinating Ropewalks Partnership was established to carry forward a plan produced by the Building Design Partnership. With European Union Objective 1 funding secured through the Government Office for the North West as well as resources from the North West Regional Development Agency, a major programme of new construction, refurbishment of historic buildings and improvements to the public realm was undertaken to cement Ropewalks as a cultural quarter between 1999 and 2004. The anchor building for this programme was the FACT Centre (Foundation for Art and Creative Technology). Established in 1988 as 'Moviola', FACT opened a new building in 2003 boasting exhibition and work spaces, training courses and a state of the art cinema with 70mm projection and THX sound (Figure 6.9). Ropewalks was one of the developments flagged in the ECoC bid, to indicate that 'culture' in Liverpool was not merely trading on the city's historic legacies.

There is some irony that one of Liverpool's more interesting, grass-roots cultural institutions, Quiggins, came out rather badly from the redevelopment of the city centre. Founded in the mid-1980s, Quiggins occupied a large, somewhat ramshackle building on School Lane, a then low-rent area just behind the city's main shopping axis. Home to a variety of 'alternative' traders, Quiggins served as a central city business incubator for small craft designers and other micro-businesses. Quiggins was approximately 200 metres outside the boundary of the Ropewalks cultural cluster, but within the Paradise Street Development Area and was threatened with a compulsory purchase order in 2004 which persuaded its owners to sell up. Many of the traders moved to a new home, 'Grand Central', housed in the old Methodist Central Hall, although this is somewhat further out from the city core. The façade of the Quiggins building was retained in the new development and converted into a branch of clothing chain, Jigsaw. Quiggins itself was, effectively, the wrong kind of culture in the wrong place, not in keeping with the high-end retail that the developers Grosvenor sought to bring to what became the Liverpool One shopping centre.

The Quiggins issue was a very minor distraction in the rapid pace of change in central Liverpool. In the run-up to 2008 there were claims that the Capital of Culture would bring 12,000 new jobs to Liverpool while doubling visitor numbers to 38 million per annum and generating £2bn of extra spending in the local economy. The bid team's consultants, ERM Economics, had in fact painted a much less rosy picture. They estimated approximately 720,000 extra visitors per year, rather than 19 million. Indeed, though the report did talk about an extra 13,200 new jobs, this was a projection of general growth in the creative industry sector – jobs directly created by the ECoC were estimated at fewer than 1,400 (Jones and Wilks-Heeg, 2004). One can, however, understand the boosterist claims given that Liverpool has been experiencing chronic unemployment and population loss for decades.

Figure 6.9 FACT, Liverpool, acts as the key anchor in the city's Ropewalks development and has been fitted sensitively into the existing narrow streetscape.

ECoC was clearly a stimulus to a major programme of investment in the city, including Liverpool One and the arena and conference centre on the Kings Waterfront site next to the Albert Dock. The £146m development was designed to play a key part in the ECoC celebrations and consists of the 10,600 seat Echo Arena (named after a local newspaper) and 7,000m² of exhibition space in the BT Conference Centre (Edwards, 2007). European Union Objective 1 funding was a major source of finance for this, although the arena and conference centre scheme also levered in a significant amount of private capital for apartments, a hotel and other developments anchored by this key cultural resource.

There is little doubt that central Liverpool saw a dramatic transformation around its year as Capital of Culture. What is harder to untangle is the extent to which ECoC itself was the catalyst for this – after all, the run-up to 2008 was one of fevered development activity in UK cities, with major new apartment blocks, retail developments and cultural venues springing up across the country. In an attempt to evaluate the impact of its ECoC year, Liverpool City Council commissioned a five-year research project from the Institute of Cultural Capital, a joint venture between the two main universities in Liverpool. The Impacts 08 project was an impressive attempt to evaluate a variety of indicators before and after the ECoC year (Garcia et al., 2010). Thus in 2008, there were an additional 9.7 million visits to the city, bringing approximately £753m of extra tourist spending – considerably below the initial boosterist estimates. There was a dip in people coming to the city in 2009, as would be expected, but it was still significantly above previous years. The city's main attractions in 2009 were still 24% up on visitor numbers from 2004. There were also increases in positive perceptions of Liverpool in surveys of the general population, suggesting a successful re-imaging. The extent to which these changes will be sustained over time is yet to be seen; however, the ECoC year can be seen as having had a generally positive impact on the regeneration of the city. It should be noted, however, that in the period 2004–08 the number of creative industry enterprises in Liverpool increased by just 8%, during a period of sustained economic growth. This does not bode particularly well for an economic recovery which is supposed to be driven by the creative sector.

Sports-led regeneration

The Echo Arena Liverpool gives the city a major venue for hosting indoor sporting events and reflects a trend which considers sport not as a cultural phenomenon in its own right, but as a major potential source of urban regeneration activity. When discussing the potential benefits of sport, the examples of Barcelona and Sydney are often cited. A decade on from the Barcelona Olympics, hotel capacity and tourist numbers in the city were still virtually double the pre-Games figures. Yet as Gratton et al. (2005) have argued, neither Barcelona nor Sydney had the problems of declining industrial economies that typify many of the areas targeted in the UK for sports-led regeneration. Indeed, both cities were already major tourist destinations that did not need to be drastically re-imaged and so the validity of the comparison is somewhat suspect. In any case, the Olympic Games operates on a much bigger scale than most sports-based regeneration projects and it is for this reason that we will be discussing the London Olympics in Chapter 8. Instead, we focus here on the smaller projects that individual cities attempt with a view to sports acting as a catalyst for wider redevelopment.

One of the first cities in the UK to explicitly see a sporting event as an opportunity to undertake regeneration activity was Sheffield, which played host to the 1991 World Student Games. The steel industry for which the city was famous was in a state of collapse by the mid-1980s, leaving large swathes of the Don Valley derelict. Key members of the city council's ruling Labour group at this time became committed to the idea that sports and leisure activities could be one way of rebuilding the city's shattered economy (Henry and Paramio-Salcines, 1999). The successful bid to host the World Student Games was seen as the jewel of this strategy, though it was not uncontroversial in the city. With caps on local government spending imposed in 1990, some Labour councillors in Sheffield were unhappy at resources being diverted to this new sports-led strategy at the expense of conventional social programmes, as most of the £147m capital costs were being met by the council. Indeed, although the city has ended up with world-class sports facilities clustered in the Don Valley, this was at the expense of some community-level facilities, particularly for swimming, which were closed to help pay for the centralised resources (Henry and Dulac, 2001).

The Sheffield experience was somewhat problematic in regeneration terms partly because the focus was on delivering the sporting event, rather than the broader legacy. In this context, the Manchester Commonwealth Games of 2002 provides a more interesting example. The spend on sporting infrastructure in Manchester was around £200m making it the largest ever investment in sports hosting in the UK prior to the London Olympics. In addition, however, a further £470m was spent on non-sports infrastructure as part of a major redevelopment programme in east Manchester.

The 2002 Commonwealth Games set the standard for UK sports-led regeneration by attempting to ensure that there should be clear, long-term benefits to the economy of east Manchester once the event was over. In order to achieve this, the Commonwealth Games Opportunities and Legacy Partnership Board was set up in 1999 to manage the legacy of the programme. After the Games were complete, the sporting facilities were branded as Sportcity – the stadium became the main ground for Manchester City football club while the other sporting venues have been used to establish the English Institute of Sport, providing elite training facilities and generating an ongoing revenue stream in the area. This careful planning has avoided the problem of 'white elephant' facilities with no clear post-Games purpose – a lesson that the Olympics in Athens could well have learned from.

In addition to securing a use for the Sportcity facilities, the New East Manchester urban regeneration company (URC) was established in 1999 to coordinate the regeneration of east Manchester more generally, an area covering some 1,100 hectares. The URC's initial aims were to:

- double the population to 60,000 over 10–15 years;
- build up to 12,500 new homes offering a range of tenure and type;
- improve 7,000 existing homes;
- create a 160-hectare business park;
- create a new town centre with 11,000 m² of retail provision;
- produce an integrated public transport system;
- create a new regional park system; and
- bring educational attainment above the city average. (New East Manchester, 2001)

In order to realise these broader aims, New East Manchester URC attracted £25m from SRB round 5; £52m from New Deal for Communities; and around £3m from SureStart. In addition, the URC has attracted private capital to bring new facilities to the area, including a regional-sized Asda supermarket. In 1999 the housing market in the area had some severe structural problems and, in some districts, the market had completely collapsed. The value of the Sportcity brand as a marker of redevelopment in the area helped the URC to bring in developers Countryside Properties who produced a residential masterplan and have worked on a series of new housing schemes. East Manchester is still an area suffering from multiple deprivation, but there can be no doubt that the sporting event and associated infrastructure have been used as a catalyst for a more general economic and social regeneration in the decade since the Games, involving a mix of public and private resources.

One of the interesting differences between the UK and the United States is that sporting teams in the UK tend to be far less 'footloose'. Middle-ranking cities in the US frequently compete to attract sports team franchises to their cities, offering tax breaks, large new stadium complexes and other incentives. The economic benefit to the community of this kind of investment is somewhat dubious, particularly as there is little to stop teams moving once again if another city offers an even better deal (Crompton, 2001). The UK has therefore, by and large, escaped the phenomenon of cash-strapped local authorities giving subsidies to multi-million-pound sports businesses – the move of the MK Dons football club from London to Milton Keynes being very much the exception rather than the rule. Indeed, there have been some examples of individual sports teams engaging in regeneration activity, such as when Arsenal Football Club moved to a new stadium. The club teamed up with the local authority and other partners to undertake a series of new developments. Newlon Housing, a social housing provider, was brought in to help meet a target for 25% of 2,500 new homes built in the developments to be affordable – attempting to tackle an acute shortage of affordable homes in the club's neighbourhood. Some of the developments took place on the site of the old stadium, part of which was listed for preservation and has since been converted into new homes. The old pitch was not built on – partly because it was the site where so many fans' ashes had been scattered. It is, however, a gated development, meaning that locals do not have a right to access the pitch-sized park at its heart. Nonetheless, along with the Emirates Stadium (completed in 2006), the Arsenal Regeneration Team oversaw the creation of small and medium business units and have promoted some community development projects. This kind of activity goes beyond trying to maximise land value to service the massive debts incurred in building the new stadium.

Considering that the new Wembley Stadium was completed in 2007, surrounding redevelopments have been relatively slow to materialise. Given that the stadium and neighbouring Arena were Olympic venues, much of the regeneration activity seems to have been tied to this event, with new hotels, apartments, shopping centre and new Civic Centre for Brent Council starting to materialise some five years after the stadium opened. Indeed, visitors arriving by car could be forgiven for thinking that the stadium had been tacked onto the back of an industrial estate. Here the stadium was very much seen as a *national* venue and the local authority was therefore a less important factor, making it harder to put a coherent package of developments together. With the stadium in place, Brent Council have been able to attract a series of developers, and a number of projects are ongoing in the area, which had been a somewhat run-down and forgotten corner of the capital.

The story of the National Football Museum is interesting, tying together heritage- and sports-based regeneration activity (Moore, 2008). It is also a story of failure. Perhaps curiously for such a popular sport with a long history, a national museum celebrating the game was not established until 2001. It was initially based in Preston, part-funded by a £7.5m Heritage Lottery grant and integrated into Preston North End's rebuilt Deepdale Stadium. Although the team was struggling by the 1990s its status as one of the football league's founder members and the fact that the club has been on the same site longer than any other meant that there was a good heritage rationale for the museum being located in Preston. More importantly, the location of a major tourist attraction in Preston offered the town a potential cultural catalyst to anchor further development.

Although the museum received praise for the quality of its collections, it struggled financially for the first few years before the North West Regional Development Agency stepped in with additional funding. At its height, the Preston museum attracted over 100,000 visitors a year and, unlike most publicly funded museums, its audience was not predominantly middle class. But a cultural resource does not necessarily owe any loyalty to the place in which it is located, particularly in the case of the National Football Museum, which received just £10,000 toward its capital costs from the local authority in Preston. In 2010 the museum's trustees took the decision to move it to a location in Manchester with a view to substantially increasing visitor numbers. Although Preston as a location clearly has the heritage, internationally Manchester United is a rather better known team and the city has a stronger tourist infrastructure. Preston failed to capitalise on having this major sporting heritage asset, which subsequently reopened in the URBIS centre in 2011, just a short walk from Manchester Piccadilly train station. What the Preston case demonstrates is that the main focus of a cultural resource – quite rightly – is in giving as many people as possible access to it, rather than necessarily catalysing development in its immediate vicinity.

Key points

i) There is a tension between culture as an aesthetic phenomenon, such as buildings and artistic performances, and culture as a way of life.

ii) The transition to a post-industrial economy has opened up major redevelopment opportunities on former industrial sites, with dockland redevelopment having become almost a cliché of urban regeneration.

iii) The re-use of historical buildings can give a redevelopment significant character but it is also expensive and subject to the whims of fashion in terms of which kinds of architecture are valued at any given time.

iv) An expensive signature building can be an embarrassment, rather than an anchor to new development, if the resource it houses is not successful.

v) Cultural quarters have become quite fashionable among those promoting regional economic development attempting to foster creative industries, but there is a risk that non-officially sanctioned cultural expressions will be forced out through a combination of gentrification and mainstreaming.

vi) Sports events and facilities have been successfully used to anchor urban regeneration schemes, but it is crucial to consider legacy uses.

Conclusion

There is a tension in this chapter, and in regeneration more generally, between 'culture' as something which can be exploited for economic development and something which is of value in its own right as part of a diverse and healthy society. This in part comes because the word culture has such diverse meanings, that a cultural regeneration can contain contradictory claims for how it promotes and uses culture.

When thinking about culture as representing a way of life for individuals and communities, regeneration does not always treat cultures particularly well. The 'wrong' kinds of cultural expressions located in an area which has been earmarked for redevelopment can find themselves being squeezed out, even if they were the source of the area's attractiveness for development in the first place. As was demonstrated by the example of gay villages, sub-cultural characteristics can become threatened as elements of that sub-culture start to be co-opted by the mainstream.

Notions of culture are also frequently wrapped up in the notion of the knowledge economy, with cities competing to attract workers and businesses in IT, the media, arts and similar sectors. Partly this is manifested through attempts to improve the public realm and attract flagship cultural functions to make the city more appealing to the so-called 'creative class', as well as to tourists. The other key manifestation of this is the creation of cultural quarters, attempting to cluster business working in the creative sector in order to produce a hothouse of talent built on face-to-face networking. Here culture is specifically defined as that which will be economically productive within the post-industrial model. As these quarters mature, more financially marginal arts and enterprises will be driven out, except where an external body such as a local authority or regional development agency deems them worthy of subsidy.

Aesthetics plays an important role in ideas of culture. Attractive, flagship buildings produced by internationally renowned architects have become a feature of many regeneration projects, with the hope that they will create an image of a district which is innovative, exciting and worthy of investment, acting as an anchor to further commercial development. In some regards, however, the buildings are only as successful as the uses to which they are put, and high-profile flops have left some areas with embarrassing and very expensive white elephants for which new uses have to be found. The same is true of historic buildings which are put to new uses, with the added complexity that an insensitive conversion can destroy some of the coherence of that building as a manifestation of the culture that originally built it.

Another problem with aesthetics is that the attractiveness of a development is entirely subjective, with changing tastes making it very difficult to audit the 'quality' of an aesthetic design. Some attempts have been made to regulate both the functioning of urban design (for instance, asking if the road layout encourages car use) and also its aesthetics. Design coding is one tool, developed by the new urbanists, for producing more coherence between the architecture and the character of an area at the district scale. Although design coding is now in the policy mainstream, it is no guarantee of a 'good' aesthetic product.

The complexities and contradictions of cultural regeneration aside, culture is in the mainstream of policy discourse and will likely play an ever more important role. Undoubtedly some cultures – both ways of life and aesthetic products – will be more valued than others by decision-makers undertaking regeneration projects, and one should question the kinds of cultures that end up being emphasised. As a final note, it is worth reflecting that the authors of this book are both middle-class, professional, white men in their 30s, which gives us a very specific, subjective position on the kinds of cultures that we value and discuss.

Further reading

A great deal has been written on urban design, culture and regeneration. Richard Simmons' essay, written while chief executive of CABE, sets out the case for the importance of high-quality urban design, while John Punter's edited collection gives a more critical review of urban design's role in regeneration. Smith and Garcia Ferrari's review of the EU-funded Waterfront Communities project provides excellent case studies of waterfront regeneration across Europe. It is also worth revisiting Richard Florida to understand some of the economic ideas which underpin the whole notion of cultural clustering and the creative city. The special issue of the journal *Urban Studies* on culture-led urban regeneration contains a number of high-quality academic papers on the topic, generally with a UK focus. Chris Gratton has written extensively on the role of sport in society and has edited a collection of essays with Ian Henry, examining sport and regeneration. Although not limited to UK examples, it provides robust case study material and analysis.

Florida, R. (2002) *The Rise of the Creative Class and How it's Transforming Work, Leisure, Community and Everyday Life* (Basic Books, New York).

Gratton, C. and Henry, I. (2001) *Sport in the City: The Role of Sport in Economic and Social Regeneration* (Routledge, London).

Punter, J. (ed.) (2010) *Urban Design and the British Urban Renaissance* (Routledge, London).

Simmons, R. (2008) *Good Design: The Fundamentals* (CABE, London).

'Special Issue: The rise and rise of culture-led urban regeneration' (2005) *Urban Studies*, 42: 5–6.

Smith, H. and Garcia Ferrari, M.S. (eds) (2012) *Waterfront Regeneration: Experiences in City-Building* (Routledge, London).

7 Regeneration Beyond the City Centre

OVERVIEW

Policy and academic focus has hitherto concentrated on the city centre. This chapter charts the extension of the urban regeneration agenda from central cities, to the suburbs and beyond.

- *The suburban question*: how suburbs have developed historically, the different types of suburbs and the challenges they pose.

- *Regenerating social housing suburbs*: focusing on those suburbs in greatest need of regeneration because of crumbling infrastructure and social deprivation.

- *New build suburbs*: how the private sector is responding to demands to build new suburbs that are environmentally and socially sustainable.

- *The great eco-towns disaster*: exploring the failed attempt to revive the post-war new town model with an environmentally friendly twist.

Introduction

The definition of what comprises a suburb can be somewhat fuzzy. In North America the word is often used to refer to those outer parts of a built-up area which are beyond the political administration of central city authorities. In the UK, 'suburb' has become a catch-all phrase referring in general terms to the outer city or that which is beyond the city core though normally within the same political territory (Whitehand and Carr, 2001). Thus defined, suburbs are home to around 86% of the UK's population and make for an exceedingly heterogeneous collection of urban environments and communities.

Where it tends to be regeneration of city centres that grabs the headlines, many suburban areas are also in need of revitalisation. Since the mid-2000s some attempt has been made to examine the specific regeneration challenges facing areas away from the city core. The Royal Institute of Chartered Surveyors and the Commission for the Built Environment, for example, jointly commissioned a report asking how suburbs can be sustained, acknowledging that suburbs function differently from urban centres (Johar and Maguire, 2007). A number of academic studies, such as the Adaptable Suburbs project based at UCL, have been investigating whether suburbs are ready for the challenges they will face during the twenty-first century. It is telling, however, that even the team behind the Adaptable Suburbs project admit suburbs are still poorly understood (Adaptable Suburbs, 2010).

The suburban question

Historically in the UK the idea of suburbia has had some rather negative connotations. Prior to the development of rapid transportation in the nineteenth century, people lived in suburbs because they were too poor to live in the town proper. With changes in transport technology, suburbs became the place where the well-to-do could escape from the noise and smell of the central city. As cities expanded so negative images began to be associated with them, suburbs becoming characterised as a sprawling cancer of bricks spreading out across the British landscape. Where trams and railways fuelled the growth of suburbs in the nineteenth century, in the 1920s and 1930s there was a new wave of expansion based around a developing road network built to service the motor car and omnibus. Indeed, the Campaign for the Protection of Rural England (CPRE), an influential lobby group, was founded in the 1920s in direct response to this expansion. The spreading town was held in opposition to an image of an unspoiled rural idyll, an image which still affects a great deal of our understandings of the tension between town and country in the UK today. Suburban expansion triggered the widespread use of greenbelts, formalised in a government circular of 1955, to restrict further outward growth, although suburban development continued post-war, filling in the gaps between the edge of towns and their greenbelts. The greenbelts constitute one of the most long-lived, popular and well understood aspects of the UK planning system, remaining sacrosanct even in the new National Planning Policy Framework (CLG, 2012e), which is otherwise orientated to serving a pro-growth agenda.

It must be emphasised, however, that both during the inter-war and post-war building booms, it was not just spacious houses for the middle classes that were being built, but also very large estates of council housing, which had a particular demographic profile and posed distinct challenges for urban regeneration today. The way that towns have developed historically means that the suburbs form an exceedingly heterogeneous group of different land uses, house types, demographic groups and environmental qualities. One of the most useful studies of suburbs and regeneration was produced for the Joseph Rowntree Foundation (Gwilliam et al., 1999) and attempted to give some critical form to this heterogeneity by producing a typology:

- historic inner suburb;
- planned suburb;
- social housing suburb;
- suburban town;
- public transport suburb; and
- car suburb.

This typology is far from perfect: both wealthy gentrified areas and poorly maintained districts housing large numbers of socially deprived people could fall under the category of 'historic inner suburb' and yet require very different degrees of regeneration intervention. The typology is useful, however, in breaking down the idea that suburbia is a monolithic category, with suburbs home solely to the white middle classes.

The short-lived In Suburbia Partnership led by Hampshire County Council was an innovative attempt to bring together the expertise of local authorities and the now defunct Civic Trust to produce guidance on more sustainable approaches to suburbia. While the Partnership might not have lasted, the materials it produced remain very useful and build on the typology from the Joseph Rowntree Foundation report reflecting the diversity of the suburban experience. Examining the specific needs of suburban areas, the Partnership set out principles for ensuring sustainability and a high quality of life for residents:

- an appropriate and stable context;
- continuous improvements in environmental sustainability;
- good quality, affordable housing, with more choice in tenure and type of house for people of all ages and social groups;
- choice in mode of transport, so that walking, cycling and public transport become more viable;
- access to good quality local services and facilities;
- a community hub or heart;

- a diverse local economy with jobs for local people; and
- social inclusion and community safety. (In Suburbia Partnership, 2005: 5)

There is a clear stress here on transport infrastructure, in particular transport choices beyond the private car. Similarly, there is an emphasis on local employment to reduce the dependence on commuting outside the area. There are clear commonalities here with the North American idea of 'smart growth'. The context for development in the US is somewhat different, with uncontrolled outward sprawl of cities still a major problem and the principle of state intervention to better regulate development not as well established as in the UK (Krueger and Gibbs, 2008). Nonetheless, the smart growth emphasis on community, mixed uses, compact building design, walkability and public transport options are part of mainstream policy discourse in the UK. As the building industry starts to recover from the credit crunch, there is once again pressure to increase house-building on the edges of UK towns and cities, making the lessons of smart growth ever more important.

The smart growth model of local services combined with good connectivity fits closely with the 'suburban town' type identified by the Joseph Rowntree Foundation report. As towns and cities have grown outward over time, smaller settlements on the edge of the urban area tend to be absorbed. London is sometimes described as a city of villages because of the way that historically distinct settlements have retained their identities since being swallowed up by the expanding conurbation (URBED, 2002). Places like Camden, Greenwich and Kew were all urban settlements in their own right before they became buried in London's middle suburbs. These areas have retained their own identities and retain much of their independent functions, acting as towns within towns, with shops, services and sources of employment as well as good public transport links. At the same time, because these areas are still on a relatively small scale, they can function as walkable settlements. In a sense, therefore, the holy grail of urban regeneration – the small scale, sustainable mixed development – is already partially in place. This is true not only of London; in all of the major cities it is easy to identify local sub-centres that have developed from historically distinct settlements. These areas provide good models on which suburban regeneration can build.

The idea that an urban area can contain multiple centres, each self-contained to a degree, is sometimes described as the polycentric or polynucleated city within contemporary planning discourse. The provision of local services is critical, however, because suburban areas lack the competition for service provision that, theoretically at least, helps maintain quality and price in central areas. The major challenge for the polycentric city of suburban towns is the threat posed to local services by large, out-of-town shopping centres which, at the same time, increase dependence on the private car. There has been a reaction in the UK against the planning policy of the late 1980s which encouraged out-of-town development, and the value of suburban centres has been recognised. Unfortunately, however, there is a tension here with the current direction of planning policy which places an emphasis on growth and a more market-driven approach to allocating development land. Indeed, even before the Coalition government's pro-growth reforms, the *Barker Review of Land Use Planning* (Barker, 2006) was calling for the selective release of development land on the edge of existing areas to meet demands for growth. There are sound economic reasons for this and, indeed, there is some environmental justification to reduce commutes for people who otherwise choose to live beyond the greenbelt. The risk is that, without strong oversight, unfettered, market-driven development on the fringes of urban areas will prompt a return to car-dependent models which out-compete provision in local centres.

Suburbia does possess a particular set of associations in the English psyche. Where continental Europe, and, indeed, Scotland, are more comfortable with the notion of apartment-dwelling throughout the whole lifecourse, in England there is a sense that families with children should be based in a house with a garden. As a result, the surburban 'semi' remains a general aspiration. This has meant that although the city-living model has taken off since the late 1990s, it is as a distinct 'young' phase of the lifecourse, with city-centre residents twice as likely to be single as the national average and two-thirds of whom are aged 18–34 compared to the national average of a quarter (Nathan and Unsworth, 2006). This has been a factor encouraging the relatively rapid turnover of central city populations, as against the comparative stability of communities in many suburban areas.

Max Nathan and Rachel Unsworth (2006) have identified historic inner suburbs as representing a key opportunity to smooth the churn of city-centre residents moving out of the inner city as they get older and plan families. Indeed, churn was one of the problems that the Housing Market Renewal Pathfinder initiative (2002–11) was attempting to resolve by creating attractive family housing in inner-urban areas which had become run-down. Particularly at the height of the boom, some developers were trying to apply the successful city-centre model to suburban areas, building high-density blocks of studio and one-bedroom flats. This raised questions about sustainability, given that inner suburbs are often slightly too far from the centre to truly give walkable access to central resources and therefore lose one of the key selling points of the city-centre experience. Similarly, the larger properties, typically Victorian terraces, that characterise the inner suburbs can act as much-needed comparatively inexpensive accommodation in the inner city for less affluent families. Demolition of such properties to be replaced with smaller flats or houses for wealthy incomers damages the potential for demographic mixing within these areas and this was a key critique of the Housing Market Renewal Pathfinders. At the same time there are broader issues to consider, such as the quality of local schools, which is often a major determining factor for location among middle-class families. Regeneration which seeks to attract a proportion of wealthier residents to run-down areas therefore needs to take account of local social needs as well as market potential.

Developers can still make money selling apartments, even in the aftermath of the credit crunch, but the market for these in suburban areas is now highly limited. Further, trying to apply the city centre small apartment model to the suburbs is unlikely to tackle the broader social needs that regeneration seeks to address because of the UK's overwhelming cultural preference for raising children in houses rather than flats. The question, then, is whether the UK can find models of suburban regeneration which tackle the divergent needs of these heterogeneous areas which face very different challenges from the city core.

Regenerating social housing suburbs

The stereotypical affluent, white, middle-class suburb is not a priority for regeneration activity. By and large these areas can look after themselves. But there are areas of considerable deprivation beyond the inner cities which require a more active approach. Social housing suburbs, as identified in the Joseph Rowntree Foundation typology, constitute a diverse group. Some of these areas are relatively stable, with a mix of tenure types, thriving local services, well maintained open spaces and excellent public transport connections. Others are sinks of poverty and desperation. Those estates built before or just after World War II generally comprise large three-bedroom houses, often now in private ownership after they were sold under the right-to-buy legislation of the early 1980s. Many of these estates are simply not a target for major regeneration projects, though it is worth noting that even here there can be problems. The Speke estate on the southern edge of Liverpool, for example, had the dubious honour of containing the most deprived area in England according to the 2007 index of multiple deprivation despite comprising large, well-built houses from the late 1940s.

Nonetheless, the estates built in the 1950s and 1960s are more likely to suffer problems, particularly given that these are even further out from central city services and employment and were often built with experimental techniques and unpopular building types such as the maisonette[1] and tower block (Jones, 2005). Because of their isolated location and the physical defects of the dwellings, many of these estates became difficult to let, meaning that only the poorest and most vulnerable accept the offer of accommodation in them. As a result, many larger city councils have been left with sink estates on their peripheries, although some of these are now run by housing associations following tenant votes to leave local authority control under the Large Scale Voluntary Transfer mechanism. Regardless of the built form or tenure patterns, however, a great many suburban social housing estates suffer acute social, economic and environmental problems and pose some of the greatest regeneration challenges in the UK.

Clyde Gateway

Glasgow's East End, far from the regenerated city centre, hosts some of the most appalling social deprivation in the entire European Union. Estates such as Drumchapel, Easterhouse and Red Road became notorious for chronic unemployment, ill health, drug addiction, crime and poverty. Many of these areas received central government funding in the 1980s and 1990s for large-scale demolition and refurbishment programmes, but problems persisted. In 2002, Glasgow City Council successfully transferred ownership of its housing stock to the Glasgow Housing Association (GHA) which operates through 62 local housing organisations. Stock transfer unlocked a number of funding routes, including private sector finance, and the degree of local control offers the possibility of better targeted regeneration activity involving the local community, which has representatives on the boards of the local housing organisations (Daly et al., 2005).

The Dalmarnock area of the city has its fair share of the social and economic problems that plague the east end. A successful bid to host the 2014 Commonwealth Games was the catalyst for a series of major infrastructure investments in this part of the city, levering in a large amount of funding from the Scottish Government. The controversial M74 extension (which opened in 2011) completed the city's motorway box. This was accompanied by a commitment to complete the East End Regeneration Route, a new arterial road, the aim being to better connect the East End to the rest of Glasgow. The demolition of a number of high-rise and other housing blocks owned by the GHA provided an opportunity to build a major new suburban settlement.

Regeneration activity in the area is being coordinated by the Clyde Gateway Urban Regeneration Company which was established in 2007. The Clyde Gateway site is a roughly triangular 866-hectare area straddling the River Clyde, close to the Celtic Park football stadium and about 4km from the city centre. The M74 extension passes through its southern edge meaning that the site sits across the border of Glasgow and South Lanarkshire councils. It is precisely this kind of organisational complexity, coordinating local and national government priorities, strategic infrastructure and operating with social housing providers and private developers that the urban regeneration company (URC) model was set up to tackle.

A phased series of developments is being undertaken, starting with accommodation for participants in the 2014 Commonwealth Games, which will subsequently be converted to residential use. RMJM architects designed the Athletes' Village, which received planning permission in 2010. The plans for the 32.5-hectare site were for 700 homes, including 400 rental properties built to the BRE EcoHomes 'Excellent' standard (Glasgow Architecture, 2010). The URC anticipates that a further 765 homes will eventually be added to this initial development. The ongoing Oatland development, which began in 2005, has also been wrapped into the URC's remit, with the intention being to produce 1,300 dwellings. Progress has been relatively slow, however, with only 370 homes built by mid-2011. Nonetheless, the scheme will be accompanied by a considerable improvement to the public realm, including a new riverside walk along the Clyde. In terms of economic regeneration, considerable work has been undertaken in acquiring former industrial sites and decontaminating them in anticipation of future business park development. Development of these is most advanced on the Clyde Gateway East, a 14.6-hectare site with planning permission for 40,000 square metres of business premises. This is a classic business park site sitting at junction 2A of the M74, where infrastructure works began in 2010. Work has also started on other sites and there are plans for a 27-hectare arboretum on Cuningar Loop just across the river from the Athletes' Village.

The 2014 deadline has clearly galvanised action and, like Manchester's 2002 Commonwealth Games, a long-neglected area has received some focused activity. The hope with such developments is that with the public sector having started the process, private developers will be keen to take up further opportunities on the site. The advantage that Scotland has over England is the greater willingness among Scots to consider apartments as an acceptable housing type for families with children. This gives the designers looking at the Clyde Gateway area more freedom to use the kinds of apartment developments familiar from city-centre regenerations. It should be emphasised, however, that in Scotland, as in England, city-centre projects have still tended towards producing relatively small units for households without children so the model does not directly transfer to the suburbs.

Where city-centre developments can rely on proximity to central services, sub-urban projects need to think carefully about the kinds of facilities that are available in the local area. The Clyde Gateway redevelopment will need to consider whether shops, schools and other services in the local area are of sufficiently high quality to appeal to the middle-class families which it hopes to attract to buy the private housing. If these facilities are not up to standard, the development runs the risk of simply becoming a car-based commuter settlement, with all the resultant implications for sustainability. Indeed, critics of the M74 extension and the East End Regeneration Route argue that there is already too much focus on the private car in contemporary redevelopment schemes. Regardless, the Clyde Gateway project gives an interesting example of how a major event can be used to lever regeneration activity into an outer-urban area characterised by high levels of social housing and deprivation.

North Solihull

Solihull is a divided town. Most of Solihull is quite wealthy, its suburbs falling into the cliché of leafy, middle-class enclaves. The northern part of Solihull is, however, quite different. Following the reorganisation of local authority boundaries in the mid-1970s, Solihull was given control over a very large suburban housing estate which had been built by Birmingham City Council in the late 1960s. The estate was built very quickly – at the time the local authority proudly boasted that it was the size of a Mark I new town, but built in just five years. Unlike the new towns, however, the careful mix of shops, services, sources of employment and demographics was somewhat lacking. Although, quite innovatively for the time, a proportion of the houses were built for sale, the majority were for local authority tenants. The estate was served by a number of small shopping centres and retained a somewhat isolated feel, fenced in to the north and east by the new M6 motorway and to the south by Birmingham International Airport.

While parts of this vast estate have fared well, others have experienced the classic symptoms of areas with large concentrations of socially deprived residents housed in crumbling properties built with experimental techniques.

In order to tackle the problems of this area, Solihull Metropolitan Borough Council has established the North Solihull Partnership. A 15-year regeneration project is being undertaken, covering an area containing more than 15,000 households. The local authority has taken the lead on this, bringing in Bellway Homes, Inpartnership Ltd and the Whitefriars Housing Group as part of a public–private partnership to undertake the redevelopment. The stated aims of the project are quite interesting:

- More than 8,000 (4,000 net) new homes.
- A tenure mix of 60% private, 30% social and 10% shared ownership.
- Ten new, state-of-the-art primary schools.
- Five vibrant new village centres.
- New health-care facilities.
- New leisure facilities.
- Employment and training opportunities.
- A positive change to almost 40,000 people's lives.
- Mixed-use developments.
- Local environment and transport improvements.
- Massive employment opportunities. (North Solihull Partnership, 2011)

While there is clearly a move to undertake a major programme of changes to the built environment, the fact that improving people's lives is listed as a core aim is an unusual (and welcome) emphasis in the rhetoric surrounding a project like this. Large-scale demolition of tower blocks – originally the site had 34 of these – and small town houses has already taken place, with a substantial number of new homes being built.

The proposed tenure mix involves a significant change to the character of the area. At the 2001 census, the Chelmsley Wood portion of the site was over 50% socially rented. The stated aim to reduce this to 30% is in line with a great deal of housing policy not just in the UK but across Europe which seeks to dilute concentrations of poverty by attracting wealthier incomers to buy new private housing. The Dutch, for example, have been pursuing a policy of housing 'redifferentiation' on large socially rented estates since 1990 to try to reduce segregation by income (Priemus, 1998).

North Solihull was built on a greenfield site and so did not absorb older settlements which might have been used to form a suburban town type community hub. The development was originally broken down into a series of sub-settlements, nominally with their own identity, but these were quite large and not particularly distinctive. The solution adopted by the North Solihull Partnership is to create a series of 'village centres' in the area. This is a profound shift away from seeing north Solihull as a series of monolithic housing estates and instead trying to repackage and rebuild the area into distinctive settlements. Given the physical isolation of the site, both from Birmingham and Solihull centres, this notion of villages has a great deal of appeal and draws somewhat upon the smart growth model of polycentric cities. The new village centres will create walkable, mixed-use communities with greater accessibility to services and some forms of local employment. This is clearly in tune with planning discourses of mixed-use, sustainable developments and is something quite clearly different from the central-city model of small apartment development.

In terms of how this project is being carried out, the North Solihull Partnership has engaged in an extensive and sophisticated programme of involving the local community in decision-making. A series of public consultations were undertaken in each of the villages with the overall masterplans for each area subsequently revised in accordance with some of the recommendations by local residents. By drawing on local knowledges, some homes that might otherwise have ended up on the demolition list were retained because they are actually popular with people living there. While this kind of process will inevitably have winners and losers, Solihull did not feel pressure to deliver 'early wins' by demolishing and rebuilding areas without effective local consultation. Instead a longer-term partnership was established, taking seriously the idea of the community as a stakeholder in this process and trying to improve lives rather than simply cleaning up the area to attract wealthier incomers.

Key points

i) Social housing suburbs are key targets for regeneration beyond the city core with many such areas suffering from the indicators of social deprivation.

ii) While apartments are more culturally accepted as family housing in Scotland than in England, simply applying the metrocentric model of small flats will not produce demographically mixed communities.

iii) Locally available shops and services are crucial to attracting wealthier residents to regenerated areas and reducing car dependence.

iv) The introduction of village-style community hubs is one mechanism for providing identity and coherence in the redevelopment of very large social housing estates, reproducing the suburban town model.

New build suburbs

Regenerating social housing suburbs means dealing with a complex set of legacies, particularly in dealing with an often deprived existing resident population coping with an obsolete built environment. Building a new suburb on a greenfield or previously non-residential brownfield site brings a different set of challenges. Such sites can be tremendously attractive to developers, but careful thought needs to be given to transport infrastructure and the availability of local services. The first two case studies described here, indicate some of the problems that can be generated by car-dependent, wealthy suburban developments, while the third suggests ways of over-coming these disadvantages.

Port Marine

Portishead is situated on the Bristol Channel about 13km west of Bristol and 30km from Bath. The town's two power stations fell into disuse during the 1980s, with neighbouring docks and factories similarly declining, producing a large waterside brownfield site for redevelopment. Being within 5km of the M5 motorway, Portishead is strategically well located within the economically dynamic south west region, making these brownfield sites a prime redevelopment opportunity. Outline planning permission was granted in 1997 and the former dock district has been branded Port Marine, with the lead taken by Crest Nicholson, a major UK devel-oper which has focused its core business on regeneration activity (Figure 7.1).

In 1992, 13,000 people lived in Portishead, but Port Marine was intended to increase this to 30,000 with the development contributing some 4,000 new homes, although the pace of development was slowed by the 2008 property crash. One can

Figure 7.1   Though a large-scale development, Port Marine has created a very attractive and varied new waterfront for Portishead. This brownfield development is anchored by a Waitrose supermarket, giving some indication of the wealthier social demographic being targeted.

consider this new development to be a suburb of Portishead; it is perhaps more significant, however, to think of it in terms of its relationship to Bristol. It can thus be thought of as an ex-urb – a settlement outside the boundaries of a major town but highly dependent upon it, especially for sources of employment. This kind of arrangement is more common in North America than in the UK, with many small settlements looking out toward a larger city. Port Marine is well placed for this and has primarily been marketed at people wanting access to Bristol and the strategic motorway network in the region.

In the centre of a large town or city, the classic dockland conversion comprises large numbers of small apartments for relatively wealthy couples without children. But Port Marine is, functionally, a suburb and Crest Nicholson have avoided relying solely on the metrocentric small apartment model, providing a mix of three- to five-bedroom houses alongside the more familiar apartment blocks. There is a clear recognition that this development is targeting a suburban market, attempting to attract an older demographic of professional families with children as well as the standard waterside apartment market.

The development is not unproblematic, particularly because it is, in effect, largely serving Bristol rather than Portishead. One risk with a development of this kind is that where larger local authorities have more experience in squeezing concessions from developers – for example on affordable housing, or contributions to community facilities – smaller authorities may find they have less bargaining power. Similarly, with a new residential population that tends to look beyond the town, the development may not contribute as much to the economic and social well-being of the host town as its size might suggest. There have been some rumblings of discontent, even among the newcomers who moved to Port Marine, that promised social facilities and public realm improvements have not yet materialised. The town also now has major traffic problems, particularly on the key A369 which links the town into Bristol, but there is no prospect of reopening the old rail link that once served Portishead (Anon., 2007).

Nonetheless, Portishead is interesting because it indicates that developers see the possibilities offered by towns which, in and of themselves, would struggle to attract a large residential population. Even following its dramatic expansion, Portishead is still a small town, in pleasant rural surroundings with, as a result of the redevelopment, an attractive waterfront. Its strategic location is critical, however, because developers like Crest Nicholson would not look at, for example, an isolated village on the west coast of Scotland, as a major development opportunity. With the new National Planning Policy Framework in England placing an emphasis on growth and a more liberal approach to releasing greenfield sites for development, these kind of ex-urban suburbs may look like increasingly attractive prospects around major transportation corridors. While Port Marine itself is far from being a bad example of regeneration activity, when considering its impact on the regional transport infrastructure, it is clear that if there is to be an increase in these kinds of developments, more thought will have to be given at government level to strategic transport improvements.

Waterfront Edinburgh

Waterfront Edinburgh reiterates the problems of not clearly considering transport issues before development takes place. The site is itself within the political boundaries of Edinburgh, but at some distance from the city core. Historically Edinburgh was not located on the waterfront and it was neighbouring Leith that was the main port of the Firth of Forth. Leith was absorbed into Edinburgh as the city grew during the inter-war period, but the area retains a detached feel, with the capital turning its back on the waterfront. The decline of the port has produced opportunities for a whole series of brownfield developments along the waterfront, west from Leith docks. In 1999 a masterplan was drawn up by Llewelyn-Davies Architects for the area around Granton Harbour. This masterplan was subsequently adopted by Edinburgh City Council in 2001 as the development framework for 'Waterfront Edinburgh'. Although this area is only 4km from central Edinburgh, it has a distinct identity while poor transport connections make it somewhat isolated.

The Waterfront Edinburgh masterplan had a number of key objectives:

- to deliver a comprehensive and viable regeneration plan to reinforce Edinburgh's role as a major international city;
- to produce a high-density live/work environment to produce a 'buzz' in the area; and
- to socially and physically integrate the development with neighbouring communities and contribute to their regeneration. (Edinburgh City Council, 2007)

Clearly, although the development is seen as part of the wider regeneration of Edinburgh, there is an emphasis on the area having distinctive character and function, rather than simply being another one of Edinburgh's suburbs. North Edinburgh is a rather deprived area with a great deal of social housing. Unlike the plans for a mix of socially rented and private accommodation in the Clyde Gateway redevelopment, the development around Granton Harbour has been very much driven by the private sector. Granton now sits in stark juxtaposition against the surrounding social housing and it is unclear how proximity to the Waterfront Edinburgh area will help regenerate neighbouring estates.

The emphasis on high-density living/working to create a 'buzz' is also interesting. There are clear parallels to the metrocentric model of development, attracting busy young professionals without children to live in this area, but here without the major sources of professional employment that locate in the central city. While some of the new residents will doubtless work in the new business parks built as part of the development, it is clear that many of the people who move to the area will still be dependent on the city centre for employment.

The masterplan covers 57 hectares, which is a large site, but the somewhat deprived demographic of the surrounding areas suggests that it may be difficult to generate the kind of critical mass to give the waterfront district real independence from the central city. Although a new link road was built to the site, the jewel in the crown of its planning was that Granton was intended to be connected to the city's new tram network. But the tale of the Edinburgh tram system is a depressing one. Conceived at the height of the boom, the Scottish National Party was committed to scrapping the scheme in its 2007 manifesto, but, forming a minority administration at Holyrood, found itself allowing the project to continue. Critically, the scoping of the scheme proved woefully optimistic, particularly failing to anticipate the scale of costs involved in moving buried infrastructure, such as gas and water mains. In a complex, historic city centre like Edinburgh, this was always going to be a major task. A subsequent legal dispute with the main construction contractor over the hold-ups moving the infrastructure led to the scheme being delayed even further.

In the first edition of this book, we noted that the link west along the waterfront from Leith to the Granton site would likely be dropped if the scheme got into financial difficulties. This proved to be the case. Even more dramatically, however, the main section from the city centre to Leith has since also been unceremoniously cancelled. This meant that the city did not need anything like the number of trams that it had ordered, meaning that the completed vehicles were left sitting in a Spanish warehouse while Edinburgh tried to find some other city to take them off their hands at a knockdown price. Thus a tram scheme that should have been completed by the time we started writing the second edition has now been halved in length and is predicted to come in at just over £1bn – twice the original estimate for the whole scheme (BBC, 2011).

This somewhat depressing tale means that developments at Granton and plans for a new ocean liner terminal and associated development at Leith Docks will remain heavily dependent on the private car, putting additional pressure onto the already heavily congested road network heading into central Edinburgh. The architecture at Granton is dominated by uninspired off-the-shelf small apartments although a handful of developments, such as Granton Studios, have attracted praise from the Architecture Scotland Annual (Urban Realm, 2008). Indeed, there has been some quite innovative urban planning undertaken at Granton. Part of the site comprised the seventeenth-century Caroline Park which had disappeared under subsequent developments and there has been some attempt to recreate this. Similarly, some of the street layouts have sought to create interesting aesthetic effects with the underlying topography.

Ultimately a major part of this project's appeal is its waterfront status, but the fact that Edinburgh was not traditionally a port has meant that the waterfront is some way outside the centre, in contrast to the situation in neighbouring Glasgow where the Clyde runs through the city. Thus despite the beautiful views across the Firth of Forth, the developments are cut off from the city by a ring of deprived suburban social housing and a lack of adequate transport. For the time being, Edinburgh's waterfront remains a large, car-based, socially segregated settlement located next to a business park. The development therefore appears to miss some of the key aims of contemporary regeneration – integration, mixed use and sustainability.

Lightmoor

The irony of this final case study is that though it is built on a greenfield site it is probably closer to the ideals of sustainability and mixed development than the brownfield projects described above. Lightmoor is being built just beyond the urban fringe of Telford, a 1960s/1970s new town built to take the overspill of people and businesses from the overcrowded West Midlands. Where Waterfront Edinburgh was built as a middle-class outpost, Lightmoor is a partnership between private sector developers and Bournville Village Trust, a major housing association in the region. The project also had significant input from English Partnerships (now the Homes and Communities Agency) because the site was part of the land bank it inherited from the old Commission for New Towns. When the project started, prior to the deep cuts to public spending after 2010, English Partnerships were able to commit significant resources to it. Combined with the social mission of Bournville Village Trust, this has produced quite a unique settlement. Building work began in summer 2005 on the 72-hectare greenfield site, with a project cost of £31m. Certain historic features on the site, including hedgerows, lanes and parts of a canal, have been integrated into the design in an attempt to give the new development some character. Planning permission was granted for 800 homes, of which at least 25% will be affordable, provided and managed by Bournville Village Trust. Permission was also granted for a primary school, community centre and small amount of local retail suitable for a 'village'. The guidelines underpinning the development include:

- A well-defined compact village surrounded by landscape.
- A strong distinction between the recreational open spaces encircling the village and the protected rural wildlife site.
- A mixed-use centre arranged around the High Street and a village green, located so that foot access is promoted.
- Higher residential densities clustered around the village centre, with areas of lowest density at the edges of the village where transformations between urban and rural character are made.
- The character of the existing lanes is retained and they are integrated into the movement network as recreational routes for pedestrians and cyclists. (Lightmoor, 2007)

Essentially what is being produced is a planned village with walkable local services and a mixed demographic, which ties in very closely with both the new urbanist and smart growth agendas. Private developers were brought in to actually build the properties in each of the different phases of the development, sticking closely to the overall masterplan. Thus the advantages of both private capital and public sector coordination were brought to bear on the project. The development is something of a modern Bournville in that it is a planned settlement, beyond the urban fringe, with a strong sense of social mission. Technologically the development is quite advanced and even before the government set targets for low carbon domestic buildings in 2006 the decision was taken that all houses in the development should meet EcoHomes 'excellent' standard. The buildings are also designed to be flexible, so that houses can be altered and extended as future needs arise, ensuring that the buildings have a longer lifespan. Other environmentally friendly features, such as sustainable drainage systems (SuDS) for surface water runoff have also been integrated into the design of the development.

Bournville Village Trust has a very good 'brand' in terms of social mission and for being able to deliver high-quality developments. This reputation is important when putting together a project of this kind, which would otherwise seem comparatively high risk to private developers because it is so innovative. The Trust also has a long-standing commitment to use innovative environmental technologies, having experimented in orientating houses to let in maximum sunlight as early as the 1920s. This reduces the costs of heating houses and has become a central principle used by contemporary sustainability gurus ZedFactory, who used solar orientation for their BedZED development (see Chapter 5 and Figure 5.11). Lightmoor does, however, somewhat have the feel of a demonstration project, rather like Poundbury discussed in Chapter 6. Indeed, even the design of the new development has some parallels with Poundbury (see Figure 6.1), with high-density building cover, attempts to subordinate the car and a postmodern pastiche of historic building styles (Figure 7.2). One indication of the project's somewhat pioneering character is that 'Croppings', one of the later development phases, was selected by the government as one of six test sites for a new housing financing strategy. The Homes and Communities Agency is allowing development company Keepmoat to build – and sell – houses on the site before actually paying for the land (Estates Gazette, 2011). This kind of approach is attractive to developers as they no longer need to raise a great deal of capital up front, therefore securing faster progress on schemes like this, particularly in an era where developers are finding it harder to secure loans to cover the cost of projects.

Lightmoor responds to its location on the urban fringe, producing a modern version of the rural village. Unlike Edinburgh Waterfront, Lightmoor cannot be accused of trying to apply the metrocentric model to a location at some distance from the central city and does seem much more in tune with contemporary policy on questions of social integration and environmental sustainability. Despite the presence of some local services in the village centre, the development is essentially a commuter settlement for people working in Telford and so significant questions remain about its reliance on the private car by virtue of location on the urban fringe. At least in this case, however, the generously proportioned road network in the area – a legacy of its new town origins – has sufficient capacity to cope with the increase in traffic that the development will generate.

Figure 7.2 Lightmoor, just outside Telford, has been designed with a similar density of housing and narrow winding streets as at Poundbury, though without the same degree of *faux*-historic buildings.

Key points

i) New suburban developments on the edge of existing towns and cities remain highly dependent on the urban core for employment and services.

ii) Where public transport infrastructure is not of a sufficiently high standard, new suburban developments can put serious pressure on already heavily loaded road networks.

iii) Without giving careful thought to the provision of affordable housing, these kinds of developments can end up being somewhat monocultural and contributing little to the regeneration of neighbouring areas.

iv) Attempts to produce a specific response to a suburban site, such as the village model at Lightmoor, appear to be more closely allied to policy discourses on mixed use and sustainability.

The great eco-towns disaster

In 2007 Gordon Brown, at the briefly optimistic start of his short-lived premiership, announced proposals to build a series of eco-towns across England. This looked a little like a return to the new towns policy of the post-war years that delivered settlements like Harlow and Telford, but the decision to describe these settlements as eco-towns was significant. The 'eco' tag not only made this old strategy seem new and progressive, but it also served as an attempt to defuse criticism from the environmental lobby that this new programme of building would lead to the destruction of the countryside. A significant difference from the original new town policy, however, came with the commitment to using brownfield sites wherever possible. Many of the proposed sites that emerged in the subsequent bidding process were former military bases deemed surplus to requirements – unsurprising, given that military sites are nearly the only large-scale 'brown' land use outside of existing urban areas.

The preference for brownfield sites, although giving a boost to the 'eco' credentials of these development proposals, meant that the eco-towns were not strategically located in terms of transport infrastructure and sources of employment. Military land, by its nature, tends to be located in somewhat isolated areas. The lack of a strategic approach to location meant the eco-towns were quite different from the original new towns, which were predicated on upgraded transport links and relocation of industries. The risk of the chosen approach was that while paying lip service to environmental needs through re-use of previously developed land, microgeneration and highly insulated housing, the eco-towns could be accused of being merely car-based commuter settlements.

Nonetheless, of 57 bids submitted in 2008, eventually 12 sites were shortlisted with a proposal that the size of each be doubled to 20,000 homes (Figure 7.3). In many ways this was a sensible response to the shortage of houses in England. Unfortunately the intention was for the eco-towns to be built by the private sector and, following the credit crunch of 2008, private developers were unwilling to commit to schemes of this scale, particularly on sites where there was no clear market nor any commitment to invest in strategic infrastructure or employment relocation. At the same time, local opposition to the schemes grew and became vociferous, with only the Whitehill-Bordon and Rackheath proposals facing anything less than hostility at a local level (Morad and Plummer, 2010).

The eco-towns remained a central element in late period New Labour planning policy, with an eco-towns supplement to Planning Policy Statement 1 issued in July 2009 (CLG, 2009). This document, as with all the planning policy statements, was scrapped as part of the Coalition government's simplification of planning guidance into the single English National Planning Policy Framework in 2012. As originally conceived, the eco-towns project is now effectively dead. Even the label 'eco-town' is now being downplayed, with the focus instead being on eco-friendly developments added to existing towns, rather than full-blown new settlements.

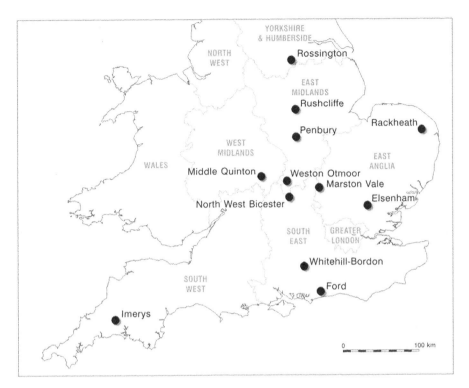

Figure 7.3 Sites initially selected for eco-towns. This controversial scheme generated rather more heat than light, sparking local protests and failing to deliver any major expansion in house-building. Drawn by Graham Bowden.

The case of the Middle Quinton proposals gives an illustration of the muddled thinking that underpinned and eventually killed the eco-town concept. The conceptual diagrams produced showed a vibrant, leafy small town with a rail link, town centre and business district. Much was made of the shortage of affordable housing in the region, particularly in nearby Stratford-upon-Avon. One third of the 6,000 planned homes were to be affordable and the whole project was to be built on a brownfield site, formerly a Ministry of Defence Engineers' depot (Shelter, n.d. ~2008). Unfortunately the rail line is freight only and there were no firm plans in place to upgrade it into a passenger service and to make the link into Stratford. Neither was it clear what kinds of employment were going to be attracted to the site. While there is a definite shortage of affordable housing in the region, placing 2,000 affordable homes at some distance from sources of employment would not necessarily address *local* housing need in, say, Stratford. The likelihood was, therefore, that residents would have to commute by car to jobs at some distance away. This in itself was a significant problem because the site is around 20 miles away from the nearest motorway and served only by minor roads, guaranteeing high levels of congestion.

As a planning concept, the eco-towns project was sound, but the implementation was appallingly botched. Without very high levels of financial commitment from the state and strategic investments in transport infrastructure, they were never going to work. The ideological commitment to using brownfield land made success even less likely as there was not the freedom to locate on sites that made sense in terms of links to existing infrastructure and sources of employment. Indeed, the one scheme which seems likely to be built in something like the originally planned form is, in effect, an extension to Bicester, a town with good road and rail links, sources of employment and solid growth prospects that are attractive to private sector developers. And this, if it does go ahead, will be on greenfield land.

Key points

i) The eco-towns strategy revived the model of new towns but without providing the capital for much needed strategic infrastructure.

ii) Brownfield sites and green housing technologies cannot, of themselves, make a development eco-friendly.

Conclusion

There is no such thing as a typical suburb; those areas beyond the urban core pose a variety of regeneration challenges. Much of the policy rhetoric that has developed around walkability, local services and compact urban form points towards something which already exists in many cities, polycentric development, where historic centres have been absorbed into the wider city yet retain their identity as independent settlements. Such polycentric development can be created through careful planning, which is one of the things that schemes like north Solihull are attempting to achieve through the creation of semi-independent village centres. This is very much in line with North American ideas of smart growth.

Large social housing suburbs like north Solihull pose some of the greatest challenges for suburban regeneration. The main approach that has developed since the 1990s has been to change the tenure mix in these types of suburbs, reducing the proportion of socially rented properties. The hope is that by diluting concentrations of poverty, new services and new employment opportunities will be attracted to the area, although such an approach opens itself to the charge of simply representing state-sponsored gentrification.

Distance from the jobs and services of the city core is the key disadvantage of suburban location for deprived communities, making local opportunities and good transport infrastructure an absolute priority. The Clyde Gateway combines good existing rail infrastructure with a major strategic upgrade of the city's road network and new business park development. Conversely, developments along the water-front at Edinburgh have been stymied by the failure of the tram scheme and pro-tracted wrangling over the future of Leith docks as a location for new sources of employment. This is in stark contrast to developments elsewhere in Europe, for example Amsterdam's IJburg, where creating a new tram line was a crucial element in developing the site.

The re-use of brownfield land became a totem of regeneration during the New Labour period. Brownfield is not, however, a guarantee of environmental friendli-ness and, as the eco-towns debacle demonstrates, can actually be a hindrance to strategically locating developments in order to secure other environmental gains. Well-planned greenfield developments such as Lightmoor can have the edge over poorly thought out brownfield projects. But the key phrase is 'well planned'. The new National Planning Policy Framework places an emphasis on growth and a presumption of development where it is deemed 'sustainable'. The danger with such an approach is that it leaves areas vulnerable to poorly planned, poorly integrated additions to existing settlements reliant upon car-based travel.

What is clear, however, is that in the UK the suburbs are still seen as a key loca-tion for families with children. While the model of small apartment development worked spectacularly well in city centres, particularly during the boom years, it caters to a very specific, young demographic. Attempts to apply this metrocentric model to suburban developments hold some real risks. The suburban experience is one which is qualitatively different from that in the central city and it is clear that to apply city-centre models in outer-urban areas will not be sustainable either in terms of mixed communities or in attempting to reduce car dependence. The relatively small amount of research and policy that responds specifically to the chal-lenge of regeneration beyond the city core indicates that these issues have not yet been carefully thought out. The suburbs, home to most of the UK population, remain a regeneration puzzle.

Further reading

Suburban redevelopment is a fascinating topic which has not really had the specific attention that it deserves. The article by Vaughan et al. is an excellent summary of the state of the art in research into suburbs more generally; their origins, function and future. Nathan and Unsworth's article is a good introduction to the tension implicit in attempting to apply city-centre models of regeneration to suburban areas, although their work focuses specifically on the inner suburbs. The report by the Civic Trust gives some indication of how the challenges of suburban regeneration might be tackled. The *Built Environment* special issue explores some of the ideas underpinning compact city development and what this means in terms of suburban development.

Built Environment Special Issue (2010) 'Revisiting the compact city', *Built Environment*, 36(1).

Civic Trust (2002) *In Suburbia* http://web.archive.org/web/20060515203401/http://www.hants.gov.uk/urbanliving/new_html/suburbia_html/assets/suburbia_brochure.pdf [accessed 23 August 2011].

Nathan, M. and Unsworth, R. (2006) 'Beyond city living: remaking the inner suburbs', *Built Environment*, 32(3): 235–249.

Vaughan, L., Griffiths, S., Haklay, M. and Jones, C.E. (2009) 'Do the suburbs exist? Discovering complexity and specificity in suburban built form', *Transactions of the Institute of British Geographers*, 34(4): 475–488.

Note

1 In the context of post-war council housing the maisonette was a distinctive type where two-storey flats were stacked one on top of another. These flats were specifically designed for families. Four- and six-storey blocks of this type were built without lifts, making them a nightmare for the elderly or those with small children.

8 Scaling Up

OVERVIEW

This chapter examines how regeneration operates when considering very large schemes with long time horizons.

- *London Olympics 2012*: how can a global mega-event be translated into a win for regeneration? Examines the delivery of the Olympic Park and legacy planning.
- *Mega-regeneration in the Thames Gateway*: examining the project to undertake a massive redevelopment of the area east of London.

Introduction

The schemes we have discussed so far in this book have varied in scale from relatively small housing projects, to large-scale reconfigurations of entire districts. In this chapter we consider two schemes with altogether grander ambitions. Both are in south east England – a region generally seen as the engine of the UK's economic growth – and both spring from London's status as a world city.

A glance at the websites of global firms like Atkins or Arup will reveal a variety of incredibly ambitious projects built or planned in different parts of China, the Middle East, Brazil and elsewhere. From famous schemes such as the palm-tree-shaped islands off the coast of Dubai to lesser known projects such as the masterplanning of a giant new port on Meishan Island in Ningbo, China, mega-projects have been a feature of the regeneration landscape for at least two decades. In fast-growing economies with high degrees of state control over land-use planning, some quite astonishing schemes can be produced very quickly in a way that is simply not possible in mature economies. In China, for example, the central state owns all the land and it is relatively straightforward to remove businesses and homes and ignore negative environmental consequences in order to make way for large prestige schemes (Ren, 2011).

This kind of large-scale, state-led *tabula rasa* ('clean slate') planning was a feature of the UK's post-war reconstruction, particularly with the new towns programme, if on a somewhat smaller scale. New towns were masterplanned by state corporations, largely built on greenfield sites, sometimes absorbing one or more smaller settlements, with private developers brought in to build some of the residential and commercial districts. The age where the state intervenes on a grand scale in the UK has, however, now largely passed, just as the mode of governance under which urban regeneration operates has shifted from state-led to partnership-led (see Chapter 2). Nonetheless, there are currently two UK regeneration mega-projects, both based in and around London and both with significant planning and financial input from the state: the Olympic Games regeneration and the redevelopment of the Thames Gateway.

London Olympics 2012

July 2005 was a strange month. On 6 July, London just edged out Paris to win the right to host the 2012 Olympic Games. A day later, London suffered a terrorist attack by a group of young British men sympathetic to the aims of Al Qaeda, killing 52 people and injuring over 700. Out of this tragedy the 2012 Olympic Games suddenly became a very good news story for the security industry and others who make a living out of the threats posed by terrorism. The rise in the projected cost of security was, however, just the first of a series of increases to the original budget. By 2007 the then Culture Secretary Tessa Jowell admitted that the initial estimates of £2.4bn had ballooned to £9.3bn (some sources put the final cost as high as £11bn; House of Commons Public Accounts Committee, 2012). The escalating costs meant cuts to other agencies, including Sport England, which meant reduced funding for programmes to increase sporting participation at the community level – which had been a key target in social regeneration (Bond, 2007).

The British media loves a good disaster story. Disappointingly then, all the buildings for the London Olympics materialised with very little drama. The UK demonstrated itself capable of delivering a global sporting mega-event on time (if not on budget). The actual sporting part of the Olympic Games is, however, only a small part of the story. One of the reasons why London won the right to hold the 2012 Olympics was that the city's bid placed a great deal of emphasis on legacy and regeneration – issues which seemed particularly imperative in the aftermath of the Athens Games, which left an embarrassing legacy of white elephant facilities and large debts.

Governance

On any project where in excess of £9bn of public resource is being spent, there will be a complex web of different actors and agencies involved. The governance arrangements were therefore crucial to ensuring both that the facilities were available to host the Olympic Games and that the legacy outputs were in place. As a national event, with a great deal of central government money at stake, the Department for Culture, Media and Sport were the lead agency, with Tessa Jowell under Labour and Jeremy Hunt under the Coalition government being the responsible Ministers for the Olympics. The scale of the event meant that the Treasury also had a significant input into the planning, as did the Department for Communities and Local Government, which fed into discussions on the regeneration side. Because the Games were going to be hosted in London, the Mayor and London Assembly were heavily involved, particularly in coordinating work by Transport for London. The regional development agency for London had a significant role in the initial stages of land assembly. A specialist body, the Olympic Development Agency (ODA) was established in 2006 to coordinate activity in building the Games while the Olympic Park Legacy Company (OPLC) was established in 2009 to manage the post-Games development of the site. The ODA will be wound up in 2014, where the OPLC was a victim of the bonfire of the quangos, reconstituted as a Mayoral Development Agency, reporting to the London Assembly rather than central government, and given a wider remit to look at development across the city. In addition, a number of London Boroughs (Barking and Dagenham, Greenwich, Hackney, Newham, Tower Hamlets, Waltham Forest) who are involved in hosting also fed into the development process. This is before one considers all the private and third sector bodies involved in delivering the site, let alone those agencies concerned with the actual sporting event hosted at the Olympic site!

Despite the complexity of the governance arrangements, some quite powerful tools were made available to those planning the Games. In addition to the brute force that a large amount of public money can wield, there were also legislative changes. The Planning and Compulsory Purchase Act, 2004, was passed in anticipation of a successful bid in order to expedite the land assembly that was needed on the Lower Lea Valley site chosen to become the Olympic Park. Compulsory purchase is a very time-consuming and controversial process meaning that local authorities and those development agencies granted these powers generally prefer to negotiate with landowners, with compulsory purchase seen as a threat and last resort. Although a number of extremely positive changes were contained within the 2004 Act, perhaps the most significant reform was an amendment to section 226 of the Town and Country Planning Act, 1990, to include a general 'well-being' clause. Compulsory purchase can be justified under the Act if the purchase can be demonstrated to improve one or all of the economic, social or environmental 'well-being' of the area (section 99, 3). The rather hazy idea of 'economic well-being' gives local authorities more leeway when it comes to securing compulsory purchase. For the 306-hectare Olympic site, compulsory purchase powers were granted to the London Development Agency. The vast majority of residents and businesses were moved through negotiation, but a hardcore of individuals resisted. The last of these, two groups of Gypsies and Irish Travellers who had been long-term residents of the area, lost their appeal against the compulsory purchase order in May 2007 (Williams, 2007). It should be noted that, although the Olympics was the catalyst, the changes to compulsory purchase legislation apply across England and Wales. Thus, thanks to the Olympics, the reformed legislation makes the threat of compulsory purchase a much more potent bargaining counter when local authorities are negotiating with reluctant landowners on large development projects.

Legacy

The lower Lea Valley site has been subject to intense regeneration activity aiming to secure the continued worth of the site in the aftermath of the Olympic Games. Located immediately to the south of the new Stratford International Station, in the heart of the Olympic Park, developers Westfield have been building 'Stratford City'. This is a classic mixed-use development with nearly half a million square metres of office space, 270,000 square metres of retail and leisure, 120,000 square metres of hotel space as well as new homes and public realm (for details, see Chapter 5). Westfield marketed the site as the 'Gateway to London's Olympic Park' (Westfield, 2011). The initial planning application for this development was actually submitted in 2003, prior to the decision to bid for the Olympics. Similarly, the major public project which leveraged private development into this run-down part of east London was in fact the second phase of the Channel Tunnel Rail link, which created Stratford International Station, where building work started in 2001. Again, although services on this line have been rebranded as 'Javelin' trains, this scheme had absolutely nothing to do with the Olympics. Even the extension of the East London underground and Docklands light railway lines were already in progress prior to finding out that the bid was successful (Gilligan, 2007). Nonetheless, it would be churlish to say that the Olympics had no impact on the £1.45bn Stratford City development, as it helped build confidence in different companies leasing space within it and probably hastened its development such that this truly enormous new retail development opened in 2011, despite the unfavourable economic climate. Of the 1,000 jobs created, 200 went to locals who had never worked before (Wallop, 2011). Indeed, where the Olympics site is more about an international rebranding of London and the wider UK, Stratford City will have a much more direct and lasting impact in Newham. But looked at on a map of the wider Olympic Park scheme (Figure 8.1), Stratford City is a relatively small component.

As with Manchester's Commonwealth Games in 2002, a great degree of thought went into planning what to do with the facilities and the site once the Olympics was over. But the Olympics is on a much larger scale than the Commonwealth Games and that larger scale tends to bring greater scope for conflict. Where it was comparatively straightforward to persuade Manchester City Football Club to take on the Commonwealth stadium as its new home ground, the process of getting a tenant for the Olympic stadium was a hugely contentious element of the Games' fraught legacy process. Different football clubs presented rival plans for taking over the Olympic stadium. West Ham ended up as the preferred bidder, partly because they intended to retain the running track around the pitch, even though UK football fans generally feel that this kind of arrangement places the spectator too far from the sporting action. A series of legal challenges from bid rivals resulted in the original deal collapsing, partly because Newham council had offered to guarantee a £40m loan to assist West Ham's move to the ground, interpreted in some quarters as a breach of European law which bans state aid to private companies (Kelso, 2011).

Regardless of the wrangling, the stadium was designed to be partially dismantable, allowing the top tiers of seating to be removed to reduce its capacity from 80,000 to 60,000 or even 25,000. This flexibility has meant that the aesthetic design of the stadium was compromised, leaving it far from iconic, particularly when compared to the astonishing 'Birds Nest' built in Beijing for the 2008 Games. In an attempt to ensure that there were plenty of photogenic buildings ready for the attention of the world's media, a series of star architects were brought in to design the more permanent buildings on the site. Most notable of these is the Zaha Hadid-designed Aquatic Centre which, as often seems the case for Hadid's work, creates an astonishing interior space housed in a somewhat uninspired exterior shell (see Glasgow's Riverside Museum for another example of this quality in her designs).

Some of the facilities on the Olympic park site were housed in temporary buildings, such as the basketball stadium which were earmarked for removal and redevelopment once the Games were over. Other buildings are intended for more permanent use. The velodrome, for example, will continue as a cycling centre and was shortlisted for the 2011 Stirling Prize, winning praise for a thoughtful and elegant design by Hopkins Architects which brought cyclist Sir Chris Hoy in as a consultant. Indeed, the fact that it stuck to its £90m budget is in stark contrast to the £180m overspend on the higher profile Aquatic Centre (Williams, 2011). Next to the stadium is another iconic structure, the 115-metre ArcelorMittal Orbit, designed by Anish Kapoor and commissioned by London's Mayor, Boris Johnson. This spiralling latticework of steel acts as a vertical feature for the site, with viewing platforms and a staircase giving dramatic panoramas across the city. These kinds of high-quality designs not only functioned to

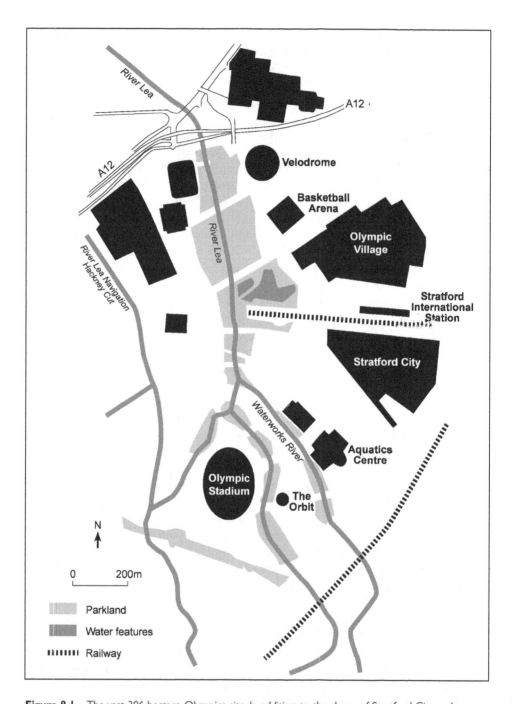

Figure 8.1   The vast 306-hectare Olympics site. In addition to the shops of Stratford City and sporting facilities, this corner of east London has been given a large new park along the Lea Valley corridor and will be the site for an ongoing programme of new housing developments. Drawn by Anne Ankcorn.

showcase London during the Games, but also to re-image this part of the city as part of a longer-term legacy programme for the Olympic Park site.

One of the simplest elements of generating a post-Games use for the site should, in theory, be the conversion of the Athletes' Village. Athletes needed somewhere to stay during the Games, and so it made sense to build a new apartment complex which could subsequently be sold. Prior to the credit crunch this would have been a profitable opportunity for private developers. Unfortunately the market for apartments flat-lined after 2008, meaning that the Olympic Development Authority had to step in and spend £1.1bn up front building the complex. Built just to the north of the new railway station, the village consists of 9- and 10-storey blocks and has a rather high-density, barracks-like appearance, with severe grey façades.

Part of the complex was sold to Triathlon Homes for £268m in 2009 to provide 1,379 affordable homes post-Games. The remainder was sold to a joint venture of Delancey and Qatari Diar in 2011 for £557m to provide 1,439 apartments for sale or rent (Kortekass, 2011). Although there will be some ongoing financial return to the state from the private joint venture, the sale has effectively left the state shouldering a quarter billion pound loss just on this one element of the Olympic park. The new owners will have to retrofit the apartments somewhat post-Games, given that the athletes were eating in communal canteens. Interestingly the Delancy/Qatari Diar post-Games business plan is not to sell individual apartments but instead to keep their half of the complex entirely as rental property to create an ongoing revenue stream. This suggests that, in the medium term at least, they do not anticipate a particularly buoyant and profitable market for housing in the Stratford area.

This is significant because there is a major plan in place for redeveloping the Olympic Park Site after 2012 coordinated initially by the Olympic Park Legacy Company (OPLC), a national quango which was converted into a Development Agency run by the London Mayor's office. The OPLC took a long view on the post-Games redevelopment, outlining developments into the 2030s. In an interview, Eleanor Fawcett, the OPLC's head of design, tacitly acknowledged that the high-density apartment development of the Athlete's Village was counter to their preferred approach to redeveloping the site (Long, 2011). The OPLC's (n.d.) prospectus about the redevelopment plans places a great deal of emphasis on producing different kinds of residential character across the site. Five 'villages', or development sites, have been identified, given names like Pudding Mill and East Wick, drawing on historical associations in the area. Work on the first of these villages, Chobham Manor, is scheduled to begin in 2013. Built on the site of the temporary Basketball Arena, Chobham Manor is intended to consist of terraces with mews-style cottages behind, reflecting the traditional urban design of some of London's most popular (and expensive) districts. Designs for the four remaining sites will be refined as the development proceeds over the next two decades.

London is a city with an acute shortage of affordable housing. The Olympic Park site, now with excellent public transport connections (just 20 minutes from Oxford Street), offers a major strategic opportunity. If the plans for its post-Games life come to fruition, the site should be home to over 20,000 people by 2030. Putting on the Olympic Games is certainly not the cheapest way to develop a scheme to house this many people and bring sources of economic activity such as Stratford City into a deprived part of London, but it certainly represents a grand project. Many of the infrastructural and employment developments would have happened without the Games, but there can be no doubt that the Olympics sped things up and released a deluge of public money. With any scheme on this scale, however, there will be winners and losers. People were thrown out of their homes and businesses forced to move. Private developers would have redeveloped this site, but more slowly, waiting for the market to recover from the credit crunch and doubtless in a more piecemeal, less integrated fashion. What it does demonstrate, however, is that where the state is willing to spend heavily, mega-projects can happen even in mature democracies with tangled property markets. The difference is that, in the UK, this kind of scheme is now rather rare, where in states like China they have become a familiar part of the development landscape.

Key points

i)   Large-scale projects require a high degree of state involvement.

ii)   The governance structure of regeneration in the UK means that any large project will involve a huge number of state agencies operating at different tiers.

iii)   The Olympics has catalysed and accelerated a series of existing schemes to redevelop the lower Lea Valley.

iv)   Although the Olympic Park site has already been dramatically transformed, a new phase of post-Games development will be required to reap the regeneration benefits of hosting this mega-event.

Mega-regeneration in the Thames Gateway

In 1995 the Thames Gateway Planning Guidance Framework identified the region directly to the east of London as a key location for new development. The Thames Gateway is a truly massive area, consisting of some 100,000 hectares running east along the River Thames from Canary Wharf in London to Margate on the coast (Figure 8.2). Plans for the area were given weight by the Sustainable Communities Plan of 2003, in which the government set out a strategy to build 200,000 new homes in south east England by 2016, 120,000 of which would be in the Thames Gateway. To put this development in context, just in terms of housing alone the

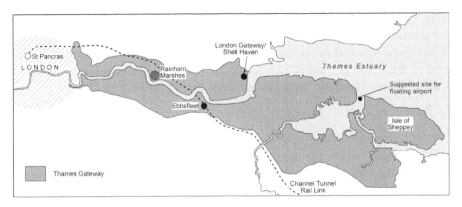

Figure 8.2 The Thames Gateway is a massive regeneration area that covers a range of land-use types and jurisdictional areas. Its size raises serious questions about whether it is possible to regenerate an area of this scale in an integrated manner. Drawn by Kevin Burkhill.

project is around 12 times bigger than that conceived for the Clyde Gateway (see Chapter 7). The Thames Gateway is truly mega-regeneration.

This area has been targeted for major development for three primary reasons (ODPM, 2005a):

- it contains 3,000 hectares, or one fifth, of all brownfield land in south east England;
- it is located in the area of the UK with the highest demand for new housing; and
- it is argued that the Thames Gateway has the potential to link London and the regions to Europe.

In light of these factors, the government believes that the area has major economic potential, and alongside the 120,000 new homes it is hoped to create up to 200,000 jobs, making the Thames Gateway the largest and most ambitious regeneration project in the UK (and many claim, Western Europe). But while characterised by similar policy goals to urban regeneration in general, it is possible to identify a number of distinct challenges related to the scale of the proposed development:

- Strategic – the challenge of planning across a large area that contains urban, suburban and rural land-uses.
- Governance – the organisational challenges of coordinating and delivering physical and social infrastructure.
- Sustainability – the environmental challenges associated with building a massive new development in a floodplain.

The idea of undertaking regeneration on such a grand scale is clear – to allow greater coordination and integration of the different elements of development – however, making this work in practice is another matter. The National Audit Office (2007) issued a damning report on the progress of the Thames Gateway, claiming that very little had been achieved in the 12 years since the project began. The three challenges identified above will be examined in turn, considering both the proposals themselves and the problems that have been encountered putting them into practice.

Strategic

The government's vision for the area is to create 'a world-class environment' (CLG, 2007c), and there is no doubt that the scale of the project presents an opportunity to implement cutting edge design and planning principles in order to create a conurbation that could act as an example of best practice for the rest of Europe.

As Figure 8.2 shows, the Thames Gateway area includes a series of pre-existing urban areas, such as Barking and Ebbsfleet, and is already home to some 1.45 million people. Its boundary reflects the area alongside the Thames that was previously home to a number of industries, whose decline has left a legacy of dereliction and contaminated land. Covering 15 different local authorities it contains some of the most deprived wards in the country and is characterised by a lack of services, unemployment and poor housing provision.

The strategic vision is to enhance existing urban conurbations and develop brownfield land, marshland and farmland across the sub-region, investing in major transport infrastructure to create a well-connected network of cities. The policy rhetoric framing the project mirrors that of urban regeneration more widely, aiming to attract business, provide high-quality housing, and improve the environment. The Thames Gateway's three areas – London, Kent and Essex – are complemented by four specific development sites, identified by the government as 'transformal locations' (Thames Gateway, 2007). These four locations represent the focus of regeneration activities and are large-scale versions of the area-based initiatives discussed in Chapter 4. They are intended to drive growth in the surrounding areas and are located where there is a concentration of available land. It is worth considering three specific developments to understand how this process is intended to work.

One of the key economic developments is the London Gateway Development, a collaborative venture between DP World and Shell, to construct an international port and establish a major logistics and business park. The London Gateway Port will be located at the existing 600-hectare Shell Haven oil refinery in Thurrock and will be capable of handling the largest container ships in the world. Approved in 2007 and begun in 2010, current plans anticipate that the port will be operational within a few years, with the first phase of an attached business park opening earlier. The business park, known as London Gateway Park, will cover 300 hectares and aims to attract the distribution and logistics industries in addition to the usual high-tech sector. The development itself is intended to create up to 16,500 new jobs, and more importantly to act as a growth pole for the Thames Gateway regeneration initiative in Thurrock (Hammerton, 2005).

A number of major mixed-use developments are also planned. For example, the area around Ebbsfleet International Station (some 790,000 m²), adjacent to the Bluewater shopping centre, is being developed with housing, retail, residential, hotel and leisure sites. A masterplan for Springhead Park was produced by major developer Land Securities, with the intention to produce 10,000 new houses, five schools, leisure uses and transport links, along with leaving 40% of the site as open space to create a sustainable community.

Governance

As discussed in Chapter 3, delivering integrated urban regeneration projects involves forming partnerships between a range of organisations from the public and private sectors. The task of coordinating these partnerships is amplified dramatically when regeneration is scaled up to a project the size of the Thames Gateway development. Increasingly, the complexity of these partnerships is being blamed for a lack of coherent action on the Thames Gateway.

Taking economic regeneration as an example, until their abolition, the Thames Gateway development area fell under the jurisdictions of three RDAs: the London Development Agency (LDA), the South East England Development Agency (SEEDA) and the East of England Development Agency (EEDA). Each of these RDAs set up sub-regional agencies (that have subsequently outlived them) to attract inward investment to their respective parts of the Thames Gateway. 'Gateway to London' deals with the Thames Gateway London area, 'Locate in Kent' is responsible for the Thames Gateway North Kent area, and the 'Thames Gateway South Essex Partnership' handles queries relating to the Thames Gateway South Essex area. The government body UK Trade and Investment also has an 'Invest in Thames Gateway Team' which aims to 'progress the region's international agenda' for competitiveness, supported by the Homes and Communities Agency. These woes are to some extent a microcosm of the wider lack of coherent governance afflicting south east England (Cochrane, 2012), which functions as a London mega-region but is governed separately as a city and surrounding region (John et al., 2005). The development of the Thames Gateway is dependent upon the involvement of the private sector, but the complexity of the network of agencies, public bodies and partnerships involved has created confusion amongst would-be investors, acting as a barrier to regeneration (National Audit Office, 2007).

Confusion plagues the delivery of new physical and social infrastructure too, with some 30 coordinating bodies involved, ranging from the Highways Agency, to the Strategic Health Authority. The glacial pace of progress seems to slow further as new agencies and partnerships enter the fray, and where individual developments do take place they often appear to be rather isolated. The Thames Gateway Forum (rebranded the East London Summit in 2011) provides the annual meeting place for all those involved in the regeneration of the Thames Gateway and Olympic region. In 2006 the event included 160 top-level speakers, and was rather grandiosely billed as 'the largest ever gathering of the people and organisations responsible for delivering the most exciting regeneration project in the world' (Olympic Delivery Authority, 2006). But although the government has spent over £7bn on the area since 2003, the NAO report found that ministers did not have so much as a costed plan for the programme to join up local initiatives (National Audit Office, 2007).

Health provision provides an apposite example of governance failure. Despite the massive potential population growth in the area, no major new hospital is planned, and in relation to health the grey literature associated with the project mentions little more than a new specialist cardiothoracic centre in Basildon, the Gravesham Healthy Living Centre and the Boleyn Medical Centre in Newham. In terms of transport, the only major new infrastructure project is the Channel Tunnel Rail Link, opened in late 2007 to create a high-speed railway line from London through Kent to the Channel Tunnel. A high-speed Javelin train service links Ebbsfleet Station to London St Pancras in 17 minutes, but beyond this the plans have been criticised for offering little more that the opening of a few new bus routes. Sir Terry Farrell, the architect responsible amongst other things for the MI6 building, remarked about the Thames Gateway project that the government seem to 'have handed out the jigsaw pieces, but there is no picture on the box' (Cavendish, 2007: 17). Unlike the Olympic Development Authority, which had a clear deadline to deliver the venues and infrastructure for the Olympic and Paralympic Games, the wider Thames Gateway development has no deadline for completion and a largely opaque and leaderless governance system.

A number of implications can be drawn from the institutional impasse that the Thames Gateway project appears to have run into: it may be that the area is simply too large to be planned in an integrated way; or it may be that the dominant models of urban regeneration are simply not suited to being scaled up on this magnitude. The partnership approach, for example, may become so complex that no action is possible when so many organisations are involved. Equally, the logic of private investment alone may not be capable of delivering the massive new infrastructure projects that are needed to create a new metropolitan region. Whichever explanation one chooses to accept, the problem of scaling regeneration up to the regional level remains pressing, and it is possible that radically different (i.e. more powerful) political bodies are needed to make regeneration work on this scale.

Sustainability

Decisions about where and how development takes place must be taken in the context of sustainability in order to minimise negative environmental impacts and maximise social and economic benefits. In light of the threat of environmental change, major developments in the Thames Gateway will be seen as a blueprint for the government's approach to housing over the next 15–20 years.

Two key elements of sustainability are worth considering in the context of the Thames Gateway:

- Flood risk issues associated with building in a floodplain.
- Environmental protection of areas of conservation value.

Many of the new homes being built in the Thames Gateway area will be built in flood-risk locations, adding to the number of properties currently at risk of flooding in the UK. The wisdom of this can be questioned, given recent high-profile debates concerning the problems of obtaining home insurance in areas prone to flooding, and the National Planning Policy Framework which seeks to privilege sustainable developments. It has obviously been deemed that the area's advantageous location outweighs the inevitable flood risk to homes, but given the scale of the development, the potentially severe problems of flooding associated with sea-level rise and increased storminess demand consideration.

Surprisingly, the Thames Estuary is one of the least understood and researched estuaries in the country. The current tidal defences for the Estuary were built in the 1970s to protect against a 1-in-2,000-year flood (or a 0.05% risk of flooding). With sea-level rise this level of resilience will gradually decline, as planned, to give protection against a 1-in-1,000-year flood (or 0.1% risk of flooding) by the year 2030. Rather ominously, the region has experienced some of the worst floods on record in recent years. One of the worst affected areas was Kent, where 310mm of rain fell in October of 2002 – the monthly average is normally 80mm.

In light of these risks, it is imperative that homes are constructed to be able to withstand flooding. For example, 2,250 new homes are planned within the tidal floodplain of the Swanscombe Peninsula (Kent Thameside Delivery Board, 2005). There is a need to protect the line around the western edge of the site, possibly through staging a managed retreat. In terms of heavy rainfall and runoff from impervious surfaces such as concrete and tarmac, much of the land has been raised by spoil deposition, which minimises the potential for flood storage as the soil is contaminated. Given the scale of the development, the existing system would not cope. The project thus requires the developer to contribute to the removal of material in order to provide flood storage.

The Thames Gateway area also includes rural areas deemed to have natural value such as the North Kent Marshes, which are recognised as Environmentally Sensitive Areas and Sites of Special Scientific Interest. Concerns have been raised because the Thames Gateway project threatens to develop significant areas of the marshland habitat. For example, the government's White Paper on air transport originally included proposals for a large international airport to be built on Cliffe Marshes in Medway. These were eventually dropped in 2003 due to opposition from local residents, the council, and various NGOs. The expense of the plan was also deemed to be prohibitive as it would have involved raising the ground level by 15m, but the government has also looked at other potential locations for an airport in the area, including the feasibility of a floating airport on an inlet between the Isle of Grain and Isle of Sheppey. This plan, for which concept plans were produced by Norman Foster in November 2011, won the backing of London Mayor Boris Johnson – and the inevitable nickname 'Boris Island' (Topham, 2012).

At the same time, a 600-hectare conservation park called Wildspace is being created at Rainham Marshes, in the heart of Havering. At three times the size of Hyde Park, the unprotected marsh and landfill area is being turned into a wildlife sanctuary. But controversy reigns over the decision to spread the Thames Gateway development out over such a large area. Many commentators have suggested that new housing should be confined to the area within the M25, and that more high-quality greenspace is needed in order to lure upwardly mobile professionals into the area. In terms of the marshes, there is a danger that planners will simply 'ring-fence the best and trade-off the rest' for development (Selman, 2002: 284).

While environmental impacts are unavoidable when considering a development on the scale of the Thames Gateway, poorly conceived plans can also cause negative impacts on surrounding communities. For example, successive mayors of London have changed their minds repeatedly on the question of whether to build the £450m Thames Gateway Bridge in east London. A public inquiry in 2009 showed that the proposed six-lane urban motorway would cause major local air pollution and congestion that would impact most heavily on exactly those poor communities that the Thames Gateway project aims to help. As discussed in Chapter 5, questions of who will benefit and who will lose out characterise many regeneration projects. The scale of the Thames Gateway makes these issues harder to ignore and more awkward to resolve, as local opposition to parts of the strategy can delay or damage the overall strategic goals of the development.

Key points

i) The principles of regeneration are being applied at increasingly large scales.

ii) The Thames Gateway has clear parallels with urban regeneration, being characterised by numerous brownfield sites and deprived communities.

iii) Proximity to London makes the Thames Gateway a key strategic site to ease problems of housing supply in the south east in spite of the problems associated with development on a floodplain.

iv) Recent reports on the project suggest that is hard to coordinate effective regeneration partnerships across such a massive area, raising questions about the ability of traditional approaches to regeneration to be scaled up to the regional level.

v) Ensuring that developments on this scale adhere to the principles of sustainability involves making major trade-offs.

Conclusion

Both of the case studies discussed in this chapter show how the principles of regeneration are being applied at ever larger scales. The Olympics has catalysed and accelerated a series of existing schemes to redevelop the lower Lea Valley in London, while the Thames Gateway entails coordinating multiple redevelopment schemes across numerous brownfield sites and deprived communities to the east of London. Both schemes embody the broader shift from a regulatory style of planning that depends upon setting rules to guide general development, to a spatial style of planning that identifies a specific area in which to undertake significant change (Allmendinger and Haughton, 2009).

Some of the challenges that characterise 'normal' regeneration are familiar, if somewhat bigger. For example, the question of whether local, often disadvantaged, communities benefit from proposed regeneration schemes tends to affect larger communities, reflected in higher levels of press coverage and political debate. Environmental trade-offs like enhancing some areas of natural interest while losing others to development play out over a greater scale.

That said, some of the challenges highlighted by the Olympics and the Thames Gateway are qualitatively different in character. The governance structure of regeneration in the UK means that any large project will involve a huge number of state agencies operating at different tiers, and recent reports suggest that is hard to coordinate effective regeneration partnerships across mega-regeneration projects. The Olympics had a single body, the Olympic Delivery Authority, with a focus on ensuring that the Games were delivered on time. The Thames Gateway, meanwhile, has no coordinating body. While the fuzziness of the Thames Gateway area lends the scheme a degree of flexibility that is pragmatically useful (it is surely impossible to foresee all eventualities in such a complex scheme), it has been plagued by a lack of coordination and by inaction (Allmendinger and Haughton, 2009). The problem of scale is not only spatial, but temporal as well. Although the Olympic Park site has already been dramatically transformed, a new phase of post-Games development will be required to reap the regeneration benefits of hosting this mega-event.

Here the question of what Bob Jessop (2004) calls 'metagovernance', or the governance of governance, emerges. In schemes as large as the Thames Gateway, New Labour's emphasis on 'getting things done' and not worrying about the neatness of administrative boundaries may have run up against the limits of partnership. Whether the solution to managing such large-scale projects is to have stronger state involvement is, of course, a moot point. The inefficiencies of large-scale, top-down state control were in many ways what drove the shift away from government towards partnership in the first place. Either way, such mega-schemes undoubtedly have a role to play in addressing the grand challenges of the twenty-first century, offering intriguing insights into the strengths and weaknesses of the current models of governance in play.

Further reading

Gold and Gold's edited volume gives an excellent background to how the Olympics has helped reshape different host cities. Gratton and Preuss critically review concepts of regeneration and legacy associated with the Games. Brownhill's literature review gives a good overview of how Olympic venues can be put to new post-Games uses. In relation to the Thames Gateway, the National Audit Office Report makes for very interesting reading, focusing on the difficulties of coordinating a large partnership that covers multiple jurisdictions. Allmendinger and Haughton similarly focus on the planning and governance issues raised by the scale of the Thames Gateway regeneration, drawing on interviews with government officials to explore the pros and cons of the partnership approach.

Allmendinger, P. and Haughton, G. (2009) 'Soft spaces, fuzzy boundaries and metagovernance: the new spatial planning in the Thames Gateway', *Environment and Planning A*, 41(3): 617–633.
Brownhill, S. (2010) *Literature Review: Olympic Venues – Regeneration Legacy*. Oxford: Report submitted to the London Assembly by Oxford Brookes University.
Gold, J. and Gold, M. (eds) (2010) *Olympic Cities: City Agendas, Planning, and the World's Games, 1896 to 2016*. Second edition (Routledge, London).
Gratton, C. and Preuss, H. (2008) 'Maximizing Olympic impacts by building up legacies', *The International Journal of the History of Sport*, 25(14): 1922–1938.
National Audit Office (2007) *The Thames Gateway: Laying the Foundations* (TSO, London)

Conclusions

Challenges revisited

At the start of this book we discussed the key issues that urban regeneration seeks to address. By way of drawing together the themes that have emerged across the subsequent chapters, it is worth reconsidering our starting point. Initially, regeneration was seen as a way to reverse the decline of industrial cities associated with the loss of manufacturing industry over the second part of the twentieth century. Industrial decline had led to severe dereliction and de-population in certain areas, creating a series of social and economic problems, particularly within inner cities. A key question driving urban regeneration was how to make cities attractive places in which to live and work. More recently, the issue of providing adequate housing supply for the population has returned to the fore, as soaring house prices and increased levels of household formation have exacerbated shortages around the country. Rather than 'concreting over the countryside' with sprawling new developments, existing cities are seen as the ideal places in which to solve housing shortages by bringing derelict land back into use. This has been reflected in a rapid population growth within some cities since the late 1990s.

Given the massive scale of these challenges, it is easy to see why the urban regeneration agenda has assumed such importance in the contemporary political landscape. From Secretary of State for the Environment Michael Heseltine visiting Liverpool in the wake of the Toxteth riots in 1981, to the ongoing Olympic Games oriented regeneration of East London, the driving force behind regeneration has been primarily political in nature. There is, however, a multitude of steps between issuing political imperatives and actually getting to the stage of laying one brick on top of another. A wide variety of people and agencies need to come together to make regeneration happen in practice. Regeneration requires input from diverse sectors such as planning, development, health, environment, transport and education, with coordination and resources needed from both public and private organisations. Regeneration involves developers, government, communities, architects and planners working closely together. Partnerships and collaboration are required across different sectors in order to avoid the mistakes of the past and create quality, sustainable environments where people will want to live and work. Throw the financial crisis and climate change into the mix and it becomes clear that regeneration has become more difficult to achieve just as the need for it has never been greater, as the growing complexity of delivering sustainable developments is accompanied by a dwindling appetite for risk in the private sector.

Key themes

The preceding chapters have worked through various dimensions of urban regeneration, considering the ways in which regeneration has been undertaken and how policy and practices have evolved since the early 1980s. This section identifies the key challenges that have emerged, and considers how they are defining urban regeneration in the UK today.

Partnership working

Perhaps the most dramatic difference between urban regeneration and previous interventions in UK cities has been the emphasis put on partnership between different branches of government, the private sector and communities. Partnership is now central to urban policy – it is no longer the case that a local authority can simply decide to rebuild a run-down part of the city and then make it happen. Because the political culture of the UK has shifted to a more neoliberal position, state funding for projects is seen primarily as a means to draw private sector investment to areas which otherwise would be seen as too risky or difficult. This said, a key critique of urban regeneration in the 1980s was that this practice of drawing in private sector partners simply acted as a state subsidy to wealthy developers. As the scope of regeneration has developed to bring together social, economic and environmental components, this critique has ebbed somewhat, with a whole variety of outputs being sought from private and public sector investments. While the broader benefits and shortcomings of the shift from government to governance can be debated, it is now a largely accepted fact that top-down approaches to urban regeneration are neither desirable nor practicable (Shaw and Robinson, 2010).

Given the broadened remit of regeneration, there is a certain logic to bringing in a variety of actors with different expertise from the public, private and charitable sectors. Scholars have developed the idea of governance to help understand how different actors come together. Partnership as a mode of governance is interesting as although non-state actors have been brought into the process, critics such as Jonathan Davies (2002) have argued that the aims of the state are still dominant. The state comprises a complex series of overlapping agencies operating at a variety of geographic scales which pursue different and sometimes contradictory aims. As a result it is perhaps rather simplistic to reduce regeneration to delivering the aims of the state, particularly as the involvement of multiple partners can change the intended direction of a project. Furthermore, as the example of the Thames Gateway shows, the larger the project the more difficult it seems to be to coordinate the many different partners involved. Ironically then, it is on precisely the kinds of projects which require most input from other agents because of their complexity and the number of people being affected that the current governance structures seem least able to cope. The ability of partnership working to coordinate developments that are socially and environmentally viable on relatively short time-scales is a critical challenge in the field of regeneration.

Tackling industrial decline

Perhaps the single biggest factor driving regeneration in the UK has been the shift to a post-industrial economy. Large areas of towns and cities fell into dereliction as industrial functions moved elsewhere as part of the restructuring of the global economy. This also left a legacy of high unemployment and economic stagnation in many urban areas of the UK. Regeneration has sought to reverse the flow of higher income groups out of the city and attract new businesses and forms of economic activity. Services, tourism and leisure have become ever more important, meaning that cities can no longer function as places where people simply work before retreating to suburban enclaves each evening.

The transformation of former industrial sites and under-utilised portions of city centres is synonymous with the regeneration process. Brownfield redevelopment has allowed urban economies to expand without further sprawl into the countryside. Areas of former dockland have become high-value office spaces, and Victorian factory buildings have been converted into loft apartments. The economic disaster of industrial decline has, through regeneration, been transformed into a story of economic growth in particular sectors and particular parts of the country. Since the late 1990s, some cities have grown rapidly in population, but others continue to stagnate. One should not lose sight of the fact that not everyone has benefited equally from new economic growth, and the resulting picture of spatial unevenness has only been exacerbated by the post-2008 recession. As a political tool to direct development to where it is needed, urban regeneration runs counter to neoliberal preferences to let market forces dictate where investment occurs. In light of the gradual drift to the right that has characterised British politics this undoubtedly places it in a somewhat vulnerable position.

Pursuing the knowledge economy

Over the past quarter century the UK has seen a process of re-imaging undertaken to make cities places where people actually *want* to be. Leeds, for example, has been transformed from being seen as a grimy, northern industrial city, to being hip, fashionable and dynamic – a place where people are excited to live. Regeneration has driven this transformation, producing new public spaces, new facilities, new apartments and new jobs in new sectors of the economy.

The knowledge economy has been at the heart of this change, with brains rather than brawn providing the engine for growth. Not all regions and demographic groups have done well out of this economic restructuring, with low-paid service jobs replacing high-skill manufacturing work in many areas. There has, however, been a great deal of enthusiasm among policy-makers to attract to their cities Richard Florida's (2002) 'creative classes' – those working in the IT, media and communications sectors – through attempts to make urban environments more attractive. There is also a belief that the development of creative industries can be fostered through the establishment of clusters, where people working in these sectors can easily meet and network with each other. A number of towns and cities have used regeneration schemes to deliver creative quarters of one kind or another, anchoring nascent clusters with high-end cultural facilities, such as the FACT centre in Liverpool's Ropewalks district, or the BALTIC on the Tyne in Newcastle and Gateshead.

The headlong pursuit of the knowledge economy does, however, raise a broader question about distinctiveness; if all towns and cities are pursuing similar strategies to try to attract creative businesses, what makes an individual town stand out in a competitive market? In a tougher economic climate, bland regeneration schemes are no longer guaranteed to succeed, although the extent to which this prompts cities to adopt more organic and distinctive approaches to regeneration remains to be seen.

Recovering from the financial crisis

Approximately 20% of the UK economy is related to real estate development, and the heyday of regeneration between 1998 and 2008 represented an exceptional period of redevelopment activity, fuelled by government policies to encourage high-density city-centre living and the availability of cheap credit that allowed these homes to be bought. The credit crunch of 2008 crippled the mortgage markets and effectively halted private regeneration schemes. There is a clear geography to the credit crunch, with the areas outside of the south east feeling the pinch most. The great cities of the North represent the poster children for regeneration, and while city centres in these places are bearing up, regeneration schemes in smaller towns and areas outside of city centres are struggling. The loss of the RDAs as facilitators and funders of regeneration in the regions should also not be understated, especially when the current legacy of government-funded PFI schemes winds up.

It is hard to see how the previous levels of regeneration will be reached again, because the conditions that stimulated the previous boom are gone. But, as history shows, capitalist economies are characterised by cycles of growth and recession and while it is always hard to see where the next economic upturn will come from, it will undoubtedly come from somewhere, albeit driven by a different set of factors. Indeed, in the much beloved metaphor of economic commentators, the green shoots of economic recovery are already showing themselves in stronger consumer spending in the major global economies. In the UK, shares in major house-builders are going up, and government attempts to streamline the planning system may further stimulate development. Evidence from private sector consultancies suggests that the market for smaller regeneration projects is beginning to come back. At the same time, the emphasis on city-centre apartments has been tempered, as policy-makers realise the folly of producing socially homogeneous developments. There is a distinct possibility that this will shift the focus of development away from costlier brownfield sites, and indeed from the regeneration of declining urban areas per se. That said, a range of massive regeneration projects is going ahead, like the continuing regeneration of East London associated with the Olympics. Interestingly, though, this mega-scheme has been driven by the government, and represents a major long-term strategy to direct London's growth eastwards. Given the long road to economic recovery that lies ahead and the need for increasingly strategic regeneration, such large-scale government-driven schemes may become more common.

Addressing sustainability and climate change

The growing need for strategic regeneration brings us neatly to the topic of sustainable development and the challenges posed by climate change. Since sustainable development entered mainstream debates in the late 1980s and early 1990s, it has become a ubiquitous presence across government policy. Sustainability and regeneration are in some ways happy bedfellows; both are concerned with achieving social, economic and environmental goals and the tenets of sustainability resonate with the defining characteristics of regeneration, such as reusing brownfield sites to reduce urban sprawl, stimulating economic activity in declining regions and tackling social issues through access to affordable, quality housing.

Assessing the sustainability of regeneration schemes more often than not boils down to the question of how trade-offs are made between economic, social and environmental priorities. As discussed in Chapter 5, brownfield sites exemplify the difficulties of balancing competing agendas, often representing ecologically diverse habitats as well as potential sites for affordable homes. Getting the balance right can be difficult and, particularly in England, it is arguable that decision-making structures have swung too far toward the delivery of economic goals. In Scotland, Wales and Northern Ireland there tends to be a stronger connection between regeneration and social policy in the responsible government departments, whereas in England social issues have tended to be shunted into a separate discourse of community 'renewal'. The National Planning Policy Framework, which aims to streamline the planning system, retains sustainable development as its core goal but undoubtedly places a greater emphasis on the development part of the equation than on the sustainability part – a tendency further reinforced by the emergence of Local Enterprise Partnerships.

While these trends suggest that regeneration will retain a primarily economic remit, sustainability is perhaps at its most useful as a concept when it pushes developers to consider the costs and benefits of different building options over the entire lifetime of a development. These kinds of approaches to urban development have been given specific impetus by the emergence of climate change as a major issue facing cities. Cities are critical in addressing climate change, because most greenhouse gas emissions are produced in urban areas. The materials from which buildings are made, their design, and the planning of regeneration schemes can all contribute to lowering the carbon emissions produced by urban areas. Cities are also looking to adapt to the potential impacts of climate change, of which flooding will be the most important in the UK.

Low carbon regeneration schemes are set to become more common as cities play an increasingly leading role in addressing climate change, bypassing recalcitrant national governments and taking action even in the absence of legally binding international agreements on emissions. The climate change agenda dovetails neatly with the competitive tendencies of cities, as low carbon regeneration is seen as the way to attract the kinds of green, clean industries that will blaze a trail towards the post-carbon economy. Low carbon economic growth thus provides an emergent framework for the current round of urban regeneration schemes. As for the eco-town debacle discussed in Chapter 7, though, the degree to which low carbon schemes achieve a form of urban development that is qualitatively different from that which preceded it remains to be seen; indeed, given that the main actors and processes have remained in place it would be disingenuous to suggest that this is more than a shift in emphasis at present.

Delivering communities

One of the most profound shifts in the functioning of UK towns and cities in the last quarter century has been the return of population to central urban areas. In the 1980s city centres were not places where people lived, while today exclusive flats and apartments in urban cores are fashionable, prime real estate, with many more being built each year. Repopulation has been accompanied by a growth in leisure facilities, with the result that the days when UK city centres shut down at 6pm are a distant memory.

The model of inner city regeneration has been immensely profitable for developers and ticks a great many boxes in terms of reducing car dependence and providing accommodation for the growing number of smaller households.

There has been a renewed emphasis on high-quality design as part of the attempt to attract people back into cities. From flagship architectural statements in the city centre, to the sensitive restorations of historic buildings elsewhere, to simple improvements in the form and legibility of the public realm, cities are being made more attractive places to live. This not only applies to city centres, but also thoughtfully designed settlements elsewhere, making use of smart growth principles of walkability and high-density design alongside innovations such as design coding. It should be noted, however, that while there has been a great deal of innovative and high-quality design, particularly in the last ten years, there has also been an explosion of bland, characterless buildings, constructed to price by the major house-building firms. This kind of design does little to improve the city living experience. The city centre is not the whole city, however, and it is possible to identify cases where an overly metro-centric model has been inappropriately applied to outer urban areas.

The word gentrification is never used by those working in the regeneration sector, but almost all regeneration activity is predicated on attracting new people and new businesses into run-down areas. This undoubtedly makes it easier to bring private developers on board, who can market to a more wealthy demographic and, indeed, can allow public bodies to negotiate with developers in order to produce a proportion of affordable homes, subsidised services and other social benefits. Bringing in new people and businesses very frequently involves the displacement of existing residents – often some of the poorer and more vulnerable members of society. In some ways this approach to urban regeneration echoes a long-standing tendency of urban policy to pathologise poor and disadvantaged communities as victims in need of external assistance, who must either be civilised by a middle-class influx, or be forced to 'engage' with their largely degraded living environments in ways that wealthy residents simply are not (Cochrane, 2007).

The connection between regeneration and gentrification is an intractable issue and this book does not suggest that there are any easy answers. One of the reasons why this book has not discussed issues of community in detail is because existing communities, in practice, tend to be by far the weakest actors in programmes to physically transform urban areas, for all of the policy rhetoric about inclusion and social cohesion. While the partnership approach has sought to go beyond the largely physical interventions of traditional town planning, focusing on wider community needs relating to education, employment and culture, the issue of gentrification and the continuing dominance of economic interests casts doubts over the extent to which this has really been achieved (Shaw and Robinson, 2010).

We do not live in an ideal world and the question of gentrification brings us back to the need for trade-offs. Those existing residents who are able to remain in a dramatically regenerated area should benefit from increased value of their homes, an improved environment, better local services and a healthier local economy. Other residents will be priced or forced out of that area. There have been cases where art-ist communities have been deliberately used to make a low-rent area fashionable before being displaced by wealthier groups attracted to the very thing that their arrival then forces out. In its worst excesses, regeneration produces very bland, monocultural developments, comprising young professionals without children housed in soulless, generic buildings. This may be the opposite of the policy rheto-ric, but in the UK over the last decade, this kind of development has happened all too frequently.

Urban regeneration is dead ... Long live urban regeneration!

Like all forms of politics, regeneration is the 'art of the possible'. The overriding message that comes across from each of the chapters is one of compromise and trade-offs between different concerns. Successful urban regeneration schemes occur when collaboration has been effective and fair, while difficulties are related to fail-ures to achieve equitable balances. One of the systemic challenges to regeneration involves ameliorating the excesses of neoliberalism, which has, in cases, resulted in a rather uneven distribution of economic benefits, and the sidelining of social and environmental concerns. Both Glasgow in Chapter 4, and Salford Quays in Chapter 5 question the extent to which those people in the greatest socio-economic poverty have benefited from urban regeneration. Here, once again, an assessment of urban regeneration runs up against a wider set of structural issues concerning the way in which the UK functions, from the tendency of capitalism to generate uneven eco-nomic growth to the withdrawal of the welfare state that has exacerbated vulner-ability and alienation in some of the UK's least well-off communities. The capacity of area based initiatives (of which urban regeneration is almost inevitably com-prised) to overcome these wider economic and political forces is obviously limited (Chatterton and Bradley, 2000). If, as Cheshire (2007: 9) states, 'the problem is pov-erty, not where poor people live', then ABIs run the risk of simply displacing prob-lems elsewhere in the city rather than solving them.

These tendencies stem from the prioritisation of economic development in regeneration policy. For example, the Sustainable Communities Plan had few solid targets for social and environmental sustainability, and was probably the most con-troversial element of the CLG's work, focusing on the massive expansion of house-building in the south east combined with demolition (and gentrification) in the Pathfinder areas. The Treasury-driven Barker reviews placed more emphasis on market forces determining how land should be developed and this has subsequently fed through into planning policy, finding expression in the subsequent Coalition government's attempt to introduce a dramatically streamlined National Planning Policy Framework that assumes in favour of proposed developments.

These observations are not intended to indict regeneration in the UK as some kind of failure. It is important to remember that the initial goals of regeneration were economic, and by most indicators economic prosperity in the urban areas of the UK has increased substantially. Cities still face challenges, however. As the *State of the English Cities Report* (ODPM, 2006) claims, levels of socio-economic deprivation remain higher and more widespread in cities, reflected not least in higher levels of unemployment. The recession that hit the UK from 2008 onwards has not helped this picture, and when climate change and decimated public budgets are thrown into the pot it becomes apparent that the future holds many challenges for urban regeneration. By way of tying up the arguments of this chapter, it is worth finally reflecting on these challenges and the potential trends emerging within the sector to address them.

Not all cities can compete within the global economy to attract the most desirable industries, and individuality will become increasingly critical to the success of cities. It was perhaps excusable that planners in the 1980s and 1990s accepted relatively generic architecture and a preponderance of flats and apartments in order to kick-start regeneration and meet housing targets. Regeneration projects are often (erroneously) described as creating truly unique places and one way this can be achieved is through retaining a sense of history and local culture. Within the broader evolution of regeneration in the UK today, however, cities need to be more creative in terms of how they develop, in order to differentiate themselves from other places and achieve change in challenging economic conditions. For example, rather than demolishing vast areas in order to present developers with 'attractive' (i.e. large) land packages, cities can opt to retain characteristic features, demanding more creative and higher quality development proposals. Such an approach would also stand more chance of producing socially inclusive developments, as existing communities could be included in the regeneration process. How far this is possible, within the context of the current economic recession and the era of austerity introduced by the Coalition government, remains to be seen.

The question of how much urban regeneration will change is in no small part bound up with the question of how distinctive the regeneration agenda as we knew it was to the political project of New Labour (Bache and Catney, 2008). Urban regeneration is caught up in a broader political tussle concerning whether devolution and empowerment are actually occurring, or whether power is being centralised. On the one hand, the Coalition government has continued New Labour's policy of devolution in regeneration policy, abolishing the RDAs but empowering LEPs as part of an emphasis on local action, self-help and community ownership. On the other hand, the government has been widely criticised for not living up to this rhetoric of local empowerment and even reinforcing the powers of Whitehall in some cases. Large-scale budget cuts and the potential undermining of community powers to resist developments under the new planning framework do little to counter this view.

This tension is not unrelated to the challenges of social and environmental change. Central government is undoubtedly entering an era in which it will need an executive capacity to respond to large-scale challenges, such as housing shortages and sea-level change. Large-scale developments like the Thames Gateway require huge infrastructure building programmes to provide sustainable transport and waste systems. The need to balance increasingly strategic decision-making powers with the empowerment of local communities who may resist them represents a major political challenge that goes well beyond the regeneration agenda. Debates over the best way to govern in the twenty-first century, and issues surrounding social and environmental citizenship will frame the way regeneration unfolds in the future.

Finally, in the face of the challenges outlined above, understanding how ideas about city-building move from one place to another is critical (McCann and Ward, 2011). This book has focused on the UK, but every week there are reports in the press of various innovative developments from around the world, whether it is Masdar, the new eco-city being built in Abu Dhabi, or the totally car-free Vauben development in a suburb of Freiburg, Germany. While regeneration in the UK has generally followed trends from the US in the past, the sector is truly global and many of the challenges facing the UK are the same as those faced elsewhere. In order to meet them, and survive in a tougher economic environment, regeneration will have to innovate and learn from others. New ways to finance projects, longer-term partnerships, and more sophisticated sets of priorities will all be required if regeneration is to continue to provide the means by which we make our cities fit for the future.

Glossary

Big Society: a key part of the Conservative party's manifesto in the 2010 election which has subsequently informed the thinking of the Coalition government. Although a somewhat vague term, it has become a catch-all for policies which seek to decrease dependence on state services and increase communities taking control of their own lives. Politically it is allied with the neoliberal attack on the state.

Blairite: the adjectival form of Blair, who led the Labour government between 1997 and 2007. The word Blairite refers to the supporters and policies of Blair's government. The hallmarks of Blairite policy include the increased use of markets to deliver public services, but reined in through partnership with the public sector, and pro-European and devolutionary policies.

Bond: a bond is a financial instrument that represents a debt security, whereby the bond holder lends money at a rate of interest that is repaid at the end of the term, or when the bond 'matures'.

Bonfire of the quangos: a term used by the media to describe a review held in 2010 by the Coalition government into the executive agencies within the UK government. The headline was that 192 bodies were to be scrapped, although in many cases this simply meant the transfer of functions back into government departments. The phrase refers to the bonfire of the vanities – an event associated with renaissance Catholicism where objects thought to encourage sin were burned.

Brownfield: refers to previously used land. The word brownfield was coined in opposition to the term greenfield, which designates a development site in previously undeveloped areas. It includes the categories 'derelict land', which is previously used, and 'contaminated land', which is previously used and polluted in some way. Brownfield is synonymous with the US term brownland.

Buy-to-let: a practice where investors purchase homes and rent them out to a third party. The rent is used to cover the mortgage payments and the hope is that the property will increase in value during the period of ownership. This model was hit particularly hard by the credit crunch leading many investors exposed to high levels of debt and falling rents on devalued properties.

Capital: in a financial sense, capital is any asset that can be used or invested. It is usually taken to mean privately owned wealth. Capital has also been used in the sense of human capital or social capital, to indicate the strength of social networks, in terms of shared interests and civic engagement.

Coalition government: although this phrase could indicate any government formed through an alliance of two or more parties, in the context of this book it commonly refers to the government formed by the Conservative and Liberal Democrat parties following UK elections in 2010. The election of 2010 brought an end to the New Labour period of government.

Creative class: coined by Richard Florida, the concept of a creative class is used to signify a shift from an industrial economy to a knowledge economy. The idea is that cities should compete to attract knowledge workers who will in turn attract large employers who require the kinds of skills possessed by members of the creative class – largely comprising graduates working in the professions. One critique of the concept is that it encourages local authorities to spend scarce resources to serve the interests of the wealthy, rather than on poorer citizens.

Credit crunch: refers to the global economic collapse of 2008 which triggered a lengthy, worldwide recession. This brought an end to a period of fevered commodity price rises and a spiralling property market. A severe reduction in mortgage availability and sharp decline in house prices followed, causing many redevelopment and construction schemes to be put on hold or cancelled.

Curtilage: the area of land around a building belonging to the property.

Deindustrialisation: since the late 1970s, Western economies generally and the UK in particular have seen a rebalancing of the economy away from manufacturing and towards services. The decline of the industrial economy has had two particular impacts relevant to regeneration. First, there has been a reduction in the availability of well-paid, skilled and semi-skilled employment which has partly been responsible for an increasing wealth-gap between the richest and poorest communities. Second, large, former industrial brownfield sites within cities have become priorities for regeneration activity and transformation into new uses.

Design codes: a system of setting out prescriptive guidance about the design of buildings and streetscapes. The intention is that by producing these guidelines the process of regeneration should be sped up as developers who stick within the design codes for an area should easily get planning permission for their projects.

Discourse: a discourse is a set of specific meanings or representations that are attached to certain things. So, for example, one discourse of inner cities represents them as dangerous and crime-ridden. Because different groups often represent things in different ways, there may be different discourses about the same thing. A contesting discourse of inner cities that is becoming more dominant is that they are vibrant and diverse places to live.

Equity: the principle of fairness between groups of people, often designated as a key principle of sustainable development. Equity can also mean the share of a person's ownership in an asset when used in a financial context.

EU: abbreviation of the European Union, a political body set up by the Maastricht Treaty in 1993, and including 27 member states. The European Commission represents one of its political bodies, and forms policy on regional development, agriculture and the environment, amongst other things.

Gentrification: the process by which buildings or residential areas are improved over time, which leads to increasing house prices and an influx of wealthier residents who force out the poorer population of an area.

Globalisation: refers to the integration of economic activity across the planet. It is often associated with multinational companies, which operate on many different continents and have GDPs that exceed that of smaller countries. Globalisation is associated with the assumption that countries are at the behest of companies that will seek the best places to do business, with little consideration of the consequences of relocating large workforces. Globalisation is also used to refer to the spread of cultural patterns and products, like MTV or Coca Cola.

Glocalisation: a term derived by combining localisation and globalisation, which highlights the idea of behaviour which is simultaneously acting to an increasing degree at both a specific local level and at the global scale ('act locally, think globally'). In the specific context of governance it can be used to refer to the hollowing out of the nation state, with powers increasingly passing upward to supranational organisations and downward to local communities.

Holistic: literally means addressing the whole. It is usually used to mean an integrated approach that considers all aspects of a problem.

Infrastructure: in the context of urban regeneration, infrastructure designates the 'hard' engineered features of the urban environment, including roads, water pipes, electricity, waste systems, railways, pavements, lighting, and so forth.

Keynesian economics: named after John Maynard Keynes, an economist who fundamentally reshaped UK policy in the 1930s and 1940s. The Keynesian approach advocates the use of increased public spending to counter the self-destructive tendencies of an unrestrained free-market approach. Keynesianism is in direct opposition to neoliberal economics which argues that state intervention distorts markets that would otherwise find a 'natural' balance.

Legacy: the long-term regeneration impact of an event hosted in a particular area or city.

Leverage: used to describe the ratio of capital to debt. This word has become more familiar in the aftermath of the credit crunch as individuals and companies have become exposed to risk as the value of their assets (e.g. houses) has gone down while the cost of borrowing has increased. Highly leveraged projects (i.e. a high ratio of debt to capital) are vulnerable to collapse/bankruptcy in the event of an economic downturn.

Levering-in: a term often used to describe the process of spending public money in an area in order to encourage private investment. Typically this may include the public sector paying to clean up a contaminated area or build a new access road in order to create an attractive site for profitable development by the private sector.

Localism: not to be confused with Blairite 'new localism', Localism as a concept has been key to the operation of the Coalition government and the philosophy of the Big Society. The idea is that much greater levels of control over state services should be in the hands of people at a local level. The result has been major reforms to local government, including the Localism Act, 2012.

Managerialism: see New Localism.

Masterplan: a general term to refer to some kind of unified document which lays out the vision for the redevelopment of an area. These documents can have various levels of specificity and can cover areas of different sizes.

Metrocentric: a term used to describe a focus on urban issues and areas.

Mixed (use) development: a general term to designate developments that include more than one kind of use. Usually mixed-use developments include retail (shops), residential (homes), business premises (offices) and leisure uses (cafés, bars and so forth). The term is also sometimes used to designate a mixture of residents and users; this can include mixed tenure (i.e. some rental, some owner-occupied), mixed-income groups and mixed ethnicities.

Neoliberal: an approach that believes that markets provide the best solution to social problems. So, for example, the introduction of carbon trading as a way to curtail greenhouse gas emissions is a neoliberal policy response. The approach builds upon classic economic ideas developed by Adam Smith, and was championed by the New Right in the US during the 1980s.

Neo-vernacular architecture: an approach to architecture that makes self-conscious reference to past styles of building, attempting to capture the qualities of older styles and building techniques. One of the most complete examples in the UK is seen in the Poundbury development on the edge of Dorchester. As a style it is commonly associated with new urbanism.

New Labour: term applied to Tony Blair's Labour government that took power in the 1997 general election. They were considered 'New' as they moved away from traditional left-wing policies (such as their long-standing affiliation with the Trade Unions) towards the centre ground, or so-called 'Third Way'. The idea that they were 'New' also articulated the fact that this was the first Labour government for almost 20 years, and that they were led by a young dynamic leader.

New Localism: not to be confused with 'Localism' policies implemented by the Coalition government, New Localism was used to describe the tendency of Blairite policies to devolve the implementation of policy goals down to the local level. A key feature of this trend is the devolution of management to the local level in order to achieve policy goals more efficiently, although the political power to decide what those goals should be is generally not devolved. The New Localism is thus closely linked to the emergence of Managerialism at the local level.

New urbanism: a movement in architecture and planning seeking to make more people-friendly settlements. Although most commonly associated with neo-vernacular architectural styles, the movement has broader aims which have entered the mainstream of planning policy, including reducing car-dependence, increasing the compactness and walkability of settlements as well as creating mixed communities of different incomes and different stages in the lifecourse.

Procurement: the acquisition of goods or services for an organisation or individual at the best possible price. The EU public procurement directive requires public bodies to put all their procurements out to competitive tender, in order to reduce corruption and ensure that the cheapest services and goods are obtained.

Public realm: commonly used term meaning public spaces and activities. Sometimes applied to areas of policy that directly concern the public.

Quango: an acronym for QUasi-Autonomous Non (sometimes 'National') Government Organisation. Quangos proliferated under New Labour, as various powers and responsibilities of the state were devolved to organisations that are neither public nor private. Quangos have been criticised because they are not democratically elected, and are often not accountable to the public for their actions. The field of urban regeneration was populated by a large number of quangos, although many were closed following the election of a Coalition government in 2010.

Remediation: the process of cleaning up polluted brownfield land.

Resilience: developing out of the work of ecologist C.S. 'Buzz' Holling, the notion of resilience refers to the capacity of different systems to absorb external shocks and adapt in response to them. In the study of towns and cities this concept has been applied to a diverse range of topics from resilience to climate change – making areas less vulnerable to flooding for example – to the social and financial resilience of communities in the face of global economic changes.

Smart growth: a widely used concept in North American planning, smart growth is focused on creating high-density developments providing homes, schools, services and jobs in a walkable settlement. It is seen in direct opposition to urban sprawl.

Thatcherite: the adjectival form of Thatcher, a Conservative party politician who was Prime Minister between 1979 and 1990. She was the first female prime minister in the UK and the longest serving of the twentieth century. Her government was associated with introducing right-wing neoliberal policies from the US, and reducing the role of the state in providing for basic social needs like health and housing.

Third sector: refers to non-profit and charitable bodies that belong neither to the public nor private sector.

Urban sprawl: a pejorative term, denoting the unregulated outward growth of towns and cities, with low-density developments fostering car-dependence.

References

Adair, A., Berry, J. and McGreal, S. (2003) 'Financing property's contribution to regeneration', *Urban Studies*, 40(5/6): 1065–1080.

Adaptable Suburbs (2010) *Briefing Note: UCL Bartlett Adaptable Suburbs Project* (http://www.sstc.ucl.ac.uk/pdfs/Adaptable_suburbs_briefing_note.pdf, accessed 19 August 2011).

Aldrick, P. and Wallop, H. (2007) 'For sale: too many flats, not enough houses', *Daily Telegraph*, 29 May, p.1.

Alker, S., Joy, V., Roberts, P. and Smith, N. (2000) 'The definition of brownfield', *Journal of Environmental Planning and Management*, 43(1): 49–69.

All Party Urban Development Group (2009) *Regeneration and the Recession* (HMSO, London).

Allmendinger, P. and Haughton, G. (2009) 'Soft spaces, fuzzy boundaries, and meta-governance: the new spatial planning in the Thames Gateway', *Environment and Planning A*, 41(3): 617–633.

Alonso, W. (1970) *Location and Land Use*. Fourth edition (Harvard University Press, Cambridge, MA).

Anon. (2007) 'Boomtown stats', *Bristol Evening Post*, 17 March, p.6.

Armstrong, P. (2001) 'Science, enterprise and profit: ideology in the knowledge driven economy', *Economy and Society*, 30(4): 524–552.

Arnstein, S. (1969) 'A ladder of citizen participation', *Journal of American Institute of Planners*, 35(4): 216–224.

Atkinson, R. (1999) 'Discourses of partnership and empowerment in contemporary British urban regeneration', *Urban Studies*, 36(1): 59–72.

Atkinson, R. and Helms, G. (2007) *Securing an Urban Renaissance: Crime, Community, and British Urban Policy* (Policy Press, Bristol).

AWM (2011) *ERDF Programme 2007–13 – Priority 3 Investment Framework – v3.2 March 2011* (www.communities.gov.uk/documents/regeneration/xls/1927179.xls, accessed 18 August 2011).

Babtie (2000) *Statement of Principles* (University Hospital Birmingham NHS Trust, Birmingham).

Bache, I. and Catney, P. (2008) 'Embryonic associationalism: New Labour and urban governance', *Public Administration*, 86(2): 411–428.

Bailey, N. (2003) 'Local Strategic Partnerships in England: the continuing search for collaborative advantage, leadership and strategy in urban governance', *Planning Theory & Practice*, 4(4): 443–457.

Bailey, N. and Turok, I. (2001) 'Central Scotland as a polycentric urban region: Useful planning concept or chimera?', *Urban Studies*, 38(4): 697–715.

Barker, K. (2004) *Review of Housing Supply. Delivering Stability: Securing our Future Housing Needs. Final Report – Recommendations* (HM Treasury, London).

Barker, K. (2006) *Barker Review of Land Use Planning: Final Report – Recommendations* (HM Treasury, London).

Bartlett, E. and Howard, N. (2000) 'Informing the decision makers on the cost and value of green building', *Building Research & Information*, 28(5/6): 315–324.

BBC (2010) 'Quango list shows 192 to be axed' (http://www.bbc.co.uk/news/uk-politics-11538534, accessed 15 August 2011).

BBC (2011) 'Face the facts: mind the funding gap' (http://www.bbc.co.uk/programmes/b0132k5g, accessed 22 August 2011).

Begg, I. (2002) *Urban Competitiveness: Policies for Dynamic Cities* (Policy Press, Bristol).

Bell, D. and Jayne, M. (2003) 'Design-led urban regeneration: a critical perspective', *Local Economy*, 18(2): 121–134.

Binnie, J. and Skeggs, B. (2004) 'Cosmopolitan knowledge and the production and consumption of sexualized space: Manchester's gay village', *Sociological Review*, 52(1): 39–61.

Birmingham City Council (2002) *Selly Oak Hospital* (Department of Planning and Architecture, Birmingham).

BIS (2010) *Local Growth: Realising Every Place's Potential. Cm 7961* (The Stationery Office, London).

BIS (2011a) 'Summary of Regional Growth Fund second round bids' (http://webarchive.nationalarchives.gov.uk/+/http://www.bis.gov.uk/policies/economic-development/regional-growth-fund/summary-of-rgf-2nd-round-bids, accessed 10 April 2012).

BIS (2011b) 'Summary of RGF first round bids' (http://webarchive.nationalarchives.gov.uk/+/http://www.bis.gov.uk/policies/economic-development/regional-growth-fund/summary, accessed 10 April 2012).

Boddy, M. (2007) 'Designer neighbourhoods: new-build residential development in nonmetropolitan UK cities? The case of Bristol', *Environment and Planning A*, 39(1): 86–105.

Bond, D. (2007) 'Costs "ruining" Games legacy', *Daily Telegraph,* 16 March, p.1.

Brennan, A., Rhodes, J. and Tyler, P. (1999) 'The distribution of SRB Challenge Fund expenditure in relation to local-area need in England', *Urban Studies*, 36(12): 2069–2084.

Bridging NewcastleGateshead (2011) *Creating the Foundations for Transformation: Housing Market Renewal in NewcastleGateshead, the BNG legacy* (http://www.bridgingng.org.uk/docs/BNG-Legacy-Brochure.pdf, accessed 25 October 2011).

Brownhill, S. (2010) *Literature Review: Olympic Venues – Regeneration Legacy.* Report submitted to the London Assembly by Oxford Brookes University, Oxford.

Bryson, J. and Buttle, M. (2005) 'Enabling inclusion through alternative discursive formations: the regional development of community development loan funds in the United Kingdom', *Service Industries Journal*, 25(2): 273–288.

Bulkeley, H. and Betsill, M. (2003) *Cities and Climate Change: Urban Sustainability and Global Environmental Governance* (Routledge, New York).

CABE (2000) *By Design: Urban Design in the Planning System: Towards Better Practice* (DETR, London).

CABE (2005a) *Creating Successful Neighbourhoods: Lessons and Actions for Housing Market Renewal* (CABE, London).

CABE (2005b) *Making Design Policy Work: How to Deliver Good Design Through Your Local Development Framework* (CABE, London).

CABE (2008) *Case Studies: Bristol Harbourside* (http://web.archive.org/web/20060925233558/http://www.cabe.org.uk/default.aspx?contentitemid=227&aspectid=23, accessed 29 August 2011).

Cameron, S. (2003) 'Gentrification, housing redifferentiation and urban regeneration: "Going for growth" in Newcastle upon Tyne', *Urban Studies*, 40(12): 2367–2382.

Cameron, S. (2006) 'From low demand to rising aspirations: Housing market renewal within regional and neighbourhood regeneration policy', *Housing Studies*, 21(1): 3–16.

Cardiff Harbour Authority (2007) *Cardiff Bay Development Corporation* (http://www.cardiffharbour.co.uk/learning/about_cbdc.htm, accessed 14 July 2007).

Carpenter, J. (2009) 'Money's too tight to mention? Urban regeneration in a recession and beyond: the case of Oxford', *Journal of Urban Regeneration and Renewal,* 4(3): 228–239.

Cavendish, C. (2007) 'We're stuck at the Gateway to nowhere', *The Times*, 31 May, p.17.

Chatterton, P. (2010) 'The student city: an ongoing story of neoliberalism, gentrification, and commodification', *Environment and Planning A*, 42(3): 509–514.

Chatterton, P. and Bradley, D. (2000) 'Bringing Britain together? The limitations of area-based regeneration policies in addressing deprivation', *Local Economy*, 15(2): 98–111.

Cheshire, P. (2007) *Segregated Neighbourhoods and Mixed Communities: A Critical Analysis* (Joseph Rowntree Foundation, York).

Cities Alliance and UNEP (2007) *Liveable Cities: The Benefits of Urban Environmental Planning* (http://www.unep.org/urban_environment/PDFs/LiveableCities.pdf, accessed 8 February 2012).

CLG (2006a) *Planning Policy Statement 3: Housing* (CLG, London).

CLG (2006b) 'SRB Round 6 bidding guidance' (http://www.communities.gov.uk/index.asp?id=1128132#P80_12915, accessed 20 September 2006).

CLG (2007a) *Land Use Change in England: Residential Development to 2006 (LUCS 22)* (HMSO, London).

CLG (2007b) *New Projections of Households for England and the Regions to 2029* (http://communities.gov.uk/index.asp?id=1002882&PressNoticeID=2374, accessed 6 July 2007).

CLG (2007c) *Thames Gateway: North Kent* (http://www.communities.gov.uk/index.asp?id=1170138, accessed 17 July 2007).

CLG (2009) *Planning Policy Statement: Eco Towns. A Supplement to Planning Policy Statement 1* (CLG, London).

CLG (2010) *Household Projections, 2008 to 2033, England* (http://www.communities.gov.uk/documents/statistics/pdf/1780763.pdf, accessed 22 September 2011).

CLG (2011a) *Grant Shapps: £30 Million Lifeline for Families Trapped in Abandoned Streets* (http://www.communities.gov.uk/news/corporate/1897506, accessed 15 August 2011).

CLG (2011b) *Live Tables on House Building: Table 254: Permanent Dwellings Completed, by House and Flat, Number of Bedroom and Tenure, England* (http://www.communities.gov.uk/housing/housingresearch/housingstatistics/housingstatisticsby/housebuilding/livetables/, accessed 6 October 2011).

CLG (2011c) *Live Tables on Repossession Activity* (http://www.communities.gov.uk/housing/housingresearch/housingstatistics/housingstatisticsby/repossessions/livetablesrepossession/, accessed 6 October 2011).

CLG (2011d) *Regeneration to Enable Growth: What the Government is Doing in Support of Community-Led Regeneration* (CLG, London).

CLG (2012a) *Enterprise Zones* (http://www.communities.gov.uk/regeneration/regenerationfunding/enterprisezones/, accessed 10 April 2012).

CLG (2012b) *European Regional Development Fund (ERDF)* (http://www.communities.gov.uk/regeneration/regenerationfunding/europeanregionaldevelopment/, accessed 10 April 2012).

CLG (2012c) *Live Tables on Housebuilding: Table 254 Housebuilding: Permanent Dwellings Completed, by House and Flat, Number of Bedroom and Tenure, England* (http://www.communities.gov.uk/housing/housingresearch/housingstatistics/housingstatisticsby/housebuilding/livetables/, accessed 10 April 2012.

CLG (2012d) *Live Tables: Land Prices: Table 563 Housing Market: Average Valuations of Residential Building Land with Outline Planning Permission* (http://www.communities.gov.uk/housing/housingresearch/housingstatistics/housingstatisticsby/housingmarket/livetables/landpricestables/, accessed 10 April 2012).

CLG (2012e) *National Planning Policy Framework* (CLG, London).

Cochrane, A. (2007) *Understanding Urban Policy: A Critical Approach* (Blackwell, Oxford).

Cochrane, A. (2012) 'Making up a region: the rise and fall of the "South East of England" as a political territory', *Environment and Planning C: Government and Policy*, 30(1): 95–108.

Cole, R. (2005) 'Building green: moving beyond regulations and voluntary initiatives', *Policy Options*, 26(6): 53–60.

Collins, A. (2004) 'Sexual dissidence, enterprise and assimilation: bedfellows in urban regeneration', *Urban Studies*, 41(9): 1789–1806.

Construction Task Force (1998) *Rethinking Construction* (HMSO, London).

Cook, I. (2004) *Waterfront Regeneration, Gentrification and the Entrepreneurial State: The Redevelopment of Gunwharf Quays*, Spatial Policy Analysis Working Paper 51 (School of Geography, University of Manchester, Manchester).

Cooper, I. (2000) 'Inadequate grounds for a 'design-led' approach to urban renaissance? Towards an urban renaissance: Final report of the urban task force', *Building Research and Information*, 28(3): 212–219.

Corridor Manchester (2010) *Annual Review 2009–2010* (http://www.corridormanchester.com/downloads/COR_annual_review.pdf, accessed 10 February 2011).

Couch, C. and Denneman, A. (2000) 'Urban regeneration and sustainable development in Britain', *Cities*, 17(2): 137–147.

CPRE Oxfordshire (2006) *CPRE Oxfordshire Campaign Briefing: Planning Policy Statement 3 in Brief* (http://www.cpreoxon.org.uk/news/briefing/edition/pps3.pdf, accessed 14 July 2007).

Creativesheffield (2011) *About Creativesheffield* (http://www.creativesheffield.co.uk/aboutcreativesheffield, accessed 30 August 2011).

Crompton, J. (2001) 'Public subsidies to professional team sport facilities in the USA', in Gratton, C. (ed.), *Sport in the City: The Role of Sport in Economic and Social Regeneration* (Routledge, London) pp.15–34.

Curtis, P. (2009) 'Cutbacks could see student numbers fall', *Guardian*, 8 May, p.7.

Daly, G., Mooney, G., Poole, L. and Davis, H. (2005) 'Housing stock transfer in Birmingham and Glasgow: the contrasting experiences of two UK cities', *European Journal of Housing Policy*, 5(3): 327–341.

Danielsen, K.A., Lang, R.E. and Fulton, W. (1999) 'Retracting suburbia: smart growth and the future of housing', *Housing Policy Debate*, 10(3): 513–540.

Davies, J. (2001) *Partnerships and Regimes: The Politics of Urban Regeneration in the UK* (Ashgate, Aldershot).

Davies, J. (2002) 'The governance of urban regeneration: a critique of the "governing without government" thesis', *Public Administration*, 80(2): 301–322.

Davoudi, S. (2000) 'Sustainability: a new "vision" for the British planning system', *Planning Perspectives*, 15(2): 123–137.

Deas, I. and Giordano, B. (2002) 'Locating the competitive city in England', in Begg, I. (ed.), *Urban Competitiveness: Policies for Dynamic Cities* (Policy Press, Bristol) pp.191–210.

DEFRA (2011) *Mainstreaming Sustainable Development: The Government's Vision and What this Means in Practice* (HMSO, London).

Department of Employment (1985a) *Employment: The Challenge for the Nation* (HMSO, London).

Department of Employment (1985b) *Lifting the Burden* (HMSO, London).

Department of Employment (1992) *People, Jobs and Opportunity* (HMSO, London).

DETR (1999) *A Better Quality of Life: A Strategy for Sustainable Development for the UK* (HMSO, London).

DETR (2000) *Our Towns and Cities: The Future – Delivering an Urban Renaissance* (The Stationery Office, London).

Dicken, P. (2003) *Global Shift: Reshaping the Global Economic Map in the 21st Century* (Guilford Press, New York).

Dodman, D. (2009) 'Blaming cities for climate change? An analysis of urban greenhouse gas emissions inventories', *Environment and Urbanization*, 21(1): 185–201.

DoE (1994) *Sustainable Development: The UK Strategy* (HMSO, London).

DTI (1998) *The Competitiveness White Paper: Our Competitive Future: Building the Knowledge-Driven Economy* (HMSO, London).

DTI (2000) *Excellence and Opportunity – A Science and Innovation Policy for the 21st Century* (HMSO, London).

DTI (2001) *Opportunity for All in a World of Change* (HMSO, London).

DTI (2003a) *Competing in a Global Economy: The Innovation Challenge* (HMSO, London).

DTI (2003b) *Energy White Paper: Our Energy Future: Creating a Low Carbon Economy* (TSO, London).

DTI (2003c) *A Modern Regional Policy for the United Kingdom* (HMSO, London).

DTI (2004) *A Practical Guide to Cluster Developments* (HMSO, London).

DTI (2006) *Sustainable Construction Strategy Report* (DTI, London).

Duffy, H. (1995) *Competitive Cities: Succeeding in the Global Economy* (E & FN Spon, London).

DWP (2011) *European Social Fund in England* (http://dwp.gov.uk/esf/about-esf/, accessed 10 November 2011).

Edinburgh City Council (2007) *Waterfront Edinburgh: Granton Masterplan* (http://www.edinburgh.gov.uk/CEC/Corporate_Services/Corporate_Communications/waterfrontintro/index.html, accessed 26 June 2007).

Edwards, A. (2007) 'It's the Liverpool Echo Arena: 10,600 seat arena takes our name', *Liverpool Echo*, 1 June, p.2.

Elkin, S. (1987) *City and Regime in the American Republic* (University of Chicago Press, Chicago).

English Heritage (2005) *Regeneration and the Historic Environment* (http://www. english-heritage.org.uk/publications/regeneration-and-historic-environment/ regenerationandhistoricenvironment2005.pdf, accessed 30 August 2011).

Estates Gazette (2011) 'Build-now, pay-later housing sites unveiled', *Estates Gazette*, 2 April, p.3.

Evans, J. (2007) 'Wildlife corridors: an urban political ecology', *Local Environment*, 12(2): 129–152.

Evans, J. and Jones, P. (2008) 'Sustainable urban regeneration as a shared territory', *Environment and Planning A*, 40(6): 1416–1434.

Evans, J., Jones, P. and Krueger, R. (2009) 'Organic regeneration and sustainability or can the credit crunch save our cities?', *Local Environment: The International Journal of Justice and Sustainability*, 14(7): 683–698.

Fearnley, R. (2000) 'Regenerating the inner city: lessons from the UK's City Challenge experience', *Social Policy and Administration*, 34(5): 567–583.

Fergus, E. (2011) 'Sweet dream for the old sugar sheds: riverside regeneration, visitors to the Tall Ships race will see start of waterfront transformation', *Evening Times (Glasgow)*, 5 July, p.6.

Florida, R. (2002) *The Rise of the Creative Class and How it's Transforming Work, Leisure, Community and Everyday Life* (Basic Books, New York).

Forio, S. and Brownhill, S. (2000) 'Whatever happened to criticism? Interpreting the London Docklands Development Corporation's obituary', *CITY*, 4(1): 53–64.

Furbey, R. (1999) 'Urban "regeneration": reflections on a metaphor', *Critical Social Policy*, 19(4): 419–445.

Garcia, B., Melville, R. and Cox, T. (2010) *Creating an Impact: Liverpool's Experience as European Capital of Culture* (http://www.liv.ac.uk/impacts08/Papers/Creating_an_Impact_-_web.pdf, accessed 30 August 2011).

Giddens, A. (2009) *The Politics of Climate Change* (Polity Press, Cambridge).

Gill, S.E., Handley, J.F., Ennos, A.R. and Pauleit, S. (2007) 'Adapting cities for climate change: the role of the green infrastructure', *Built Environment*, 33(1): 115–133.

Gilligan, A. (2007) 'Spin, hype and the truth about London's Olympic legacy', *Evening Standard*, 19 March, p.19.

Ginsberg, N. (2005) 'The privatization of council housing', *Critical Social Policy*, 25(1): 115–135.

Glaeser, E.L., Saiz, A., Burtless, G. and Strange, W.C. (2004) 'The rise of the skilled city [with comments]', *Brookings-Wharton Papers on Urban Affairs*, pp.47–105.

Glancey, J. (2004) 'In for a penny', *Society Guardian*, 29 April, n.p.

Glasgow Architecture (2010) *Commonwealth Games Athletes Village, Glasgow: Information* (http://www.glasgowarchitecture.co.uk/commonwealth_games_village.htm, accessed 23 August 2011).

Gold, J. and Gold, M. (eds) (2010) *Olympic Cities: City Agendas, Planning, and the World's Games, 1896 to 2016*. Second edition (Routledge, London).

Gonzàlez, S. (2011) 'Bilbao and Barcelona "in motion". How urban regeneration "models" travel and mutate in the global flows of policy tourism', *Urban Studies*, 48(7): 1397–1418.

Gracey, H. (1973) 'The 1947 planning system: the plan-making process', in Hall, P., Gracey, H., Drewett, R. and Thomas, R. (eds), *The Containment of Urban England Volume Two: The Planning System* (George Allen and Unwin, London) pp.74–94.

Gratton, C. and Preuss, H. (2008) 'Maximizing Olympic impacts by building up legacies', *International Journal of the History of Sport*, 25(14): 1922–1938.

Gratton, C., Shibli, S. and Coleman, R. (2005) 'Sport and economic regeneration in cities', *Urban Studies*, 42(5–6): 985–999.

Guy, S. (2006) 'Designing urban knowledge: competing perspectives on energy and buildings', *Environment and Planning C: Government and Policy*, 24(5): 645–659.

Guy, S. and Shove, E. (2000) *A Sociology of Energy, Buildings and the Environment: Constructing Knowledge, Designing Practice* (Routledge, London).

Gwilliam, M., Bourne, C., Swain, C. and Prat, A. (1999) *Sustainable Renewal of Suburban Areas* (Joseph Rowntree Foundation, York).

Hall, S. and Nevin, B. (1999) 'Continuity and change: a review of English regeneration policy in the 1990s', *Regional Studies*, 33(5): 477–482.

Hammerton, F. (2005) 'Gateway to a £650m business boost and 16,500 new jobs', *Essex Chronicle*, 28 July, p.8.

Hammond, G. and Jones, C. (2008) 'Embodied energy and carbon in construction materials', *Proceedings of Institutions of Civil Engineers – Energy*, 161(2): 87–98.

Harding, A., Harloe, M. and Rees, J. (2010) 'Manchester's bust regime?', *International Journal of Urban and Regional Research*, 34(4): 981–991.

Harrison, C. and Davies, G. (2002) 'Conserving biodiversity that matters: practitioners' perspectives on brownfield development and urban nature conservation in London', *Journal of Environmental Management*, 65: 95–108.

Harrison, J. (2011) *Local Enterprise Partnerships* (Centre for Research in Identity, Governance, Society (CRIGS)/Globalization and World Cities (GaWC) research network, Loughborough University, Loughborough).

Hart, T. and Johnston, I. (2000) 'Employment, education and training', in Roberts, P. and Sykes, H. (eds), *Urban Regeneration: A Handbook* (Sage, London), pp.129–152.

Harvey, D. (1989) 'From managerialism to entrepreneurialism: the transformation of urban governance in late capitalism', *Geografiska Annaler B*, 71(1): 3–17.

HCA (2011) *Housing Market Renewal* (http://www.homesandcommunities.co.uk/ourwork/housing-market-renewal, accessed 15 August 2011).

HCA (2012a) *Kick Start Housing Programme* (http://www.homesandcommunities.co.uk/ourwork/kickstart, accessed 2 April 2012).

HCA (2012b) *National Affordable Housing Programme* (http://www.homesandcommunities.co.uk/ourwork/national-affordable-housing-programme, accessed 2 April 2012).

Healey, P. (1997) 'A strategic approach to urban regeneration', *Journal of Property Development*, 1(3): 105–110.

Henry, I. and Dulac, C. (2001) 'Sport and social regulation in the city: the cases of Grenoble and Sheffield', *Loisir et Société*, 24(1): 47–78.

Henry, I. and Paramio-Salcines, J. (1999) 'Sport and the analysis of symbolic regimes: a case study of the city of Sheffield', *Urban Affairs Review*, 34(5): 641–666.

HESA (2010) *Student numbers* (http://www.hesa.ac.uk/dox/dataTables/studentsAndQualifiers/download/institution0809.xls?v=1.0, accessed 8 March 2010).

HM Government (2012) *UK Climate Change Risk Assessment: Government Report* (TSO, London).

HM Treasury (2001) *Productivity in the UK: The Regional Dimension* (HMSO, London).

HM Treasury (2005) *The Government's Response to Kate Barker's Review of Housing Supply* (HMSO, London).

Hodson, M. and Marvin, S. (2007) 'Understanding the role of the national exemplar in constructing "strategic glurbanization"', *International Journal of Urban and Regional Research*, 31(2): 303–325.

House of Commons Public Accounts Committee (2012) *74th report: Preparations for the London 2012 Olympic and Paralympic Games* (http://www.publications.parliament.uk/pa/cm201012/cmselect/cmpubacc/1716/171602.htm, accessed 9 April 2012).

Hubbard, P. (2008) 'Regulating the social impacts of studentification: a Loughborough case study', *Environment and Planning A*, 40(2): 323–341.

Hubbard, P. (2009) 'Geographies of studentification and purpose-built student accommodation: leading separate lives?', *Environment and Planning A*, 41(8): 1903–1923.

Hughes, H. (2003) 'Marketing gay tourism in Manchester: New market for urban tourism or destruction of "gay space"?', *Journal of Vacation Marketing*, 9(2): 152–163.

Hurst, W. (2010) 'Come clean on Kickstart: HCA forced to reveal details of poor housing', *Building Design*, 3: 3 December.

Imrie, R., Lees, L. and Raco, M. (2009) *Regenerating London: Governance, Sustainability and Community* (Routledge, Abingdon).

Imrie, R. and Raco, M. (2003) 'Community and the changing nature of urban policy', in Imrie, R. and Raco, M. (eds), *Urban Renaissance? New Labour, Community and Urban Policy* (Policy Press, Bristol), pp.3–36.

Imrie, R. and Thomas, H. (1993) *British Urban Policy and the Urban Development Corporations* (Paul Chapman Publishing, London).

In Suburbia Partnership (2005) *In Suburbia: Delivering Sustainable Communities* (Civic Trust, London).

Jacobs, J. (1961) *The Death and Life of Great American Cities* (Random House, New York).

Jacobs, J. (1985) *Cities and the Wealth of Nations* (Random House, Toronto).

Jessop, B. (1994) 'Post-Fordism and the state', in Amin, A. (ed.), *Post-Fordism: A Reader* (Blackwell, Oxford), pp.251–279.

Jessop, B. (2004) 'Multi-level governance and multi-level metagovernance changes in the European Union as integral moments in the transformation and reorientation of contemporary statehood', in Bache, I. and Flinders, M. (eds), *Multi-level Governance* (Oxford University Press, Oxford), pp.49–74.

Johar, I. and Maguire, C. (2007) *Sustaining our Suburbs* (www.rudi.net/system/files/paper/optional_file/40149_Sustain_Suburbs_5_0.pdf, accessed 19 August 2011).

John, P., Tickell, A. and Musson, S. (2005) 'Governing the mega-region: governance and networks across London and the South East of England', *New Political Economy*, 10(1): 91–106.

Johnstone, N. (2010) 'Homes and Communities Agency cuts £1.9bn funding for 13 schemes' (http://www.propertyweek.com/news/news-by-sector/residential/homes-and-communities-agency-cuts-%C2%A319bn-funding-for-13-schemes/5009384.article, accessed 4 August 2011).

Jones, P. (2005) 'The suburban high flat in the post-war reconstruction of Birmingham, 1945–71', *Urban History*, 32(2): 323–341.

Jones, P. (2008) 'Different but the same? Post-war slum clearance and contemporary regeneration in Birmingham, UK', *City: Analysis of Urban Trends, Culture, Theory, Policy, Action*, 12(3): 356–371.

Jones, P. and Evans, J. (2006) 'Urban regeneration, governance and the state: exploring notions of distance and proximity', *Urban Studies*, 43(9): 1491–1509.

Jones, P. and Wilks-Heeg, S. (2004) 'Capitalising culture: Liverpool 2008', *Local Economy*, 19(4): 341–360.

Karadimitriou, N. (2005) 'Changing the way UK cities are built: The shifting urban policy and the adaptation of London's housebuilders', *Journal of Housing and the Built Environment*, 20: 271–286.

Kelso, P. (2011) 'Tottenham resume Olympic Stadium fight with West Ham after High Court judge tells Spurs their case is "arguable"', *Telegraph*, 24 August (http://www. telegraph.co.uk/sport/football/teams/tottenham-hotspur/8720327/Tottenham-resume-Olympic-Stadium-fight-with-West-Ham-after-High-Court-judge-tells-Spurs-their-case-is-arguable.html, accessed 6 September 2011).

Kent Thameside Delivery Board (2005) 'Strategic flood risk assessment of Kent Thameside (http://www.kt-s.co.uk/kts02/pdfs/FR_main.pdf, accessed 4 July 2007).

Kortekass, V. (2011) 'Olympic Village sold to consortium for £557m', *Financial Times* (http://www.ft.com/cms/s/0/a4bcb88e-c4f6-11e0-9c4d-00144feabdc0. html#axzz1X9zjgeOF, accessed 6 September 2011).

Kotaji, S., Schuurmans, A. and Edwards, S. (2003) *Life-cycle Assessment in Building and Construction: A State-of-the-Art Report* (SETAC, Raleigh, NC).

Krueger, R. and Gibbs, D. (2008) '"Third wave" sustainability? Smart growth and regional development in the USA', *Regional Studies*, 42(9): 1263–1274.

Krugman, P. (1996) 'Making sense of the competitiveness debate', *Oxford Review of Economic Policy*, 12: 17–25.

Laganside Corporation (2007) *Bringing New Life to the River* (http://www.laganside. com/about.asp, accessed 8 Feburary 2007).

Layard, A. (2012) 'The Localism Act 2011: What is "local" and how do we (legally) construct it?', *Environmental Law Review* (in press).

Leather, P., Cole, I., Ferrari, E., Robinson, D., Simpson, C. and Hopley, M. (2007) *National Evaluation of the HMR Pathfinder Programme: Baseline Report* (CLG, London).

Lever, W. (2002) 'The knowledge base and the competitive city', in Begg, I. (ed.), *Urban Competitiveness: Policies for Dynamic Cities* (Policy Press, Bristol), pp.11–32.

Leyshon, A. and French, S. (2009) '"We All Live in a Robbie Fowler House": the geographies of the buy to let market in the UK', *British Journal of Politics & International Relations*, 11(3): 438–460.

Lightmoor (2007) *Development Proposals* (http://www.lightmoor.info/development_proposals.html, accessed 27 June 2007).

Long, J. (2010) *Weird City: Sense of Place and Creative Resistance in Austin, Texas* (Texas University Press, Texas).

Long, K. (2011) 'Queen of the East: Olympics head of design shares her vision', *London Evening Standard*, 24 August (http://www.thisislondon.co.uk/standard/article-23980726-queen-of-the-east-the-head-of-design-for-the-olympics-talks-about-her-vision-for-east-london.do, accessed 9 September 2011).

Lynch, K. (1960) *The Image of the City* (Technology Press, London).

MacLeod, G. (2002) 'From urban entrepreneurialism to a "revanchist city"? On the spatial injustices of Glasgow's renaissance', *Antipode*, 34(3): 602–624.

Malpass, P. (1994) 'Policy-making and local governance: How Bristol failed to secure City Challenge funding (twice)', *Policy and Politics*, 22(4): 301–312.

Manchester City Council (2009) *Manchester: A Certain Future* (Manchester City Council, Manchester).

Manchester City South Partnership (2008) *Manchester City South Partnership Strategic Development Framework* (Manchester City South Partnership, Manchester).

March, J. and Olsen, J. (1984) 'The new institutionalism: organizational factors in political life', *American Political Science Review*, 74(3): 734–749.

Marsh, P. (2011) 'China noses ahead as top goods producer', *Financial Times*, 13 March.

McCann, E. and Ward, K. (2011) *Mobile Urbanism: City Policy-making in the Global Age* (University of Minnesota Press, Minneapolis).

McCarthy, J. (2006) 'The application of policy for cultural clustering: Current practice in Scotland', *European Planning Studies*, 14(3): 397–408.

McKinsey and Company (2009) *Pathways to a Low Carbon Economy – Version 2 of the Global Abatement Cost-curve* (http://www.mckinsey.com/globalGHGcostcurve, accessed 27 November 2010).

Mebratu, D. (1998) 'Sustainability and sustainable development: historical and conceptual review', *Environmental Impact Assessment Review*, 18: 493–520.

Montgomery, J. (2003) 'Cultural quarters as mechanisms for urban regeneration, Part 1: Conceptualising cultural quarters', *Planning Practice and Research*, 18(4): 293–306.

Montgomery, J. (2005) 'Beware "the Creative Class". Creativity and wealth creation revisited', *Local Economy*, 20(4): 337–343.

Mooney, G. (2004) 'Cultural policy as urban transformation? Critical reflections on Glasgow, European City of Culture 1990', *Local Economy*, 19(4): 327–340.

Moore, K. (2008) 'Sports heritage and the re-imaged city: the National Football Museum, Preston', *International Journal of Cultural Policy*, 14(4): 445–461.

Moore, R. (2011) 'Firstsite – review', *Observer: New Review*, 18 September, p.29.

Moore, S. and Rydin, Y. (2008) 'Promoting sustainable construction: European and British networks at the Knowledge–Policy interface', *Journal of Environmental Policy and Planning*, 10(3): 233–254.

Morad, M. and Plummer, M. (2010) 'Surviving the economic crisis: can eco-towns aid economic development?', *Local Economy*, 25(3): 208–219.

Munro, M., Turok, I. and Livingston, M. (2009) 'Students in cities: a preliminary analysis of their patterns and effects', *Environment and Planning A*, 41(8): 1805–1825.

Nathan, M. and Unsworth, R. (2006) 'Beyond city living: remaking the inner suburbs', *Built Environment*, 32(3): 235–249.

National Audit Office (2007) *The Thames Gateway: Laying the Foundations* (TSO, London).

National Trust (2011) *Government Reforms Threaten Green Spaces* (http://www.nationaltrust.org.uk/main/w-global/w-news/w-latest_news/w-news-planningisforpeople.htm, accessed 15 August 2011).

Neighbourhood Renewal Unit (2007) *Neighbourhood Renewal Fund* (http://www.neighbourhood.gov.uk/page.asp?id=611, accessed 23 April).

New East Manchester (2001) *New Town in the City* (NEM, Manchester).

New Economics Foundation (2008) *A Green New Deal* (NEF, London).

Newman, J. (2001) *Modernising Governance: New Labour, Policy and Society* (Sage, London).

Newman, O. (1973) *Defensible Space: People and Design in the Violent City* (Architectural Press, London).

NISRA (2010) *Statistical Report: 2008 Based Household Projections for Areas within Northern Ireland* (http://www.nisra.gov.uk/archive/demography/population/household/NI08_House_Projs.pdf, accessed 22 September 2011).

Noon, D., Smith-Canham, J. and Eagland, M. (2000) Economic regeneration and funding, in Sykes, H. and Roberts, P. (eds), *Urban Regeneration: A Handbook* (Sage, London), pp.61–85.

North, P. (2003) 'Communities at heart? Community action and urban policy in the UK', in Imrie, R. and Raco, M. (eds), *Urban Renaissance? New Labour, Community and Urban Policy* (Policy Press, Bristol), pp.121–138.

North Solihull Partnership (2011) *The Vision* (http://northsolihull.co.uk/the-vision, accessed 26 August 2011).

Northern Ireland Assembly (2002) *Measures of Deprivation: Noble versus Robinson* (Northern Ireland Assembly Research Paper 02/02, Belfast).

Oatley, N. (1998) *Cities, Economic Competition and Urban Policy* (Sage, London).

ODPM (2002a) *Living Places: Cleaner, Safer, Greener* (ODPM, London).

ODPM (2002b) *Planning Policy Guidance 17: Planning for Open Space Sport and Recreation* (HMSO, London).

ODPM (2003) *Sustainable Communities: Building for the Future* (HMSO, London).

ODPM (2005a) *Creating Sustainable Communities: Delivering the Thames Gateway* (HMSO, London).

ODPM (2005b) *Planning Policy Statement 1: Delivering Sustainable Development* (ODPM, London).

ODPM (2005c) *Securing the Future: UK Government Sustainability Strategy* (HMSO, London).

ODPM (2005d) *Sustainable Communities: People, Places and Prosperity* (HMSO, London).

ODPM (2006) *State of the English Cities Report* (ODPM, London).

Olympic Delivery Authority (2006) *Media Release: London 2012 can be the 'Regeneration Games' – David Higgins* (http://main.london2012.com/en/news/press+room/releases/2006/November/2006-11-22-12-25.htm, accessed 4 July 2007).

ONS (2011) *ONS Construction Statistics, No. 12, 2011 Edition* (http://www.ons.gov.uk/ons/rel/construction/construction-statistics/no--12--2011-edition/index.html, accessed 21 September 2011).

OPLC (n.d.) *Queen Elizabeth Olympic Park* (http://www.scribd.com/doc/47007639/Future-of-the-Park-launch-brochure, accessed 9 September 2011).

Owens, S. (1994) 'Land, limits and sustainability – a conceptual-framework and some dilemmas for the planning system', *Transactions of the Institute of British Geographers*, 19(4): 439–456.

Pachauri, R.K. and Reisinger, A. (2007) *Contribution of Working Groups I, II and III to the Fourth Assessment Report of the Intergovernmental Panel on Climate Change* (IPCC, Geneva).

Parkinson, M., Ball, M. and Key, T. (2009) *The Credit Crunch and Regeneration: Impact and Implications* (CLG, London).

Parkinson, M., Champion, T., Evans, R., Simmie, J., Turok, I., Crookston, M., Katz, B., Park, A., Berube, A., Coombes, M., Dorling, D., Glass, N., Hutchins, M., Kearns, A., Martin, R. and Wood, P. (2006) *State of the English Cities: A Research Study* (ODPM, London).

Parliamentary Office of Science and Technology (1998) *A Brown and Pleasant Land: Household Growth and Brownfield Sites* (HMSO, London).

Partnerships UK (2011) *Project Database: A Record of all Private-Public Projects* (http://www.partnershipsuk.org.uk/PUK-Projects-Database.aspx, accessed 1 December 2011).

Pendlebury, J. (1999) 'The conservation of historic areas in the UK – a case study of "Grainger Town", Newcastle upon Tyne', *Cities*, 16(6): 423–433.

Pendlebury, J. (2002) 'Conservation and regeneration: complementary or conflicting processes? The case of Grainger Town, Newcastle upon Tyne', *Planning Practice and Research*, 17(2): 145–158.

Pierson, P. and Skocpol, T. (2002) 'Historical institutionalism in contemporary political science', in Katznelson, I. and Miller, H. (eds), *Political Science: State of the Discipline* (Norton, New York), pp.693–721.

Porter, M. (1990) *The Competitive Advantage of Nations* (Free Press, New York).

Priemus, H. (1998) 'Redifferentiation of the urban housing stock in the Netherlands: a strategy to prevent spatial segregation?', *Housing Studies*, 13(3): 301–310.

Punter, J. (2010a) 'The recession, housing quality and urban design', *International Planning Studies*, 15(3): 245–263.

Punter, J. (2010b) 'Reflecting on urban design achievements in a decade of urban renaissance', in Punter, J. (ed.), *Urban Design and the British Urban Renaissance* (Routledge, London), pp.325–352.

Raco, M. (2005) 'Sustainable development, rolled-out neo-liberalism and sustainable communities', *Antipode*, 37(2): 324–346.

Raco, M. (2012) 'A growth agenda without growth: English spatial policy, sustainable communities, and the death of the neo-liberal project?', *GeoJournal*, 77(2): 153–165.

Raco, M. and Flint, J. (2012) 'Introduction: characterising the new politics of sustainability: from managing growth to coping with crisis', in Raco, M. and Flint, J. (eds), *The Future of Sustainable Cities: Critical Reflections* (Policy Press, Bristol), pp.3–28.

Raco, M. and Henderson, S. (2005) 'From problem places to opportunity spaces: The practices of sustainable urban regeneration', Paper presented to the Sustainable Urban Brownfield Regeneration: Integrated Management Conference.

Raco, M. and Henderson, S. (2006) 'Sustainable planning and the brownfield development process in the United Kingdom', *Local Environment*, 11(5): 499–513.

Ren, X. (2011) *Building Globalization: Transnational Architecture Production in Urban China* (University of Chicago Press, Chicago).

Rhodes, J., Tyler, P. and Brennan, A. (2003) 'New developments in area based initiatives in England: the experience of the single regeneration budget', *Urban Studies*, 40(8): 1399–1426.

Rhodes, J., Tyler, P. and Brennan, A. (2005) 'Assessing the effect of area based initiatives on local area outcomes: some thoughts based on the national evaluation of the Single Regeneration Budget in England', *Urban Studies*, 42(11): 1919–1946.

Rhodes, R. (1997) *Understanding Governance: Policy Networks, Governance, Reflexivity and Accountability* (Open University Press, Buckingham).

Rice, J.L. (2010) 'Climate, carbon, and territory: greenhouse gas mitigation in Seattle, Washington', *Annals of the Association of American Geographers*, 100(4): 929–937.

Roberts, P. (2000) 'The evolution, definition and purpose of urban regeneration', in Roberts, P. and Sykes, H. (eds), *Urban Regeneration: A Handbook* (Sage, London), pp. 9–36.

Robson, B. (2002) 'Mancunian ways: the politics of regeneration', in Peck, J. and Ward, K. (eds), *City of Revolution: Restructuring Manchester* (Manchester University Press, Manchester).

Robson, B., Bradford, M., Deas, I., Hall, E., Harrison, E., Parkinson, M., Evans, R., Garside, P. and Robinson, F. (1994) *Assessing the Impact of Urban Policy* (HMSO, London).

Royal Institute of Chartered Surveyors (2005) *Green Value: Green Buildings, Growing Assets* (RICS, London).

Rydin, Y. (2010) *Governing for Sustainable Urban Development* (Earthscan, London).

Sassen, S. (1994) *Cities in a World Economy* (Pine Forge Press, London).

Saxenian, A. (1999) *Silicon Valley's New Immigrant Entrepreneurs* (Public Policy Institute of California, San Francisco).

Scottish Government (2009) *Polnoon Masterplan: Idea to Design* (http://shcs.gov.uk/Resource/Doc/292798/0090361.pdf, accessed 21 August 2011).

Scottish Government (2010) *Household Formation in Scotland: What Does it Mean for Housing Policy?* (http://www.scotland.gov.uk/Resource/Doc/318342/0101518.pdf, accessed 22 September 2011).

Scottish Government (2011) *Labour Market Monthly Briefing – July 2011. Employability, Skills and Lifelong Learning Analysis* (http://www.scotland.gov.uk/Topics/Statistics/Browse/Labour-Market/Labour-Market-Briefing, accessed 10 April 2012).

Selman, P. (2002) 'Multi-function landscape plans: a missing link in sustainability planning?', *Local Environment*, 7(3): 283–294.

Shaw, K. and Robinson, F. (2010) 'UK urban regeneration in the twenty-first century: continuity or change', *Town Planning Review*, 81(2): 123–149.

Shaw, R., Colley, M. and Connell, R. (2007) *Climate Change Adaptation by Design: A Guide for Sustainable Communities* (TCPA, London).

Shelter (n.d. ~2008) *Middle Quinton Eco-town: The Facts* (http://england.shelter.org.uk/__data/assets/pdf_file/0012/121143/Middle_Quinton.pdf, accessed 22 August 2011).

Shirley, P. and Box, J. (1998) *Biodiversity, Brownfield Sites and Housing: Quality of Life Issues for People and Wildlife* (Urban Wildlife Partnership, Newark).

Simmie, J., Carpenter, J., Chadwick, A. and Martin, R. (2006) *The Economic Performance of English Cities* (ODPM, London).

Simmie, J., Sennett, J. and Wood, P. (2002) 'Innovation and clustering in the London metropolitan region', in Begg, I. (ed.), *Urban Competitiveness: Policies for Dynamic Cities* (Policy Press, Bristol), pp.161–190.

Smets, P. (2011) 'Community development in contemporary ethnic-pluriform neighbourhoods: a critical look at social mixing', *Community Development Journal*, 46(supplement 2): ii15–ii32.

Smith, D. (2002) 'Patterns and processes of studentification in Leeds', *Regional Review*, April, pp.6–7.

Smith, D.P. (2009) 'Student geographies', *Environment and Planning A*, 41(8): 1795–1804.

Smith, D.P. and Holt, L. (2007) 'Studentification and "apprentice" gentrifiers within Britain's provincial towns and cities: extending the meaning of gentrification', *Environment and Planning A*, 39(1): 142–161.

Smith, N. (1996) *The New Urban Frontier: Gentrification and the Revanchist City* (Routledge, London).

Springings, N. (2002) 'Delivering public services under the New Public Management: The case of public housing', *Public Money & Management*, 22(4): 11–17.

Statistics for Wales (2010) *Household Projections for Wales* (http://wales.gov.uk/docs/statistics/2010/101014seminarsen.pdf, accessed 22 September 2011).

Stewart, J. (1994) 'Between Whitehall and town hall: the realignment of urban regeneration policy in England', *Policy and Politics*, 22(2): 133–145.

Stone, C. (1989) *Regime Politics: Governing Atlanta, 1946–1988* (University Press of Kansas, Lawrence, KS).

Strategic Forum for Construction (2008) *Strategy for Sustainable Construction* (http://www.bis.gov.uk/files/file46535.pdf, accessed 16 March 2012).

Stratford Renaissance Partnership (2012) *Stratford's Future* (http://www.stratfordlondon.info/developments/stratford-developments, accessed 2 April 2012).

Student Castle (2012) *About Us* (http://www.studentcastle.co.uk/about-us/, accessed 9 April 2012).

Sustainable Construction Task Group (2003) *The Construction Industry: Progress Towards More Sustainable Construction* (Sustainable Construction Task Group, London).

Swyngedouw, E. (2004) 'Globalisation or "glocalisation"? Networks, territories and rescaling', *Cambridge Review of International Affairs*, 17(1): 25–48.

Talen, E. (1999) 'Sense of community and neighbourhood form: an assessment of the social doctrine of new urbanism', *Urban Studies*, 36(8): 1361–1379.

Taxpayers' Alliance (2008) *Structure of Government No. 3: The Case for Abolishing Regional Development Agencies* (http://www.taxpayersalliance.com/structure_of_government_3_the_case_for_abolishing_rdas_e.pdf, accessed 10 April 2012).

Thames Gateway (2007) *Thames Gateway Transformal Locations* (http://www.thamesgateway.gov.uk/70_ThamesGatewayTransformalLocations.html?PHPSESSID=1803e0fdcd2177bf6556cfd4ed41482e, accessed 4 July 2007).

Thornley, A., Rydin, Y., Scanlon, K. and West, K. (2005) 'Business privilege and the strategic planning agenda of the greater London authority', *Urban Studies*, 42(11): 1947–1968.

Tickle, L. (2007) 'Here come the students – and there goes the neighbourhood: noisy parties, crowded streets and huge amounts of rubbish are driving local residents up the wall', *Guardian*, 15 May, Guardian Education Pages, p.10.

Tiesdell, S. and Macfarlane, G. (2007) 'The part and the whole: implementing masterplans in Glasgow's New Gorbals', *Journal of Urban Design*, 12(3): 407–433.

Topham, G. (2012) '"Boris Island" airport: how, what, where?', *Guardian* (http://www.guardian.co.uk/politics/2012/jan/18/boris-island-airport-what-where, accessed 12 February 2012).

Travers, T. (2002) 'Decentralization London-style: The GLA and London governance', *Regional Studies*, 36(7): 779–788.

UNECE (2006) *Bulletin of Housing Statistics for Europe and North America* (www.unece.org/hlm/prgm/hsstat/Bulletin_06.htm, accessed 16 March 2012).

United Nations (2007) *City Planning will Determine Pace of Global Warming* (http://www.un.org/News/Press/docs/2007/gaef3190.doc.htm, accessed 2 December 2008).

Urban Realm (2008) *Granton Studios* (http://www.urbanrealm.com/buildings/294/Granton_Studios.html, accessed 22 August 2011).

Urban Task Force (1999) *Towards an Urban Renaissance: Final Report of the Urban Task Force Chaired by Lord Rogers of Riverside* (DETR, London).

Urban Task Force (2005) *Towards a Strong Urban Renaissance: An Independent Report by Members of the Urban Task Force Chaired by Lord Rogers of Riverside* (http://www.urbantaskforce.org/UTF_final_report.pdf, accessed 23 May 2008).

URBED (2002) *A City of Villages: Promoting a Sustainable Future for London's Suburbs* (http://www.urbed.coop/journal_docs/City%20of%20Villages%20GLA%20report. pdf, accessed 23 August 2011).

Walburn, D. (2005) 'Trends in entrepreneurship policy', *Local Economy*, 20(1): 90–92.

Wallop, H. (2011) 'Riots won't stop Europe's biggest shopping centre', *Daily Telegraph*, 1 September, Business pages, p.3.

Wang, T. and Watson, J. (2007) *Who Owns China's Carbon Emissions? Tyndall Briefing Note No 23* (http://gesd.free.fr/wangwats.pdf, accessed 9 April 2012).

Ward, S. (1998) *Selling Places: The Marketing and Promotion of Towns and Cities 1850–2000* (Spon, London).

WEFO (2011) *Progress of 2007–2013 Programmes* (http://wefo.wales.gov.uk/programmes/ progress/?lang=en, accessed 18 August 2011).

Westfield (2011) *Westfield Stratford City* (http://uk.westfield.com/stratfordcityleasing/, accessed 6 September 2011).

While, A. (2006) 'Modernism vs urban renaissance: Negotiating post-war heritage in English city centres', *Urban Studies*, 43(13): 2399–2419.

While, A., Jonas, A.E.G. and Gibbs, D. (2004) 'The environment and the entrepreneurial city: Searching for the urban "sustainability fix" in Manchester and Leeds', *International Journal of Urban and Regional Research*, 28(3): 549–69.

While, A., Jonas, A.E.G. and Gibbs, D. (2010) 'From sustainable development to carbon control: eco-state restructuring and the politics of urban and regional development', *Transactions of the Institute of British Geographers*, 35(1): 76–93.

Whitehand, J. and Carr, C. (2001) *Twentieth-Century Suburbs: A Morphological Approach* (Routledge, London).

Williams, R. (2007) 'Gypsies lose high court battle over Olympic sites', *Guardian*, 4 May, p.7.

Williams, R. (2011) 'Olympic velodrome threatens to give London games a good name', *Guardian* online (http://www.guardian.co.uk/sport/blog/2011/feb/01/velodrome-london-2012, accessed 9 September 2011).

Wolch, J. (1990) *The Shadow State: Government and Voluntary Sector in Transition* (Foundation Centre, New York).

World Commission on Environment and Development (1987) *Brundtland Report: Our Common Future* (Oxford University Press, Oxford).

Zukin, S. (1982) *Loft Living: Culture and Capital in Urban Change* (Johns Hopkins University Press, Baltimore, MD).

Index